Gateway to Justice

Studies in the Legal History of the South

EDITED BY PAUL FINKELMAN, TIMOTHY S. HUEBNER,
AND KERMIT L. HALL

This series explores the ways in which law has affected the development of the southern United States and in turn the ways the history of the South has affected the development of American law. Volumes in the series focus on a specific aspect of the law, such as slave law or civil rights legislation, or on a broader topic of historical significance to the development of the legal system in the region, such as issues of constitutional history and of law and society, comparative analyses with other legal systems, and biographical studies of influential southern jurists and lawyers.

JENNIFER TROST

Gateway to Justice

The Juvenile Court

and Progressive Child Welfare

in a Southern City

The University of Georgia Press
Athens & London

© 2005 by the University of Georgia Press
Athens, Georgia 30602
All rights reserved
Set in Minion by Bookcomp, Inc.
Printed and bound by Thomson-Shore
The paper in this book meets the guidelines for
permanence and durability of the Committee on
Production Guidelines for Book Longevity of the
Council on Library Resources.

Printed in the United States of America

09 08 07 06 05 C 5 4 3 2 1
09 08 07 06 05 P 5 4 3 2 1

Library of Congress Cataloging-in-Publication Data

Trost, Jennifer (Jennifer Ann)
  Gateway to justice : the juvenile court and progressive
child welfare in a southern city / Jennifer Trost.
      p. cm. — (Studies in the legal history of the South)
Includes bibliographical references and index.
    ISBN 0-8203-2664-x (hardcover : alk. paper) —
ISBN 0-8203-2671-2 (pbk. : alk. paper)
    1. Juvenile justice, Administration of—Tennessee—
Memphis—History. 2. Juvenile courts—Tennessee—
Memphis—History. 3. Child welfare—Tennessee—
Memphis—History. I. Title. II. Series.
    KFX1838.T76 2005
    345.768'1908—dc22   2004018181

British Library Cataloging-in-Publication Data available

To my parents and to my sister.
With much love.

Contents

Tables

Acknowledgments

I RECEIVED EXCELLENT TRAINING from my faculty at Carnegie Mellon University. I would like to thank my adviser Steven Schlossman for his initial suggestion that I pursue the subject of juvenile justice and for his guidance as I finished my dissertation. Joe William Trotter's difficult questions helped me refine many important points about the dynamics of race and class in Memphis child welfare.

Many people in Memphis made this work possible. I would like to thank the staff of the Juvenile Court of Memphis and Shelby County for their hospitality and support of the project. Bob Martin, clerk of court, gave me permission to use the court records, and Bill Dougherty answered my many questions. The staff at the Memphis Room and History Division of the Memphis Public Library assisted me in my data gathering, answered questions, and cheered me on while I was sitting at the microfilm machine.

Colleagues at Saint Leo University have also helped my book along. Many of my students have been among my most enthusiastic supporters, and I have been touched by their interest in the project. We have so much in common, having all survived Senior Seminar. The reference librarians and interlibrary loan staff helped me find obscure articles and meet my deadlines. I would also like to thank the vice president of Academic Affairs for giving me time to complete the writing of the book. Both he and my department chair have encouraged me as a young historian.

Great friends have also supported me over the years at various stages of my life and work. Lisa Sigel, Joe and Jennifer Spillane, Loretta Lobes, Tim Haggerty, Jared Day, and Kirsten Guss have edited, advised, commiserated, consoled, or cajoled. They each know their contribution to this book. Greta Niu, Audrey Colombe, Martha Serpas, Kathryn Duncan, Carol Ann Moon, and Elna Green have all been happy for me. Finally, Jim Longhurst is my closest intellectual and emotional companion. Your book is next!

Gateway to Justice

Introduction

THIS STUDY EXPLORES the relationship between social welfare and criminal justice history by looking at juvenile justice and child welfare in a southern city. The juvenile court in Memphis, Tennessee, served as a gateway to a network of public and private agencies for both dependent and delinquent children. Using court sources makes it possible to explore the fascinating stories and complex struggles of black and white working-class families and their interaction with child welfare officials. The crimes and characteristics of the children who passed through the justice system influenced the operation of both the juvenile court and the welfare network. In addition, community members used the juvenile court as mediator of family disputes, enforcer of standards of behavior, and dispenser of welfare. Both black and white parents turned to the court to deal with their unruly children. Comparing dependency and delinquency cases that came before the court shows that while white families both benefited from the court's attempt to alleviate their dire circumstances and chafed under its intrusion, black children primarily, though not exclusively, experienced the juvenile court coercively as delinquents. This study shows that racial ideology has always affected juvenile courts and that, in the urban South, the juvenile court was a crucial component to social welfare provisions.

PROGRESSIVISM AND JUVENILE JUSTICE

Progressivism and juvenile justice coincided during the American child-saving movement, which flourished between the 1850s and the 1920s. Many institutional innovations on behalf of children embodied new concepts of childhood. As Anthony Platt has contended, the child-saving movement sought to control delinquency by significantly expanding the power of the state. The movement also expressed reformers' strong value preferences toward the nuclear family, agricultural labor, and Protestant nativism.[1] New middle-class conceptions of childhood gave rise to a wide variety of specific reforms, including juvenile courts and other institutions for delinquent and dependent children, and also produced dramatic expansions of state authority such as regulation of child labor and enforcement of compulsory schooling.

The child-saving movement incorporated G. Stanley Hall's isolation of childhood as a distinct psychological and developmental stage. Hall's theories of childhood play and self-discovery influenced a variety of Progressive Era reforms in the areas of recreation and education. His naturalistic theories emphasized that everyone in the human race went through the same set of developmental stages. Despite Hall's distinctive psychological contributions to a theory of delinquency (see chapter 5), most Progressive reformers continued to blame delinquency on bad parental or environmental circumstances. Hall's ideas were used, if at all, to justify greater separation of children from poor or unfit parents.[2]

The concept of *parens patriae,* whereby the state assumed the role of parent, provided the legal and philosophical justification for the creation of reform schools and juvenile courts. This doctrine gave judges great power in determining social policy and reaffirming the constitutionality of institutions for neglected children. In 1905, in *Commonwealth v. Fisher,* the appellate court of Pennsylvania confirmed the power of the state to intervene to protect the welfare of the child. This ruling upheld a boy's commitment by a Philadelphia juvenile court judge to the city house of refuge despite his father's attempt to have him released.[3] The juvenile court movement swept the country in the early twentieth century, and the very first court opened in Chicago in 1899. Although most proponents of the juvenile court subscribed to common legal and child welfare principles, procedures and personalities were different in each court. Because the juvenile court was more diverse in practice than in theory, it is best to think of many juvenile courts rather than *the* juvenile court.[4] During the past quarter century, the extent and effects of juvenile court jurisdiction over family matters have been a starting point for many debates among scholars about the proper role of the state in child welfare.

The juvenile court movement introduced several measures into judicial proceedings to keep children out of adult court. Probation officers often acted as mediators between a family, social welfare agencies, and law enforcement officers to determine informally whether a child should be brought to court in the first place. If a child was brought to court, separate facilities and procedures were to be used. Children were to be kept in age-segregated detention houses and were, if at all possible, to continue schoolwork while detained. Another innovation was the adult delinquency statute, which was intended to eliminate bad parenting. The most important operational component of the juvenile court (not strictly "new" but never fully popularized or institutionalized until after the turn of the century) was probation.[5] Although commitment to a custodial institution was considered a necessary treatment option, probationary supervision of a child in his or her own home was viewed as the ideal disposition. Heavy reliance on probation captured the anti-institutional strain of the Progressive movement. Probation officers, as symbols of the aspirations of the entire Progressive Era child welfare movement, were supposed to uplift clients through casework and personalize justice through therapeutic, one-on-one relationships.[6]

Juvenile courts, not surprisingly, were not fully implemented according to these ideals. One contemporary criticism of the court was its expansive jurisdiction. The court exerted its influence in all directions in order to fill a void in early-twentieth-century public child welfare services. In addition to delinquency and dependency cases, juvenile courts exercised a variety of relief duties. Many courts administered mothers' pensions and heard non-support cases because, at the time, no other agencies existed to administer these programs. By the early 1920s critics began to argue that the court should have more limited jurisdiction. Some even suggested that the court should not hear cases of neglect or dependence.[7]

The vagueness of "dependency" and its overlapping definition with "delinquency" lay at the heart of this debate. Here we have one of the most contentious issues in social welfare history: the ambivalence of social reformers toward clientele, and its corollary, the criminalization of poverty. A study done for the Russell Sage Foundation in 1921 found that children in many cities were committed to institutions for delinquents on charges such as "lack of care," "death of a mother and drunken father," or "desertion of father and drunkenness of mother."[8] The Memphis Juvenile Court, as we shall see, often committed dependent children to the Industrial School because the orphanages were full, no family members lived nearby, or no other viable placement alternative existed. The hazy relationship between delinquency and dependency in southern juvenile justice is a major concern throughout this study.

Much of the disillusionment with the juvenile court that began in the 1920s rested on differences between the theory and practice of juvenile justice. In reality, probation officers and judges were often little more than ex-police officers, untrained volunteers, or political hacks. Caseloads were much too high for officers to provide individual attention, and institutions were continually crowded and poorly run. Thus the idea of specialized and highly trained probation officers working in courts of compassion was quickly overwhelmed by lack of money and expertise.

Previous studies about juvenile courts pay special attention to the ideology of people who founded or ran the courts, emphasize the power of the court to control individuals and families, and focus mainly on delinquency cases. These institutional studies isolate the juvenile court from its social context, downplay the welfare role of the court, and assume that the court exercised degrees of social control far beyond what was actually the case. Randall Shelden, for example, argues that the founders of the Memphis Juvenile Court were from the city's upper and middle classes and that they sought to bolster their own white, upper-class hegemony over city affairs by creating new institutions of social control.[9] Steven Schlossman, while sensitive to the experiences of clientele, makes little mention of dependency and neglect but explores in great detail the dynamics of probation and delinquency. And Eric Schneider also argues that reformers in Boston used the juvenile justice system as a tool of cultural hegemony and that court officials became moral coaches for their working-class clients. Because much of the debate centers on the creators of the juvenile court and their power over the court's clientele, insufficient attention has been paid to the children and adults who came before the court, and the broader social context of the court.[10]

A family-oriented study provides fresh insight into the goals and results of welfare institutions in early-twentieth-century urban America. Historians who have cast the juvenile court as an agent of overbearing power over the working class and their delinquent children have tended to overestimate its autonomy.[11] When one looks from the inside of the juvenile court outward, a different picture of its operations emerges. The Memphis Juvenile Court case files reveal not only extensive cooperation between parents and court officials but also a court that generally lacked the resources to keep pace with community demands or engage in systematic oversight of neglected and delinquent children. The interplay between public and private actors, between the legal right of the state to intervene and familial authority, highlights the degree to which juvenile justice policy was created by a dynamic combination of multiple forces.

The degree to which the juvenile court of Memphis intruded into the lives of its clients is ambiguous. The court, to be sure, had punitive and coercive tendencies, and Chief Judge Camille Kelley occasionally overstepped her legal authority. Plenty of the parents, moreover, expressed annoyance at the intrusiveness of court officials. If the court had a larger staff, it would probably have engaged in the kind of systematic oversight of its clientele that child welfare reformers advocated. The reality, however, was that the Memphis Juvenile Court, like those in most cities, was continually underfunded and hampered in its efforts to engage in the personal, therapeutic casework that Progressive child welfare workers strongly advocated. Furthermore, family members in Memphis, not unlike those in Boston or Los Angeles described by Linda Gordon and Mary Odem, often invited court personnel to enter aggressively into their lives.[12] Community members also used the court to mediate neighborhood disputes and enforce race relations and thereby reinforced local standards of behavior. Thus the court's intrusion into the lives of families was selective. Its decision to intrude was usually a response to community-initiated demands rather than an autonomous or arbitrary action initiated on its own.

Many dimensions of American juvenile justice have not been studied systematically by social, legal, or social welfare historians. Most notably, the history of juvenile courts in the South and southern social welfare policy more generally have received limited attention.[13] A key component of a southern study is the dual racial system. The treatment of blacks in the juvenile justice system has been almost entirely ignored by historians, who have argued that reformers "invented the juvenile court" as a way to control the behavior of European immigrants crowding into American cities around the turn of the century.[14] This explanation does not apply to Memphis, however, because by the early twentieth century, much of the immigrant population had left or died during the yellow fever epidemic in the 1870s and had been replaced by white and black migrants from the surrounding countryside. Explaining the creation of the court mainly as a way for the white-dominated state to control the new black population in Memphis is not entirely persuasive either. As we shall see, leading black citizens were actors in the operation of the segregated juvenile justice system. Other scholars have argued that changing racial dynamics in the twentieth century have contributed to the transformation of the juvenile court into an explicitly punitive institution.[15] Black children, racial ideology, and the competing goals of social welfare and criminal control have shaped the operations of the juvenile court since it was founded.

The juvenile court in Memphis served as a gateway to justice for dependent and delinquent children. With the founding of the court in 1910, the city created a formal and legal structure that served to direct children into the various private charitable agencies and public correctional centers. By the end of 1920 the juvenile court in Memphis had become well-established and stable. Throughout the ensuing decade it refined its policies and procedures, hired professionals, and expanded its role as a policy-making institution. The operation of the court strengthened ties between existing private efforts and fledgling public institutions. It unified disparate community efforts and haphazard state attempts to provide a system of child welfare, turning them into a well-integrated network of juvenile justice and charity. The establishment of the juvenile court embodied the city's growing sense of responsibility to run both a criminal justice system and a social welfare system that were child oriented and separate from adults.

Historians have debated the content and timing of Progressive reform and the extent of social welfare provision in the American South. Because the early-twentieth-century South remained more rural and agricultural, and many of the problems addressed by Progressives resulted from rapid urbanization, the general chronology of the national Progressive movement was from 1890 to World War I. Recently, however, historians have extended the reform impulse into the 1920s, particularly with regard to the activities of women and social welfare. So while the hallmarks of Progressive reform, such as an activist government, professionalized social work, and environmental approaches to poverty, made their way through the South, they did so later than in places that had urbanized in the nineteenth century. Therefore, even though this story takes place in the 1920s, it is very much one of Progressivism.

MEMPHIS AND SOUTHERN SOCIAL WELFARE

As a growing city and a regional distribution center, Memphis, Tennessee, provides an excellent case study of Progressivism and urban social welfare in the South. Located on the Mississippi River in the western end of the state, Memphis has always been Tennessee's largest city. In the nineteenth century its economy was dominated by the sale and shipping of cotton and the continued availability of cheap black labor. Manufacturing and building enterprises became increasingly important, and by the early twentieth century Memphis was the South's fifth largest urban manufacturing center. Railroad, levee, and street construction, riverboats, cotton warehouses, cottonseed oil factories, gins, saw mills, and foundries provided employment for wage laborers.[16] Despite industrial growth, the Memphis economy relied mostly on cotton. Wages for industrial workers in Memphis remained lower than those in the North and were concentrated in marginal or locally based industries. Sharecropping and the cotton system undermined the development of a diversified economy and reinforced white supremacist ideology. The economic base of Memphis relegated blacks to the lowest paying and least desirable occupations and neighborhoods and reinforced racial segregation.

From the late nineteenth century onward, Memphis had a substantial black population, and the implications of the racial composition of the city were played out in the provision of charity and corrections. Unlike other juvenile courts where the religion or ethnicity of the clientele strongly shaped the welfare experience, in the Memphis Juvenile Court race was more central.[17] The city had legally segregated institutions, and private organizations, more by custom than by law, also directed their efforts toward specific racial groups. The Memphis Municipal Code specified that the city was to maintain two detention homes for children in the care of the juvenile court—one for white children and one for black children. Detention homes were still legally segregated as late as 1949.[18] However, in a city that in 1920 was about 40 percent black, there was a gap between policies that tried to enforce public segregation and the close contact that existed between whites and blacks in their private lives.

Memphis was a notable exception to the almost complete political exclusion of blacks in the South that took place during the Progressive Era. Although there is some disagreement among historians about the beginning of black disfranchisement in Tennessee, blacks managed to sustain some political participation in Memphis. In the election of 1914 Mayor E. H. Crump (also known as Boss Crump) organized a write-in campaign among black voters to help his handpicked successor. Crump and a prominent black Republican, Robert Church Jr., aligned in 1924 to defeat Ku Klux Klan candidates. In return for their support, blacks insisted on city services such as parks, hospitals, and schools. Blacks in Memphis enjoyed more political participation, even under the restrictions of Crump's voting machine, than in other southern cities.[19]

From the founding of child welfare institutions in the nineteenth century to the elaboration of these various agencies into a true welfare network in the 1920s, Memphis was linked to national developments in child welfare reform. However, the city had regional characteristics centered on the importance of race relations and the city's continued reliance on private provision of welfare. Memphis, as the main city serving a very poor, rural hinterland, experienced a continual influx of rural white and black migrants who brought with them their values of self-sufficiency, paternalism, and racial tension. Along with a commercial-civic elite that dominated Memphis government, these migrants shaped the needs of the city's social welfare system along lines very different from those in most northern cities.

For a variety of reasons, social welfare historians have downplayed developments in the South. One reason for the dearth of southern studies is the misconception among many social welfare historians that their interpretations, personalities, and issues speak to developments in the South.[20] Many studies of social welfare history focus on public systems of provision and concentrate on the northeastern United States, especially New York and Boston.[21] Since these works are mainly interested in explaining the origins of public welfare, they tend to portray volunteerism as a premodern stage of welfare rather than as an enduring strategy for meeting human need, as in the South. The relationship between voluntary and public responsibility for social welfare, in short, has not been adequately analyzed because previous scholars either do not address southern developments or do not evaluate voluntary efforts as positive expressions of mutual responsibility. Social welfare provision in Memphis represented a mixture of the cultural values of a strong community and a changing state that reflected the rural background of much of the Memphis population.[22]

Historians of the South have also slighted social welfare institutions. Older studies that focused on southern reform argued somewhat defensively that Progressivism and social justice reform did indeed have a place in the South.[23] These early studies of southern social welfare presented it as an offspring of northern philanthropy but paid scant attention to indigenous social welfare provisions. They also overlooked the role of blacks in setting up their own institutions, and the complexity of race relations by declaring that Progressivism was for "whites only." More recent studies of southern social welfare have provided a partial corrective, drawing especially on research examining the self-help efforts of black women.[24] By analyzing the gaps in welfare provision that black women tried to fill, scholars of black history have provided the most nuanced treatment of welfare issues in the South. Nevertheless, the history of social welfare institutions in the South remains incomplete.[25]

The relationship between white and black systems of social welfare in the twentieth-century South has also not been explored by historians. Black women and men established a variety of benevolent societies, orphanages, playgrounds, and schools in Memphis for their own community.[26] In addition to these, however, white charitable organizations often provided services to children of both races. Further, although blacks did not take the lead in establishing a juvenile court or custodial institutions such as the Shelby County Industrial and Training School, they did work to obtain equal access to and fair treatment from those institutions.[27] Black working-class parents in the juvenile court, as we shall see, often used it for their own purposes in much the same way as white working-class parents: to buttress their authority within the family. Thus black children were not excluded from the child welfare system in Memphis.

WOMEN AND MATERNAL JUSTICE

The juvenile court of Memphis and Shelby County was founded amid a burst of female reform efforts on behalf of the city's children and allows us to follow the development of a maternal state. Led by Suzanne Scruggs, founder of the Children's Protective Union, several middle-class white women's organizations pushed for the establishment of a juvenile court. The female influence in social welfare work continued in a more formal manner with the appointment of Camille Kelley as chief judge of the Memphis Juvenile Court in 1920. Judge Kelley was the first woman in the South to be selected for such a position, where she remained until retiring in 1950.[28] Beulah Wood Fite was named chief probation officer in 1924, and over the next twenty years, at least five other women held official positions in the court. Thus the Memphis Juvenile Court highlights the existence of a middle-class female charity network and provides an opportunity to deepen historical understanding of the implications of gender for child welfare policy. Memphis women successfully campaigned for state child welfare legislation. The Memphis branch of the Children's Bureau did not have a male director until

1950. The Memphis Juvenile Court and the social welfare network it helped create provide an opportunity to see the similarities between a female-led juvenile justice system and the male-led systems of juvenile justice created in other early-twentieth-century cities.

Recent scholarship on the role of women as creators of welfare policy has prompted analysis of what have been called the "maternal state" and "maternal justice."[29] From this vantage point, middle-class women designed policies that often discriminated against their working-class sisters. Professional women's own desires for careers rested on their public identification with and control over social policy issues that involved women and children. They tended to define social problems, such as family stability among the poor, so as to make women's actions central to a solution; in the process, they tied women inextricably to home, children, and sexuality. Women policy makers designed legislation that protected the principle of a male-headed family wage system.[30] In the Memphis Juvenile Court, moreover, women participated in reinforcing double standards of behavior by punishing adolescent girls but not boys, and poor mothers but not fathers for sexual misbehavior.[31] And finally, while Judge Kelley did not obviously punish black delinquents more harshly than white delinquents, she did very little to change the racial system of justice nor showed particular sensitivity to the needs of her black clients. Thus case file evidence that followed families and children through the juvenile court shows maternalism to have been primarily rhetorical rather than a substantive or consistent difference in policy or procedure.

To date, the historical investigation of women's roles in creating twentieth-century welfare policy has had little to say about southern developments. The Memphis Juvenile Court, with its female officers, also policed adolescent female sexuality. However, the court did not act autonomously. Working-class white and black parents both used the juvenile court to reinforce their authority within the family and to control their daughters' emerging sexual identity and behavior. Judge Kelley's court actively used the most punitive option, institutionalization, but mainly for white girls; it mostly released black girls. Thus, in Memphis, race also influenced treatment decisions in ways that add new complexity to understanding the interplay of gender, race, and sexuality in early-twentieth-century child welfare policy.

My analysis of juvenile justice and the child welfare network in Memphis relies heavily on the confidential case files of the Memphis Juvenile Court.

These documents (probation officer reports; summaries of court hearings; correspondence between court officials, other agencies, and families; and psychiatric evaluations) reveal family motivations and experiences, court goals and methods, and extensive cooperation among child welfare agencies in Memphis in unusual detail.[32] The Memphis Juvenile Court case files show the enormous efforts that the local government committed to its vulnerable children and their families. Other primary sources that shed light on community attitudes toward poverty and delinquency include minutes from the Memphis Council of Social Agencies and local newspaper accounts of child welfare issues and important personalities.

The study is divided into five chapters. Chapter 1 shows that, as an urban center, Memphis attracted many rural migrants who possessed few private connections to draw upon for assistance during the frequent economic downturns of the early twentieth century. At the same time, Progressive reformers gradually expanded the role of local government by increasing its range of public services and regulatory powers. Chapter 2 argues that Memphis reformers, like those in other American cities, established a quintessentially "Progressive" child welfare system based largely around a juvenile court. Moreover, maternal justice dominated this Progressive system and, at least rhetorically, offered a friendly model of welfare. Chapter 3 argues that because of its broad jurisdiction and the strong personality of Judge Kelley, the juvenile court served as the gateway to the city's child welfare network. Further, with the juvenile court in place, the agencies and organizations that dealt with children and made welfare policy in Memphis formed a self-conscious child welfare network. Chapter 4 demonstrates that the many community definitions of dependency shaped the court's extensive social welfare role. Dependency cases highlight the degree to which members of the white community used the juvenile court for assistance with a variety of family emergencies. Chapter 5 shows that black as well as white parents used the juvenile court to control their daughters' sexuality. It also finds that male delinquents, rather than committing status offenses, primarily engaged in criminal behavior such as petty theft, particularly of coal. The study concludes with suggestions for further research and also proposes that a juvenile court with more social services to offer entire families might be more successful than one relegated to only criminal matters.

CHAPTER ONE

The City of Memphis
and Progressive Social Reform

THE NATIONAL AND LOCAL GEOGRAPHY of Memphis shaped much of its economic and social history. Located on the Mississippi River between St. Louis and New Orleans high up on the Chickasaw Bluffs, Memphis served as a distribution center for cotton, hardwood, and other natural resources between northern and southern cities. Linking the farmers of the upper Mississippi Valley with the manufacturing centers of the Northeast, Memphis prospered because of its importance in the national trade and transportation network. Its economic diversity made Memphis a frequent destination for migrants. The assorted demographic composition of the population and cultural values of the migrants inevitably affected the city's social and political history in many ways.

A series of migrations shaped the social structures of the city. European immigrants and southerners from the Tidewater region of the United States settled in the city before the Civil War. Transients from river or rail traffic became day laborers. After the Civil War, newly freed blacks poured into the city, seeking relief from racial persecution, and new economic opportunities. In the aftermath of the yellow fever epidemics of the 1870s, rural migrants, both black and white, moved to the city. While each successive group of people had distinctive expectations and values, all shared and brought to the city a characteristic set of rural assumptions about community and state power. The city's close ties to agricultural cycles and successive waves of rural migrants helped structure local politics and the provision of social welfare.

The persistence of rural values, such as community resistance to external or bureaucratic government, explains the particular patterns of reform in early-twentieth-century Memphis. Traditions of localism and individualism flourished among whites and blacks in villages and small towns and on farms in the Mississippi Valley in the absence of any strong representation of the state. Reliance on family networks and conservative evangelical Protestantism justified a biracial society and acceptance of low living standards in the rural South.[1] For blacks, the strategies of mutuality learned under slavery were reinforced on arrival to the city. Many unskilled laborers banded together in mutual relief and burial societies. The result of this value system was self-sufficiency, religious-based community building, and resistance to the intrusion from outsiders into matters that came under community control. Social policy, therefore, evolved around strong personalities and resulted from pockets of power rather than concentrated authority.[2]

As rural migrants streamed into the city, the power of local elites increased because rural white migrants and disfranchised blacks did not ask much of government except economic opportunities. Businessmen dominated Memphis city government. Municipal reform in Memphis, as in many other Progressive Era cities, was essentially conservative and focused on improving government efficiency, reducing financial waste, and expanding municipal services, principles that reflected the goals of the business leaders.[3] Despite the new administrative duties of city government, public authority remained weak and subservient to private interests and strong leaders.

Progressivism in Memphis transformed the relationship between individuals and government and fell into two main categories: political efficiency and social justice. Political reform consisted primarily of the provision of public services such as roads, sewerage and water, a health department, a fire department, and parks. These services increased governmental power in the public sphere. Social justice reforms, such as laws to regulate child labor, compel school attendance, or remove children from adult criminal courts, were usually carried out by women. These reforms increased state power in the private sphere since they all sought to reorganize family relations using new definitions of childhood. Although this new power brought the state into the everyday lives of many people for the first time, state intrusion was selective. Social welfare provision and racial equality remained the responsibility of the community. Not only was the expansion of state power selective, but also many people resisted this new state power. Parents, for example, often protested the juvenile court decisions, compulsory vaccination, and child labor regulation. Progressivism, then, represented an uneasy new alignment between state power and individuals or their community.

ECONOMIC FOUNDATIONS AND EARLY SOCIAL HISTORY

Tennessee is one of the most diversified states in the South. It has three grand divisions, each with geographical and cultural distinctions. East Tennessee was unsuited for plantations and slavery because of its mountains and valleys. The predominance of small farmers and the control of the Republican Party led to its opposition to secession and support of the Union. The capital city of Nashville dominated middle Tennessee, and although the region shared the antebellum plantation system, its economy was more varied because of tobacco and wheat farming, and its politics were strongly Democratic. Although west Tennessee had the largest city in the state (Memphis), it was the most rural of the three divisions. It had the largest concentration of blacks and was the center of the state's cotton production. The Democratic Party controlled the region and supported secession.[4] Thus, differences in soil, crops, tenancy systems, income levels, and credit institutions determined farming systems that in turn reflected the cultural diversity of Tennessee.[5]

Since Memphis was initially dominated by the cotton economy and the use of black slave labor, issues of race and class played important roles in its history. In the early nineteenth century, poor whites, American Indians, and a few free blacks along with migrating river men made up the population of Memphis and gave it a reputation for interracial mixing. As slavery became more profitable, however, city leaders imposed regulations on the civil and political rights of blacks in ways that reinforced whites' belief in their own racial superiority.[6] These restrictions on blacks' rights and the continuation of white supremacy ideals after the Civil War translated into segregated neighborhoods and schools and relegated blacks to the lowest levels of employment.

On the eve of the Civil War, the racial and ethnic diversity of Memphis was similar to that of other southern towns. In 1860 83 percent of the city's population was white and 17 percent was black. Of the white population, 36 percent were born outside the United States, with German and Irish immigrants making up the majority of the foreign population.[7] Most of the German immigrants were skilled laborers and played an important part in the commercial life of the city. However, the unskilled Irish, brought from the North to work on railroad construction, often competed with black laborers in occupations such as dockhands, barbering, and domestic help.[8] The rest of the white population consisted of native-born whites who were mostly southerners.

In a multiracial society, these racial and ethnic divisions translated into distinct social classes. The prosperous merchants, planters, and professionals composed of native southern whites made up the top layer of the Memphis social structure. German shopkeepers (dry goods mostly) and craftsmen along with other white proprietors, clerks, and teachers formed the middle class. Before railroad construction began, the most visible members of the Irish community were small property holders, merchants, grocers, professionals, and artisans. However, after 1850 the vast majority of the Irish were unskilled and propertyless, and they, along with black slaves, made up the lower class. Even before the Civil War, Memphis began to become a city divided into racial and ethnic enclaves. Between 1850 and 1860 the city developed two distinct residential zones: one made up of Irish and German immigrants and another made up of free blacks and slaves.[9] Thus residential segregation actually began before the rapid industrialization of the late nineteenth century.

The mixture of European immigrants' hostility to slavery and the relatively small number of free blacks or slaves in Memphis prompted major conflicts between unionists and secessionists for control of the city from Lincoln's election in November 1860 until the state referendum on secession in February 1861. Economic ties to the North made many Memphis citizens initially hostile to secession. The Irish and German population opposed secession and, because of their opposition to slavery, did not support the southern political cause. Not until the fall of Fort Sumter and Lincoln's call for troops in April 1861 did the merchants in Memphis, as well as the rest of Tennessee, vote to join the Confederacy. Although its surrounding countryside was devastated, few southern cities suffered as little from the Civil War or made such a rapid economic recovery as Memphis. Because of its capture in 1862 by the Union forces after only an hour-long gunboat battle, the city landscape and civilian population remained untouched.[10] Memphis played an important role in the trade of contraband goods between North and South and profited from the federal government's need for cotton.

The influx of newly freed blacks who participated in the day-to-day business life of Memphis was the most important social change after the Civil War. From 1860 to 1870 the number of blacks in Memphis increased from three thousand to fifteen thousand. Along with political enfranchisement, a system of schools for blacks was created during Reconstruction under the auspices of the Freedmen's Bureau. A stratified black class structure with a small but stable black middle class made up of property owners, artisans, ministers, and entrepreneurs (many of whom were free before the war) emerged in the 1870s. Former slaves working on railroads and levee construction made up the bulk of the emerging working class.[11] However, race relations reached a boiling point in 1866 when members of a black troop of federal soldiers tried to prevent several white policemen from making an arrest. The rest of the police force, predominantly Irish, along with firemen and politicians rushed to the scene and, in the ensuing disorder, began shooting blacks and burning buildings. After two days of rioting, forty-four blacks and two whites were dead, and twelve black schools and more than ninety homes were burned.[12]

In contrast to many other southern cities, blacks participated in the postwar political development of Memphis. During the 1870s at least a dozen blacks won seats on the city council. In the 1880s blacks from Memphis served in the state legislature and strengthened the Republican Party in Tennessee. Along with Democratic factionalism, the significant black population provided the Republicans with political clout until the end of the decade. By the late 1880s some black career politicians and property owners had become increasingly alienated from the Republican Party. After a decade of freedom, the mass of blacks had little to show for their support, and they shifted their voting strength to the Democratic Party. Imposition of voting restrictions and enforcement of Jim Crow legislation, however, diminished the nascent black political power and contributed to renewed black distrust of whites.[13]

During the 1870s one of the most important events in Memphis's history radically altered its demographic composition and solidified its racial divisions. After a series of yellow fever epidemics between 1873 and 1878, most of the Irish and German immigrant population either died or left the city. Many Germans who could afford to escape moved up the river to St. Louis, but the Irish were generally too poor to leave, and many of them died. In the 1870s the population of Memphis decreased from 40,226 to 33,592. The foreign-born population decreased from around 36 percent in 1860 to 8 percent in 1890 and to 5 percent by the turn of the century. After the epidemics, many blacks, by contrast, migrated to Memphis from the surrounding rural areas and by 1900 made up 49 percent of the population. The effect of the yellow fever epidemics combined with the later migration of both blacks and native-born whites created a city that was almost evenly divided by race but without its previous diversity among white ethnic groups. The wave of southern European immigration around the turn of the century bypassed Memphis, as it did almost the entire South. While most northern cities became increasingly diverse ethnically, Memphis became racially bipolar.[14]

The yellow fever epidemic also had an important impact on the political power structure of Memphis. The city owed six million dollars to New York bondholders, but in the aftermath of the epidemic, Memphis could not pay its creditors. The state legislature revoked the city's charter and made it a "taxing district" to avoid the suits of creditors. A board of commissioners consisting of members of the Merchants' Cotton Exchange, other bankers, lawyers, and merchants was granted governing powers. Since Memphis did not regain the right of self-government until the turn of the century, the creation of this taxing district consolidated power in the hands of private citizens who were wealthy business and professional men.[15] Although the Reconstruction leadership had been made up of middle-class professionals (lawyers) and traders, the creation of the taxing district paved the way for the return to power of the prewar business elites. This "commercial-civic elite" continued to control the city during the first part of the twentieth century.[16]

The industrialization of Memphis was part of the larger economic expansion of the "New South" after Reconstruction. An infusion of northern and foreign capital made the initial industrialization of Memphis possible. Following the 1870s depression, the South became an outlet for investments. Spurred by federal land sales policy that ended the practice of reserving public land for homesteading and opened the way for speculators, northern capitalists and numerous English ventures such as the North American Land and Timber Company, Limited, bought up millions of acres of land. Southern railroad development also attracted investments. A wave of financial consolidation followed the railroad construction boom so that by 1890, a dozen large companies based in New York controlled more than half of the railroad mileage in the South.[17] However, most of the goods they shipped passed through Memphis.

Memphis was an important distribution and commercial center. Ten trunk line railroads, numerous barge line terminals, and two bridges crossing the Mississippi River made Memphis the "Great Southern Gateway."[18] The Illinois Central Railroad and the river linked Memphis to other industrial centers such as Chicago and Pittsburgh. Memphis served as the southern and western distribution point for Jones and Laughlin Steel, automobiles, and farm equipment and was the government's port of call between St. Louis and New Orleans. Memphis had a branch of the Federal Reserve Bank along with eighteen banks and trust companies. Its major newspaper, the *Commercial Appeal,* had one of the largest circulations in the South.[19] The marketing of cotton, however, and trade in wholesale groceries were the most important commercial enterprises.

Since Memphis was in the heart of the cotton-producing region of the country, the sale and shipment of cotton and cottonseed products were its main industries. The Chamber of Commerce boasted in 1920 that Memphis was the largest inland cotton market in America and the world's largest producer of cottonseed products. Cottonseed industries included oil for soap and lard, and cattle feed.[20] By 1929, 14 percent of the total United States cotton crop passed through Memphis.[21] Other products associated with the cotton industry formed the small textile base of Memphis and included the Tri-State Dress Company, the American Bag Company, and the Memphis Tent and Awning Company.

The hardwood forests of the Mississippi Valley near Memphis made lumber and its distribution the city's other important industry. The lumber industry consisted of sawmills and planing mills. Most of the mills were located on the riverfront since the logs were floated down the river to Memphis. By 1900 an estimated five hundred mills within a hundred-mile radius of Memphis produced over one billion feet of lumber annually. Woodworking operations formed another part of the lumber industry. Initially, furniture and cooperage companies used a small percentage of the lumber for local building. Most of the lumber, however, was exported to domestic and foreign markets, so distribution was also part of the industry. By the 1920s the manufacturing of wood products exceeded lumber production. As the forest reserves decreased, the woodworking industry became more specialized. Automobile wheels and bodies, veneer, and other manufactured products replaced the less profitable milling and planing operations.[22]

Economic growth in Memphis followed national trends. The highest rate of economic expansion in Memphis occurred between 1880 and 1890. New railroad lines entered the city and connected Memphis to the growing cotton market of the Southwest. Manufacturing investments increased by 304 percent, and the value of manufactured goods increased by more than 200 percent. In 1891 Memphis was the fifth largest wholesale grocery market. The Panic of 1893 lowered the price of cotton and slowed investments. However, between 1899 and the end of World War I, investments, construction, and the number of wage earners in industry all increased. In addition, the wartime demand for cotton brought some prosperity to white and black cotton growers.[23]

The Memphis class structure from the end of Reconstruction to the 1930s was tied to the cotton and agricultural economy and growing commercial networks. With the emancipation of slaves and breakup of the large plantations, the cotton factor replaced the planter in the control of cotton production. Cotton factors were financial intermediaries, or "the planter's banker," because they financed the plantation operator's crop, sold it, and received a commission.[24] Since much of the land was destroyed in the war, planters raised their crops on credit advanced to them by cotton factors who then acted as brokers for the planters' cotton crop. As presidents of the large banks, cotton factors controlled local finances. Cotton firms also conducted large wholesale grocery trades and as a result, according to one historian, "cotton factors ruled Memphis during the eighties and the nineties."[25]

With the economic boom of the 1880s, stratified classes among whites and blacks emerged. The native-born planter elites of antebellum Memphis dominated the city's political and social life. Other entrepreneurs who did not belong to this older group of families included a sizable group of mercantile capitalists who owned or managed railroad lines, river barges, warehouses, or timber companies. Manufacturers also made up part of the city's economic elite. They specialized in cotton and hardwood production and processing. These two major industries relied on unskilled black labor. Except for printing and publishing companies and Ford Motor (which made wooden auto bodies), nearly all manufacturers employed large numbers of blacks.[26]

The rapid industrialization and commercial expansion during the 1880s and early 1890s contributed to the city's emerging white middle class, which consisted of retail dealers, salespeople, clerks, and insurance agents. White men dominated professional occupations in government (judges, lawyers, sheriffs), the media (writers, editors), and college education.[27] The city's industrial working class included those who worked in factories, personal service, and a variety of skilled and unskilled occupations. Memphis had a stagnant industrial base during the 1920s and 1930s because cotton and commercial interests continued to dominate the economy.[28] Domestic and personal service, however, employed the largest number of workers, 25 percent of the Memphis workforce. For blacks, domestic and personal service employed 46 percent of the workforce.[29]

During the 1920s Memphis gained a reputation as a place of black capitalism. The city's black professional and middle class included undertakers, ministers, teachers, doctors and dentists, and postal carriers and porters.

Two black banks, Roddy's Citizen Cooperative Stores, the Tri-State Casket Company, several undertaking firms, insurance agencies, and retail and restaurant establishments along with black professionals in medicine and law made up the business community. Insurance companies for accident and burial were the fastest growing businesses. These insurance companies formalized some of the work of benevolent societies begun by working-class black women after the Civil War.[30] A black press was started. Black banks struggled to remain solvent, and when the Fraternal and Solvent Savings Bank and Trust Company failed in 1927, it reverberated into the entire black community, and civic and fraternal groups limited their activities. Middle-class blacks of the early twentieth century came to rely on a black clientele more than the post-Reconstruction middle class. Blacks had shown their willingness to invest in racial businesses and continued to do so as an expression of racial consciousness.[31]

The distribution of employment among different occupations in Memphis during the 1920s had noticeable racial patterns. White men dominated wholesale and retail trade, the building industry, public service, and professional and semiprofessional services. Black men predominated in saw and planing mills, domestic and personal service, hotels and restaurants, and unspecified industrial occupations. Occupational segregation was even greater among women in Memphis. White women worked in a wide range of service occupations, including telegraph and telephone, wholesale and retail trade, and other professional and semiprofessional service in addition to some manufacturing industries. In contrast, black women worked primarily in domestic and personal service, laundries and pressing shops, and hotels and restaurants. In 1930 these occupational categories accounted for 85 percent of black female wage earners. Black women also participated in the paid workforce at a higher rate than white women.[32]

In addition to the commercial nature of the Memphis economy, which linked the city to national developments, the surrounding rural Mississippi Delta also shaped the social character of Memphis. Memphis was the urban heart of the black-majority plantation region of the lower South. In 1900 Shelby County was 55 percent black. Fayette County (the next county east) was 73 percent black and, out of a population of thirty thousand, had no locality with a population of twenty-five hundred or more.[33] In 1920 Tunica, Mississippi, about 40 miles south of Memphis, was 85.8 percent black. In this region the sharecropping system of farming was nearly universal and brought blacks and whites into almost daily contact. Even though schools, churches, social clubs, and cemeteries were segregated, blacks and whites shared country stores, cotton gins, and roads. Despite ever-present class and racial hostility, the boss-hand, creditor-debtor relationship was personal and frequent. Although predominantly black, much of the countryside was racially integrated.[34] While Memphis may have been a commercial and industrial center, its outlying areas were decidedly rural, and it was these people who made up its principal labor force.[35]

Since Memphis offered more opportunities and higher wages than a rural subsistence economy, it attracted a variety of people, most of them from western Tennessee and Mississippi. Between fifty thousand and sixty thousand people moved to Memphis during the 1880s and 1890s after the yellow fever epidemics had subsided.[36] By 1915 the boll weevil had crossed the Mississippi River, devastated many farmers, and pushed many landless farmers, many of them black sharecroppers, into the cities.[37] Between 1910 and 1930 the population of Memphis as well as other larger southern cities more than doubled. The propensity to move, although intensifying after the turn of the century, was not a new phenomenon. From the end of the Civil War, landless tenants and sharecroppers moved frequently, looking for better soil, crops, housing, and landlords.[38]

In addition to economic pressures, social factors affected the decision to migrate, although the meanings and trajectory of migration were somewhat different for white and black southerners. Increased freedom or anonymity in the cities, expectations of industrial and wage employment, opportunities for schooling, and the presence of family members all influenced white and black families' decision to leave the countryside. Many migrants moved permanently, but for some, the itinerant life was a means to return to farming. They worked in mills or factories in order to buy their own land and retreat to the country.[39] Opportunities for schooling also lured black families to Memphis.[40] In addition to moving to southern cities as a final destination, the mobility of black southerners served as an assertion of freedom and a prelude to the Great Migration north.[41]

Thus migration to Memphis did not always mean a dramatic break with the countryside, because white and black farmers maintained connections between family farms and the city. The kinship and community resources supported not only trips north but also the return trips south.[42] Migration, then, was a fluid process that consisted of decisions based on a family's seasonal income needs, crop cycles, the stage in life course, and family structure. Among blacks, single young adult men and women were in the best position to migrate to nearby southern cities.[43] In contrast, whole white families moved from mill town to mill town. While some families may have had networks of support in Memphis, many had few community ties, such as church affiliation. This seasonal movement back and forth between Memphis and nearby cotton fields is evident in the Memphis Juvenile Court case files, which also indicate that many families did not belong to a church in Memphis even if they listed a religious affiliation. It was these families who often came to the attention of, or sought assistance from, social welfare agencies.

Migration to the city required some adjustments for rural white and black families. Most important, they had to adapt to neighborhood segregation and new codes of public behavior, although segregation, as opposed to outright exclusion from public accommodations, did allow some fluidity in race relations.[44] Despite increasing urban segregation, there was still potential for interracial interaction because pockets of working-class whites and blacks continued to live near one another in many southern cities at the turn of the century.[45] White and black migrants also encountered different economic opportunities once they arrived in Memphis. Despite economic expansion and experience with industrial work in rural mill towns, mines, or scattered steel plants, black men and women had few industrial opportunities in Memphis.[46] These economic and social factors contributed to the city's complex race relations.

The continual influx of rural migrants gave Memphis its distinctive southern characteristics. These migrants, who came to the city amid dispossession and various depressions in the countryside, provided cheap unskilled labor and kept Memphis wages low compared to other cities. The migrants also carried with them the assumptions of white supremacy and other traditional and rural values.[47] The use by whites and blacks of extralegal means to settle conflicts (dueling, rioting, and vigilantism) characterized the system of authority that prevailed in the rural South.[48] If rural whites believed themselves to be above the law, blacks saw themselves as outside the law, since whites had destroyed blacks' faith in the law. Black honor, therefore, fed on white injustice but was usually contained within the black community. Honor and vengeance, the acceptance of the private use of force, and self-sufficiency clashed with the constraints of urban living and helped produce in Memphis a tradition of lawlessness and violence that led one contemporary observer to call Memphis the most "rural-minded" city in the South.[49]

POLITICS AND PROGRESSIVE REFORM

The era of political and social reform in Memphis followed the economic growth and geographical expansion of the city. During the first two decades of the twentieth century, city leaders enacted many Progressive reform measures that created administrative structures to serve an increasingly industrial and densely populated city. At the turn of the century, Memphis had just over 100,000 residents and was the third largest city in the South. By 1920 Memphis had a population of 162,351 and was the sixth largest city in the South.[50] In 1929 the population was over 200,000. A series of annexations in 1909, 1913, 1917, and 1919 nearly doubled the size of Memphis. Streetcars could not meet transportation needs, and increases in automobiles overburdened the street system.[51] The city had outmoded public schools, inadequate public health measures, and deficient fire and police departments. Having grown into much more than a river town, Memphis lagged in the development of new administrative structures.

Progressive reform in Memphis selectively increased the power of the state over the private life of home and family and attempted to reform the state itself by elevating it above the sway of political interests and by increasing its responsibility for public services. Municipal reformers in Memphis, as well as the entire South, stressed efficiency and modernization; much of the reform initiative came from businessmen.[52] As part of a southern "search for order," reformers in Memphis focused on regulation of business, efficiency in politics, and control of morality.[53] These Progressive reformers did not radically seek to change the status quo, particularly regarding race relations, but simply wanted to ameliorate the worst social conditions.[54]

No one dominated the political history of Memphis as thoroughly as Edward Hull Crump. As in many other southern cities, urban reform came in the guise of a city boss, and Crump's reputation as an autocrat was unsurpassed by that of any other twentieth-century political boss.[55] Nevertheless, he led the first wave of Progressive reforms in Memphis while he was mayor and began a series of important initiatives that continued during the 1920s. Crump's veneer of big-city Progressivism masked the rural traditions of paternalism and localism. The lack of political competition that resulted from the one-party state and disfranchisement helps explain his rise to power and made it possible for him to advance Progressive innovations that increased the regulatory power and service functions of the city government.

Most portraits of Crump focus on his political power and his transformation into an urban boss in the 1930s, but his importance in the early 1900s is the example he set as a reformer. His business background and quest for efficiency had an impact on social welfare provision in Memphis. He embraced Progressive innovations such as the juvenile court that increased the power of the state, but he was a quintessential paternalist toward his city. He appealed to neighborhood ideas of community, and his subsequent power illustrates the weakness of public institutions in Memphis.

Like many people who grew up in small towns, Crump migrated from nearby Holly Springs, Mississippi, to Memphis in search of better opportunities. When he was in his early twenties, he began working as a bookkeeper for a carriage and saddlery firm and, after several years of hard work, advanced into the executive circle. In 1900 Crump became secretary and treasurer of the newly consolidated Woods-Chickasaw Manufacturing Company. Much of his early business success came from his marriage into a family of wealth and respectability. In 1902 he borrowed fifty thousand dollars from his wife's parents and bought the Woods-Chickasaw company. He later changed it to the "E.H. Crump Buggy Company."[56] His new company did well and he used it, along with his high-status marriage, to rise into the business elite of Memphis. Crump eventually became a millionaire from his own real estate and mortgage loan business.

Crump's entry into politics began with his election to the city council in 1905 as a reform candidate. While he was chairman of the electric committee, he issued a series of recommendations to make city administration more economical and to protect the public interest. His first high-profile job was that of fire and police commissioner. He gained the reputation for dramatizing issues when he led a series of raids on notorious prostitution and gambling houses to embarrass the police chief and mayor and to show the public that law enforcement under the current administration was a sham.[57] The logical next step for Crump was the mayor's office, which provided a springboard for his long involvement in city politics. He served as mayor from 1910 until 1915 and developed a reputation for political invincibility.

Crump made lasting contributions in three ways: reforming city administration, maintaining moderate race relations, and improving city services. Crump's most notable contribution to city administration was his role in establishing the commission government in Memphis to replace the mayor-council type of government. The commission was designed to overcome political factionalism by emphasizing nonpolitical and efficient administration with simplified and centralized municipal duties. The new system did result in financial savings for the city and better provision of urban services such as roads, street lighting, and sewerage.[58] Crump tightened tax assessment procedures, sought public ownership of utilities, and ran the city with businesslike fiscal efficiency.

Despite increasing racial hostility during this time, Crump maintained stable race and class relations. In 1914 his choice for sheriff had not been able to get his name on the ballot, but Crump decided to organize a write-in campaign. Counting on the black vote, the Crump forces sent large numbers into working-class black neighborhoods to teach them how to write "Riechman," the candidate's name. Riechman won by a large majority. The *Commercial Appeal*, a longtime critic of Crump, became incensed that he would teach working-class blacks to write and, fearing his power, called the write-in campaign an "exhibition of the power and evils of machine politics in Memphis."[59] Although working-class blacks did not have a real choice in candidates, they did vote because Crump paid their poll taxes, and elite black leaders bartered for favors and limited recognition. Crump showed concern about the lack of a city park for blacks. Over some objections from within his administration, Crump pushed through a plan for the purchase of land that became Douglass Park, named after Frederick Douglass.[60]

The person with equivalent political power in Memphis among African Americans was Robert Church Jr., whose father had come to Memphis during Reconstruction. From 1912 until 1940 Church provided Republicans in Tennessee with their most consistent source of black support. Church made his fortune in real estate and various small businesses. During that time he served as a delegate for the Republican Party's national convention and formed the Lincoln League. The league adopted a platform that called for "direct measures" to end discrimination in civil service appointments, to end peonage restricting free migration of labor, to enact antilynching laws, to denounce Jim Crow laws, to include more blacks in the armed services, and to provide federal and state funding for black schools. The league also educated black voters about election issues.[61]

Church's activities invigorated blacks in Memphis and created political awareness. He represented what the historian Lester Lamon describes as "black progressivism." The Progressive response of blacks was more narrow than that of whites. Instead of clinging to a heritage of individualism, middle-class and elite blacks struggled to achieve recognition of their freedom and concentrated on an expanded concept of social justice.[62] Church's power offered protection for middle- and working-class blacks in Memphis, and during the 1920s the two powers coexisted and respected each other's domain. Crump refrained from race baiting and harassment while Church worked with federal officials and avoided local affairs. Not until the decline of Republican power in Washington, D.C., did Crump challenge Church.[63]

While Crump was mayor, he presided over the transition of Memphis from a riverboat town into an urban, industrial center. The need for expanded city services was crucial. He began efforts to improve public health by regulating the city's milk supply; to expand the park system, sewerage, and roads; and to modernize the fire and police departments. The reduction of crime was one of his toughest challenges because, during the 1910s, Memphis held a national reputation as a lawless city. The high rates of crime and violence, the widespread use of drugs, prostitution, and weak law enforcement contributed to the disorder of the city. The high murder rate caused an insurance company statistician to call Memphis the "murder town" of the country.[64] The influx of rural workers with their southern codes of honor and violence accounted for much of this chaos.[65]

A combination of his refusal to enforce the prohibition law and the temperance movement's success at passing an "ouster" law stopped Crump's initial rise to power. Crump believed that prohibition could not be adequately enforced in large cities, and he knew that a majority of businesses opposed the law. The Law Enforcement League, made up of local church people, was not convinced. In 1915 prohibitionists successfully lobbied for a law that ousted public officials for neglecting to enforce any laws of the state of Tennessee. Shortly afterward, the chancery court of Shelby County announced that Crump could no longer hold office. Crump believed that powerful utility interests were behind his ouster suit.[66] Thus Crump's formal political career, but not his political power, ended.

After his ouster, Crump still retained the confidence of businessmen and held sufficient political power to name city managers and influence policies. In 1916 he was elected the county trustee and was in charge of collecting state and county taxes, which provided considerable remunerative returns because the trustee received a percentage of the taxes he collected. He continued to exercise power by filling county and city offices with men who were loyal to him. Crump's main concern in this era was his difficulty with incumbent mayors.

The election and tenure of Rowlett Paine as mayor was important for three reasons. First, it represented an era of a politically independent mayor. Paine, a wholesale grocer and native of Memphis, was mayor from 1920 until

1928, when Crump did not have a strong voice in city government. Indeed, one of Paine's problems was Crump's frequent opposition to his administration's policies. During Paine's first six months in office, he failed to reappoint a well-respected and qualified Crump protégé to the Park Commission, and Paine and Crump broke off personal relations.[67] Crump devoted most of this time period to the consolidation of his political machine and business affairs.[68]

Second, Paine's 1923 election was important because it was a decisive political defeat for the Ku Klux Klan in Memphis. The newspapers billed the election as a choice between "Paine or Klan" and came out squarely for Paine, claiming that he worked to advance the welfare of Memphis, whereas the Klan members were "political mannikins dressed in the regalia of religious intolerance." If the Klan won, the Memphis News Scimitar predicted, the city would be "shackled in the chains of intolerance and sacrificed on the altar of un-American hate." The editor of the other Memphis paper, the Commercial Appeal, C. P. J. Mooney, a Catholic, also relentlessly attacked the Klan. The Commercial Appeal was the region's largest paper, and the Klan publication, the Kourier, called it one of "the most vicious anti-Klan newspapers in the country."[69] During the election campaign, Paine and the other candidate distanced themselves from the Klan and actively courted the black votes. At the last minute, Crump intervened to help Paine, who won reelection by five thousand votes. The historian William Miller writes that according to a lifelong Crump supporter, the 1923 mayor's election was evidently a stolen election. Had it been an honest election, the Klan candidates would have won. Crump feared the disruption of civic order and political stability if the Klan won; he opposed the Klan's ideas about race and religion in politics.[70] The loss of this election effectively ended the power of the Ku Klux Klan in Memphis politics, and by middecade, membership had decreased to the point where the Klan virtually disappeared.[71] This quick rise and fall of Klan influence in Memphis was typical of the movement in southern cities during the 1920s.

The significance of the Klan's defeat in Memphis lay in its potentially destabilizing effect on the city's political, class, and racial structure. Urban Klansmen focused on winning elective offices in order to advance their cause since they were not as free as their rural counterparts to demonstrate publicly and achieve their goals through intimidation. Warnings about undisciplined immigrants, the Catholic conspiracy, the Jewish internationalists, black depravity, and the call for "one hundred per cent American" appealed to alienated lower middle-class whites.[72] However, political stability in Memphis rested on the relationship between the long-term working-class black vote bartered through influential black middle-class politicians and Crump's nascent machine patronage system. A *News Scimitar* editorial portrayed the Klan candidates as outsiders who had played no part in the progress of Memphis, saying that even if they were not candidates of an order with repulsive ideals, they had no claim on the voters of Memphis.[73] A coalition of those with vested interests, elite and working-class members of minority groups, elite and middle-class liberal Protestants, and the newspapers came together to defeat the Klan and to preserve political and racial stability in Memphis.

Finally, during the 1920s Paine's administration continued the municipal improvement programs begun by Crump and expanded the power of city government by increasing its regulatory duties. The city schoolteachers were on the verge of striking, and the city's firemen did strike because of low wages.[74] Paine raised the salaries of teachers and firemen and instituted civil service exams for firemen and policemen. The administration reorganized the health department by making all employees full time, establishing a record-keeping system, adopting a new health code, and adding new internal divisions. Paine continued Crump's efforts to regulate the city milk supply, where he ran into stiff opposition from milk suppliers. The superintendent of health threatened to revoke milk licenses in order to gain compliance with new sanitary and pasteurization standards. With cleaner milk, consumption went up and the number of privately owned cows in the city decreased. The city built a new waterworks plant, municipal auditorium, high school, swimming pool, and modern river terminal.[75]

Despite the development of public services, some citizens in Memphis remained tied to traditional rural values that regarded centralized and impersonal authority with suspicion. An example of resistance to this new state power involved a mother's fight against the city ordinance mandating vaccines for public school children. In 1925 a Mrs. Allen was arrested and fined and her children adjudged dependent and neglected when she refused to allow them to be vaccinated with what she termed "the poisonous pus of an ailing cow." Her children were barred from attending school, and two years later the state supreme court decided against her, saying that the school board could refuse to admit children if they were not vaccinated.[76] Even though the city accepted increasing responsibility for the public health, most social policy evolved largely through the work of private citizens, especially women, through benign neglect, or through conflict between tradition and progress.

While the diversity of the Memphis economy insulated it from the harshest effects of the weak southern economy, the surrounding countryside remained poor. During the 1920s the depressed cotton industry exposed the vulnerability of a region that relied on a single crop. Foreign competition in cotton growing and milling and large cotton yields in the United States contributed to the decline in cotton prices below the cost of production. Profits from northern industries, lured by free sites and tax waivers, flowed out of the region, and much of the South resembled an economic colony.[77] The resulting poverty of the surrounding Mississippi Delta created the need for welfare services for the many people who moved to Memphis. As we shall see in a later chapter, many of those who sought welfare services, including access to the juvenile court, were either unemployed or chronically underemployed.

SOUTHERN PROGRESSIVISM AND SOCIAL WELFARE

Progressive reform in Memphis was similar to that in other southern cities at the time. Key elements of southern Progressivism included modernization and increased efficiency of city services and government; expansion of regulatory and bureaucratic powers of the state; and concern for social justice for blacks and urban workers by improving public health, schools, and conditions inside prisons. Southern Progressivism embodied numerous tensions between reformers and local communities, between old traditions of regional identity, race control, and patronage. It also made new progress toward Americanization, the interracial movement, and meritocracy.[78]

Early reform efforts to improve social justice by increasing state regulation of prisons, education, and child labor were loosely organized by the 1890s. Hoping to coordinate the variety of social welfare efforts, the Southern Sociological Congress was founded in 1911 in Nashville as an advocacy organization for social justice and public welfare reform. Its program included the abolition of child labor and the convict lease system, better standards for public health and child welfare, and improved race relations. The development of the Southern Sociological Congress illuminates several distinctive characteristics of southern social reform. Southern reformers, whether they were ministers, social workers, civic leaders, teachers, or wealthy wives, cooperated extensively with northern philanthropists and foundations. At the first meeting of the congress in Nashville, about half of the speakers were from northern cities, and throughout the congress's eight-year existence, northern delegates continued to make up between one-third and one-half of the group.[79] Important northern social reformers such as Hastings H. Hart of the Russell Sage Foundation, James Hardy Dillard of the Anna T. Jeanes Fund, and Julia Lathrop of the U.S. Children's Bureau made significant contributions to both individual sessions and the overall character of the congress.

Since the founding members of the congress did not believe that there were social problems peculiar to southern states, they struggled to define their relationship to the National Conference of Charities and Corrections. Unlike the National Conference, the congress spent considerable energy on improving race relations, and according to E. Charles Chatfield Jr., it exercised a liberalizing effect on southern attitudes. The congress was also heavily influenced by religious and evangelical activities. However, by 1920 it had been overtaken by national debates and focused on reform instead of welfare and apparently no longer served a regional need. Although the congress never became an agent for the coordination of social work in the South, it was partially successful as a "vehicle of challenging social ideas."[80]

The battle to regulate child labor and to raise the age of sexual consent was particularly complicated in the South because of enduring poverty, the excessive number of children over adults, rural resistance to reform, and the dual racial system.[81] Deep-seated differences between reformers and traditionalists characterized efforts to regulate child labor in the South. For instance, the child labor crusade, influenced by Christian humanitarianism, advanced concepts of childhood that emphasized the nurturing and protection of children, such as extending their schooling. Mill owners and family members resisted this alien philosophy by insisting that child labor was part of the family labor, continuing to employ children under age twelve as "helpers" and neglecting to enforce legislation.[82]

The dichotomy between rural and urban life in the South is a recurring theme in southern Progressivism. William Link, in *The Paradox of Southern Progressivism*, argues that Progressive reformers had limited success in changing the behavior of the South's rural population because of the urban middle-class origins of the reform agendas. The paternalistic reformers believed many of the social problems resulted from an inadequate structure of government and attempted to increase state power and intervention. However, they confronted what Link calls the "southern traditionalists," who had a different view of community and the social contract. Traditionalists were generally isolated and rural and clung to local, personal means of governance. They resisted outside interference and the reformers' attempts to professionalize public welfare.[83]

While Link is mostly concerned with the resistance of rural southern communities to urban reformers, he raises important questions about the limitations of reform ideology and institutional solutions to social problems. In many ways, Memphis, as an urban locality, had more in common with other northern cities than its predominantly rural and agricultural surroundings. As shown in a later chapter, however, the cultural isolation of professional reformers (and their institutions) from the community was not so great in Memphis. In the city, professionalism did not undermine reform or the development of long-term personal relationships.

Along with child labor regulation, efforts to raise the age of consent also rested on new interpretations of state power and its role in protecting children. As part of the social purity movement that began in the late nineteenth century, reformers (mostly middle-class white women) convinced the "government to enforce their vision of moral order by making sexual relations with young women a criminal offense."[84] They aimed to amend the rape statute by raising the age of consent for women from ten to eighteen years. To protect women and girls and undermine the sexual double standard, the legislation imposed criminal charges against men who had sexual intercourse with underage women. Although they encountered resistance, particularly in the South, from male legislators and medical authorities, by 1920 every state had raised the age to either sixteen or eighteen years.

White and black women responded differently to the age-of-consent campaign. Southern white women waged their own campaign to raise the age of consent. In Tennessee, during the 1880s and 1890s, the Memphis branch of the Woman's Christian Temperance Union worked to raise the age from ten to sixteen and eventually eighteen years old. Building on these successes and overcoming the indifference of rural districts, the reformers next attempted to raise the legal age of marriage to twenty-one for men and eighteen for women and impose a five-day notice clause for those underage.[85] While black women supported a single standard of morality, they did not participate in the campaign to impose criminal penalties on male sex offenders. They feared that it would be used unfairly against black men and would do little to protect young black women. Instead, black women worked to counter stereotypes of black female immorality and to combat sexual exploitation by white men.[86] They were concerned about sexual vulnerability in a racist society.

The preoccupation with race is a defining element of southern Progressivism, and the extent of racist intent in Progressive reform is highly contentious among historians. Some argue that the movement was "conservative, elitist, and above all racist" and that black disfranchisement and segregation made all other reforms possible. Others downplay racism and argue that regulatory zeal was partisan rather than racial. Still others assert that black segregation in the urban public sphere was an improvement over the exclusion they endured before freedom. Among these historians many document ongoing resistance to discrimination and note that black expectations often outran their capacity to influence social change.[87] Of course, the white South did not have a monopoly on racism. Ohio and Indiana had the most Ku Klux Klan members, and most of the race riots in the summer of 1919 happened outside of the South. Reform and race relations in Tennessee encompassed both optimism and moderation along with hostility and segregation.

Memphis businessmen and politicians developed new ways of coping with the social problems of urban growth in the early twentieth century. From social welfare to municipal government, reformers changed the relationship between individuals, their community, and the government. Progressives used the restricted political environment in the South to advance reform because political conformity in a one-party region and disfranchisement allowed sweeping changes in social policy.[88] However, this new role of political society and governmental institutions did not necessarily weaken civil society and private institutions. Traditional rural values in which individualism and local authority predominated mediated these changes.[89] This ideology resulted in a city where a combination of voluntary organizations and strong personalities created social policy.

Southern Progressivism had much in common with the national movement. The Progressive movement in the South, like that in the North, sought to increase state regulation of industries, social services, and morality. Railroad regulation, social justice reform, and the prohibition movement dominated the state legislatures until World War I. Yet none of these campaigns attempted to alter the basic structure of southern society. Hence, reformers did not try to end segregated facilities but rather sought to improve existing ones. Herein lay the tension in southern Progressivism: reconciling past traditions with new progress.

CHAPTER TWO

Child Welfare and the Establishment of the Juvenile Court

EXPANSION OF THE REGULATORY FUNCTIONS of Memphis city government during the 1910s laid the basis for new social policy in the 1920s. The child-saving movement successfully redefined certain social conditions as social and political problems subject to state action. Children who sold newspapers, played in streets and alleys, and loitered in the neighborhood alarmed child welfare advocates. The opening of a reform school and a juvenile court served to increase the power of the state over family life. This new state power, however, did not take over the work of voluntary welfare or diminish the importance of private charities. Indeed, private organizations carried most of the responsibility for the care of dependent children until after World War II; institutions for delinquent children were funded almost entirely by the state or county. The continual interplay between new public institutions and existing private agencies characterizes not only the development of social policy but also the economic and political history of Memphis.

The establishment of a juvenile court in Memphis was very much a part of the national movement toward a separate system of justice for children in early-twentieth-century America. It followed patterns of Progressive development similar to those in other cities. First, women's organizations provided much of the reform initiative. Second, the court had to be wrested from control of political interests. Third, the court was initially staffed with police officers instead of child welfare workers or probation officers. And fourth, Memphis reformers sought to remove children from adult criminal procedures and detain them before and after trial in separate jails. The juvenile court formed part of a wider attempt to introduce centralized control and planning to diverse aspects of urban life and child welfare.[1] In Memphis, the creation of a juvenile court eventually unified the disparate child welfare efforts of private charities, orphanages, and the reform school.

The Memphis Juvenile Court had two important and distinctive characteristics: first, its domination by women, including the thirty-year tenure of a female chief judge, and second, the effects of racial ideology on court procedures and operations. A strong upper- and middle-class female power network sought to improve social welfare in the city mainly by advocating child welfare legislation, founding the court, and ultimately pushing for a female chief judge. Judge Camille Kelley had a clear vision of how she wanted her court to work. She recruited professional social workers and was a member of numerous national child welfare organizations. She spoke extensively about child welfare and used her position to advance legislative issues of importance to her. Known locally and nationally as a "municipal mother," she dealt with children and their parents in an informal manner, often in her chambers, so as to gain their confidence. This friendly approach characterized her court and reinforced the importance of her gender.

Racial ideology also distinguished Kelley's court from many better-known juvenile courts in the first half of the twentieth century. Despite many innovative features, the Memphis Juvenile Court operated within the constraints of contemporary southern race relations. The judge heard black and white cases on different days of the week. The two detention homes and the responsibilities of court personnel were legally segregated by race.[2] The court also did not devote the same resources to black and white children. Only one probation officer handled blacks' casework. The city spent less money on facilities for blacks and instead relied more on private citizens, thus limiting the institutional options for black dependent children. The court did not exclude black children but rather segregated them. The Memphis Juvenile Court embodied a conflict between incorporating an innovative approach to juvenile justice while upholding traditional race relations that reflected tensions within southern Progressivism more generally.

EARLY CHILD WELFARE AND JUVENILE JUSTICE

In Tennessee, as in the rest of the South, during the nineteenth and early twentieth century, private institutions assumed most of the responsibility of caring for dependent children, while public institutions cared for delinquent children. During the early twentieth century, private philanthropies operated more than thirty institutions for children throughout the state. The state maintained five institutions of various kinds for children (none in Memphis), while three counties (including Shelby County) operated reform schools.[3] Along with the state institutions and county-operated reform schools, public responsibility consisted primarily of a Board of State Charities and two juvenile courts.[4] The Board of State Charities was created in 1895 to inspect, license, and supervise all public and private institutions in the state that cared for children, both dependents and delinquents.[5] Not until 1905, when Tennessee passed its juvenile court law, did the state attempt to deal systematically and comprehensively with delinquency and dependency.

State institutions primarily cared for disabled and delinquent children. The School for the Blind, founded in 1844, and the School for Deaf and Dumb, founded in 1845, operated only during the school year. The latter had a department for black children.[6] The Tennessee Industrial School opened in 1886 for dependent, neglected, and wayward (i.e., delinquent) children and admitted boys between eight and eighteen and girls between eight and sixteen. Beginning in 1918 the school accepted commitments only from courts, whereas before it had also accepted children brought in by parents or guardians. The Tennessee Reformatory for Boys opened in 1907, but its name was changed to the State Training and Agricultural School in 1917 when it added a "negro department." The school admitted boys between ten and eighteen who were committed by courts throughout the state. The Tennessee Vocational School for Girls opened in 1918 and admitted all classes of delinquent girls, including blacks, under the age of eighteen. However, it was not until 1923 that the state opened the Tennessee Vocational School for Colored Girls in Tullahoma to house delinquent black girls. Before the school at Tullahoma opened, black girls who were eligible for commitment to the vocational school were boarded in detention homes at state expense. The vast majority of black and white girls were sent to the reform schools for "associating with vicious and immoral persons."[7]

In addition to these state institutions for delinquent children, the city of Memphis relied on local voluntary welfare efforts to care for dependent children. The oldest organizations, established in the 1800s, were religious affiliates such as St. Peter's Orphanage, Protestant Widows and Orphans Asylum, the Church Home, and the Convent of the Good Shepherd. The Old Ladies and Orphans Home was for blacks and was the only nonreligious institution founded before 1900. Many of these institutions did receive state subsidies, but they relied primarily on private donations and fund-raising efforts. These efforts to address the problems of dependent children in Memphis preceded those on behalf of delinquent children by more than fifty years. Before the opening of the Shelby County Industrial and Training School or the juvenile court, only private orphanages or religious institutions took care of children. All of these early institutions remained important parts of the child welfare network in the 1920s. Their longevity revealed the vital role played by voluntary organizations even as the city broadened its legal responsibility for child welfare in the form of the juvenile court.

Reformers perceived the problem of juvenile crime as an integral and inevitable result of urban poverty. They associated delinquency with slum living, lack of education for children, evil companions, and lack of parental authority. More specifically, they categorized male delinquents into two broad types. Delinquents were described as "hardened," "tough," or "vicious," on the one hand, while predelinquents were "poor," "helpless," or unfortunate victims, on the other. These two groups of children required different approaches: treatment for the predelinquent and punishment for the delinquent youth.[8] Reformers in Memphis saw the solution to the problem of juvenile delinquency mainly in the combination of a reform school for the mature delinquents and a system of playgrounds for the predelinquents.

Government responsibility for juvenile delinquents in Memphis began in 1904 with the opening of the Shelby County Industrial and Training School. The Industrial School was an essential part of the juvenile justice system in Memphis until its closing in 1935. William LaCroix, a city councilman, first presented the idea for an industrial school, and the local press heartily endorsed it. LaCroix wrote to the *Commercial Appeal* in 1900 that Memphis needed a proper institution to care for young criminals, and he suggested a reform or industrial school.[9] The newspaper played a role in galvanizing public opinion in favor of a reform school by expounding on the benefits of such a school. It pointed to the large number of boys who emerged from other reform schools around the country and became good citizens, developed self-respect, and learned to find interest in their work. Once the idea of a reform school gained political and popular legitimacy in Memphis, another group of people began the practical work of actually creating the institution.

Along with a group of businessmen and lawyers, a club of white, upper- and middle-class women, the Friends of the Needy Circle, began the movement to raise money to establish a reform school for delinquent boys.[10] The activists petitioned the Shelby County Court to approve a building and authorize funding. The county court appropriated twenty-five thousand dollars for the project. The Friends of the Needy Circle and the Shelby County Court then presented a bill asking the state legislature to approve funds. In March 1903 the state gave seventy-five thousand dollars in addition to the local funds.[11] A committee of the county court purchased a site east of the city.

Problems with the location for the Industrial School emerged immediately. It turned out that one member of the county court, N. C. Perkins, owned the piece of land that the committee purchased. The county attorney said that the committee could not buy from a member of the court. Perkins resigned from the court and said the property was still for sale. The county attorney insisted that a trusteeship be set up with members of the court and the Friends of the Needy Circle. The women trustees disliked the suspect Perkins deal and, to the annoyance and exasperation of the county court officials, blocked the sale. The *Commercial Appeal* concurred with the women trustees and scolded the court for its corruption. Finally, the next year, the county court purchased a tract of farmland fifteen miles east of Memphis in Bartlett, Tennessee.[12]

The Shelby County Industrial and Training School opened in 1904 with high ideals. The president of the Friends of the Needy Circle, Mrs. Knowlton, wanted the Industrial School to be "a place where we could educate the youths confined there in the practice, as well as the science, of agriculture . . . a place where from whence they could go with a technical knowledge which would enable them to take a position in the world as useful citizens."[13] The founders also hoped that the sale of farm goods would make the school financially self-sufficient. The *Commercial Appeal* continued to laud the treatment and respect for the boys and claimed that the boys appeared satisfied with their surroundings.[14]

However, all was not well inside the Industrial School. Within the first few years, it was overcrowded and frequently refused to accept new commitments because there was no space. The school was also poorly administered. Records did not exist for some inmates, and other inmates who had files could not even be located at the institution. No one knew what happened to the boys on their release. The school did not separate boys according to age, mentality, or criminal tendencies. As late as 1920 the school still did not offer vocational or industrial training, although it did have some academic schooling.[15] Despite its weaknesses, the Industrial School formed an important part of the juvenile justice system in Memphis because it was the only local institution for delinquent young boys.

The Industrial School did not admit black boys until 1914 but was segregated by race.[16] From the time William LaCroix first proposed the idea of a reform school in 1900, various people, including LaCroix, mentioned the need for a place for black children. A member of the Friends of the Needy Circle and a *Commercial Appeal* editor praised the efforts of black citizens to open a segregated reform school for blacks. When the county Industrial School opened, its superintendent declared that room would soon be available for black youths, but the county court voted against a tax that would have established an area for blacks in the school.[17] Since the city, county, and state all refused to appropriate any money, the financial support had to come privately from the black community of Memphis.

A group of middle-class black clergymen, bankers, lawyers, and teachers organized the Negro Reform Association in 1908 to open a reform school for black children or to make space for them in the county Industrial School. A reform school was especially important for black children because, in the absence of other facilities, they were often sent to adult prisons or jails.[18] Some leaders of the Negro Reform Association included Dr. Cleveland Terrell, superintendent of the Negro Baptist Hospital; Dr. Ernest Irving, physician and vice president of Solvent Savings, the largest black-owned bank in Tennessee; and Thomas Hayes, undertaker and also vice president at the bank. For the next several years, while the Negro Reform Association raised about five hundred dollars and pressed for a black department, the county court pleaded lack of money for black facilities. Finally, in 1914, the county court created a "negro department," saying that black boys should do the general farmwork while white boys should receive industrial training.[19]

Conditions for black children remained inadequate. In 1920 the Tennessee Child Welfare Commission found that sanitation was bad and that before their visit there was no sewerage. Water and plumbing had just been connected on the day of their visit.[20] While the school paid for teachers for white boys, it did not provide any educational facilities for black boys.[21] Since members of the county court believed that black boys were particularly suited for farmwork, blacks probably suffered the most from the school's practice of paroling boys to local citizens for agricultural labor. Thus the racial ideology that dictated separate spheres and relegated blacks to isolated agricultural labor thoroughly permeated juvenile justice in Memphis.

Charges of peonage eventually surfaced. One black parent claimed that her son was "paroled" to a member of the county court who took the boy to work on his farm. The boy was still on the farm a year later, and his mother claimed he worked as a common laborer, received no pay, was inadequately clothed, and lived in abject slavery. Numerous other cases emerged in which the school released boys, both black and white, to prominent citizens. The boys worked on farms for more than a year without educational opportunities, and the school did not conduct follow-up investigations of their well-being. Indeed, the school lost track of several boys once they left. By 1920 the increase in the number of petitions for a writ of habeas corpus seeking the release of delinquent children resulted in an investigation of the conditions in the school.[22] In March a Shelby County grand jury began investigating charges of peonage and mismanagement.[23] The results of this particular grand jury investigation are unknown, but the juvenile court continued to send boys to the Industrial School. Over the next fifteen years, however, numerous other grand juries investigated the Industrial School. They found that overcrowding persisted and that the county never appropriated enough money to run the school properly. The building was declared a fire trap, and in 1935 a grand jury began efforts to close the school. One former member of the board of trustees worried that the school's closure would cause great hardship for child welfare in Memphis. Despite the obvious need for a local reform school, all inmates were transferred to state institutions by 1936, and the Shelby County Industrial and Training School was closed.[24]

Public playgrounds, along with the Shelby County Industrial and Training School, formed the foundation of a child welfare system in Memphis and linked the city to the Progressive reform agendas in other cities. Bemoaning the lack of suitable recreation space, reformers sought to have a playground within walking distance of every child in Memphis. Suzanne Scruggs, the wife of a local judge, headed the Memphis Playground Association, which was founded in 1908 under the guidance of the Playground Association of America. Its purpose was to "establish, equip and maintain public playgrounds and social centers in and about the City of Memphis in cooperation with the Park Commission, Board of Education or other department of City Government [and] to secure legislation on matters relating to the welfare of children."[25] The Playground Association served as an intermediary organization and prodded the city into action. Scruggs took the lead in publicizing the need for public playgrounds.

In a letter to the *Memphis Press*, Scruggs outlined plans for creating a system of public playgrounds. She declared that there was an urgent need for public playgrounds, since the one hundred largest cities in the country had park systems and Memphis should not be left behind. To keep costs low, the Playground Association planned to begin a playground program in the summer and use school facilities and teachers as supervisors. Since the school board already had the grounds and the people to supervise, the plan would not cost any more money. Scruggs promised that the Playground Association and other public-spirited citizens would help buy equipment and secure the loan of convenient lots. She hoped that the city commissioners would provide shower baths to make life more "comfortable for the hot, dirty little citizens of the tenements." The plan would ensure the "moral and physical uplift of the city's children."[26] The playground movement sought to mitigate the harshest aspects of urban life by creating safe refuges for children.

Designed also to help prevent delinquency, public playgrounds supplemented parental and school authority. Scruggs noted that playgrounds would accommodate "the thousands of active children just liberated from the confinement of schools for the long summer vacation." The playground programs would "train the boundless energy of its youth toward useful and loyal citizenship." They were " 'schools of democracy' in which our future citizens learn the lessons of good government by respecting the rights of others . . . the children would be made to feel that the parks are their 'very own.' "[27] The reformers viewed the playgrounds as multipurpose, citizen-building institutions.

Like other national leaders, Scruggs saw the parks as a way to structure the play of children; the key to successful playgrounds was supervision.[28] "Under proper guidance and control [the children are] carefully guarded from contact with the wretched ills and debasing temptations that lie in wait for little ones who know no other play ground but the soiling atmosphere of streets and alleys," she stated. "These playgrounds are week-day [S]unday schools of great practical character. They are eliminants [sic] of bad habits."[29] Playgrounds would not only remove children from harmful environments but also intervene in children's lives before they became delinquent. Scruggs's philosophy mirrored national trends toward increasing supervision of play and ameliorating conditions of life for working-class children, especially those who lived in substandard housing.[30]

The Memphis Playground Association operated within the confines of a racial ideology that segregated public spaces by race. Therefore, black citizens mounted a parallel campaign for playgrounds for black children. Julia Hooks, a longtime social welfare reformer in Memphis, petitioned the

Memphis Park Commission in 1908 for help in establishing playgrounds for black children. Scruggs praised the efforts and said, "we may regard it as a matter of self congratulation that colored citizens of the type represented by Julia Hooks, who won such high respect in her many years work for the moral uplifting of her own race, are interested in an effort to do something for the moral and physical betterment of the colored children of the city." Scruggs went on to point out that other cities that had large percentages of blacks, such as Washington, D.C., Richmond, and Kansas City, maintained municipal playgrounds.[31] This initial attempt for a park was unsuccessful; it was not until 1913 that the city grudgingly provided the first public park for black children.[32]

Child welfare reformers in Memphis saw juvenile delinquency as the most obvious sign of urban social disintegration and viewed children as an avenue into broader investigation of family lives.[33] To upper- and middle-class reformers such as Suzanne Scruggs, playing in the streets, begging, selling newspapers, and stealing represented not only lax parental control but also urban poverty. To keep pace with trends in other cities and make separate provisions for children, the Playground Association established a system of supervised public playgrounds, while another group of activists founded the Shelby County Industrial and Training School. These two innovations were merely the first parts of an emerging child welfare system that eventually included a juvenile court and a network of private child-caring agencies.

ESTABLISHMENT OF THE MEMPHIS JUVENILE COURT

Efforts to establish a court for juveniles in Memphis were part of the nationwide juvenile court movement. Questions about which court should have primary jurisdiction over juveniles, the use of the police as probation officers, and the influence of political patronage on court appointments plagued many other juvenile courts in the country as well.[34] Reformers and court officials in Memphis were very much aware of national trends and scrutinized their court according to the national standards.

While public debates about the structure of the court occupied most of the reformers' time, racial politics also affected its character in less openly articulated ways. City officials initially neglected to concern themselves about facilities or separate policies for black children. Rather than have black children excluded from a juvenile justice system that embodied

Progressive child welfare ideals, black reformers took up the cause themselves and spent their own money to provide a detention home for black
children. From the time Memphis's court opened, it embodied assumptions
about racial segregation that distinguished it from most northern urban
courts in the country.

The urban locations and continual shifting of jurisdiction between
county and city courts characterize the legislative history of juvenile courts
in Tennessee. The first juvenile court act in Tennessee was passed in 1905
and applied only to the three most populous counties: Shelby, Davidson,
and Knox. The next year, the minimal population requirement necessary
to establish a juvenile court was raised to one hundred thousand. Thereafter the act applied only to Shelby and Davidson counties.[35] The initial act
was quite limited. It merely forbade holding children under age fourteen
in jail and required county courts to provide detention homes. If a child
was charged with a felony, he or she was still prosecuted in criminal courts.
The act did not provide for probation service or for separate hearings for
children. Moreover, any judge of any criminal, circuit, or county court could
exercise jurisdiction.

In 1909 a clause was added that gave jurisdiction over juveniles in Shelby
and Davidson counties exclusively to their largest city courts in Memphis
and Nashville, respectively. Formerly, any court in these two counties could
handle juvenile matters. This clause also provided compensation for probation officers. Thus, although the judge was a city official, the court's jurisdiction included the entire county. For administrative purposes, it was
unclear whether the juvenile court was a city or county court.[36] This ambiguity set the stage for numerous lawsuits challenging the legality of the
Memphis Juvenile Court.

Serious efforts to comply with the first juvenile court law were apparently
ignored in Memphis until the Playground Association, the most influential
child welfare reform organization in the city, began working to establish a
juvenile court in 1908. The movement took concrete shape when the Juvenile Court Committee of the Playground Association, after consulting with
national experts, drew up a bill that ultimately created the juvenile court
and made it part of the probate court.[37] However, the Legislative Council
of Memphis modified the original bill. Despite great opposition from the
bill's original authors, the juvenile court became part of both the city court
and the police department. Although the exact structure took several years
to finalize, originally the clerk of the city court was designated to become

the ex-officio judge of the juvenile court at a salary of $750. The Fire and Police Commission was authorized to appoint two patrolmen as the first probation officers, and to make arrangements for a separate place of detention for children. No action was taken until 1910, when an advisory board was created to find a suitable location for a detention home and to devise operational procedures. The juvenile court finally opened in 1910 in a part of the old city hall.[38]

A network of middle-class and elite white female organizations and individual women activists played a crucial role in the development of the child welfare system in early-twentieth-century Memphis.[39] The Nineteenth Century Club, the Women's Christian Association, and the Woman's Public School Association formed the heart of this female network. In 1893 the establishment of the Woman's Council formalized the coordination of women's organizations in Memphis and two years later had forty-eight member organizations. At the same time, Memphis women also allied themselves with national organizations such as the National Congress of Mothers and Parent-Teacher Associations and the Federation of Women's Clubs. Many Memphis women headed national committees. They worked for legislation protecting women and children, expanding compulsory education, and raising the legal age for marriage. Locally they founded a normal school and numerous homes for working girls and unwed mothers and sought female representation on the Board of Education. During the early twentieth century, these women were motivated by concepts of moral guardianship and being good neighbors in their community.[40]

The most prominent child welfare activist in Memphis during the early Progressive years was a middle-class white woman, Suzanne Scruggs. She was president of the Playground Association and a member of the Woman's Public School Association and the Nineteenth Century Club. She corresponded extensively with national welfare leaders in her campaign for a juvenile court. She also helped draft the original juvenile court bill and served on the first Juvenile Court Advisory Board. Along with members of several women's organizations and the Shelby County Court, she also began the movement to establish a reform school for delinquent boys.[41]

Black women in Memphis also had a long history of establishing autonomous institutions and providing social services and child welfare programs. Since the end of the Civil War, black women, primarily unskilled laundresses, founded and sustained benevolent societies such as lodges, mutual relief societies, trade associations, and self-improvement associations.

Black congregations served as the organizational base for the various chapters of these benevolent societies. The United Daughters of Ham, the Sisters of Zion, and the Daughters of Zion sponsored mission and educational work. Building on the early self-help societies of these working-class women, the National Association of Colored Women, founded in 1896, consisted of middle-class women whose priorities were similar to those of the benevolent societies but whose networks were secular. Their projects included day nurseries, orphanages, hospitals, and scholarship funds. The NACW became the leading national organization for social change among black women and embraced the local activities of Memphis women.[42]

The focus of social service activity by these female benevolent associations and clubs differed by race. White middle-class and elite women lobbied for increased state responsibility for social welfare and increased their own participation in Memphis politics and the public sphere. Similar to women in other cities in the South, Memphis women used volunteer work to expand their professional opportunities. Black women, however, focused on raising money, creating their own institutions, and providing for themselves what the white state would not, particularly schools. While white women saw themselves as helping the "other" (particularly working-class women or immigrants), black middle-class and working-class women sought to help each other. The realities of racism somewhat muted class tensions among black women.[43]

In addition to the work of female clubs, men and mixed gender organizations also continued to establish parallel organizations and institutions for black children. T. O. Fuller, president of Howe Junior College, and Sutton E. Griggs, who later founded the Public Welfare League, were both Baptist ministers and headed efforts to raise money for black charity. Clubs such as the Ruth Circle, the True Hearted Gleaners, and the Child's Welfare Club contributed to the support of the Old Ladies and Orphans Home, the Charles Wilson Home for children, the Orange Mound Negro Orphanage, and other organized black charities. Doctors, funeral directors, and the headwaiter at the Peabody Hotel also raised money.[44] Since the city refused to spend public money on facilities for black children, and for that matter very little for white children, black citizens paid operating expenses in order to try to keep apace of changes in the white child welfare system.

Clubwomen effectively used the press to advance their campaign for a juvenile court and commanded considerable press attention. Scruggs bombarded the papers with letters advocating playgrounds, a juvenile court, and more general child welfare legislation. She also corresponded privately with writers for the local city newspapers. As a result, the local newspapers, the *Commercial Appeal* and *Memphis Press*, loudly endorsed the idea of a juvenile court and provided almost daily coverage of initial efforts to establish one. As early as 1904 the *Commercial Appeal* had begun popularizing the idea of a juvenile court by running editorials and reprinting an early juvenile court bill that came before the state legislature. As the momentum for the court increased, the pitch of editorials intensified. The newspaper not only complained that "kids, smoking cigarettes, gather in the park and shoot craps for hours" but also worried that a child treated as an adult criminal would become "one of the skulking and utterly abhorred creatures who must live in fear of law officers and detested by the honest and upright portion of mankind." Before the opening of the juvenile court, boys were put in jail at the police station with adults because there was no place else for them. [45]

White women's clubs complained about the structure of the court almost immediately after its founding. Scruggs wrote to the *Commercial Appeal* that partisan politics had made the judge of the city court, rather than the clerk as proposed earlier, the ex-officio judge of the juvenile court. She said, "After this bill had been passed by the lower house of the general assembly and recommended for passage by the judiciary committee . . . partisan politics was brought to bear on its passage, and it was only by permitting the bill to be amended into its present absurd form, making the judge of the city court ex-officio judge of the juvenile court and other wholly unsuitable provisions, that those in charge of the bill could secure its passage." [46] Scruggs felt that the juvenile court should have been part of the county probate court, which already handled guardianship and orphan cases. The decision to give the city court jurisdiction was motivated by politics rather than what was best for children, she contended, because the city judge had no experience in interpreting juvenile laws. She implied that members within city court sought control over the juvenile court to preserve their power in city government.

More damaging, according to Scruggs, was that by being integrated into the city court, the juvenile court was part of the police department. Policemen serving as "so-called 'probation officers'" only did police service, she complained; the probation work actually done was by volunteers. [47] Since the juvenile court judge also had to hear cases for the city court, he was often too busy to hear all juvenile cases. As a result, the police officer assigned as a probation officer was sometimes called on to handle an entire case, including its adjudication. On this uncertain foundation, the juvenile court lurched forward.[48]

The next important change in juvenile court legislation was the Public Act of 1911, which did three things. First, it raised the age of children protected from fourteen to include sixteen-year-olds. Second, it provided separate definitions of delinquent and dependent children. Third, with the exception of the courts of Memphis and Nashville, the judges or chairmen of the county court were given jurisdiction over children's cases in all other counties of the state.[49] Therefore, when they dealt with children's issues, the county courts became juvenile courts. The act, theoretically, created a uniform and comprehensive legal system of juvenile courts for Tennessee. In practice, local legislative acts determined the specific details of individual juvenile courts.

The legislation in 1911 affected Memphis by making the city court judge fully responsible for the juvenile court without assistance from the police department, and requiring the children's hearings to be held at a place and time separate from adult offenders. The city commissioners were authorized to appoint persons of "good moral character" as probation officers and to pay them a salary. In practice, the judge of the juvenile court was someone appointed by the mayor and elected by the city commissioners for a one-year term.[50]

Women's clubs in Memphis mobilized in the 1910s to help correct specific problems with the court and to advance other general child welfare legislation. The Memphis and Shelby County Union of Mothers and Parent-Teacher Associations drew up a set of bills and had the Tennessee Congress of Mothers submit them to the state legislature. The bills included, among other things, the separation of the juvenile court from police or other criminal courts, and the prohibition of policemen from being probation officers.[51] Scruggs was chairman of the committee of the Tennessee Congress of Mothers, which was responsible for submitting the bills. In all likelihood, Camille Kelley also worked on this legislation. At this time, Kelley was a leader in the Memphis Parent-Teacher Associations and organized the first branches in Memphis. The outcome of this lobby appears to have been unsuccessful, because references to the lack of properly trained court officials persisted over the next few years, and the juvenile court was not separated from the police department until 1920.

Conditions in the detention facilities remained dirty and inadequate. The first report of the Juvenile Court Advisory Board, filed in February 1910, noted that the facility had only four beds and no kitchen outfit. The building needed electrical and carpentry work and also a gas heater for hot water. Scruggs herself paid for the phone service. The report recommended that "as soon as possible arrangement be made by which dependent children and delinquents may be kept apart." It also said that delinquent girls should be sent to the Convent of the Good Shepherd, while dependent girls should go to St. Catherine's School of Industry. In addition, the Advisory Board recommended that school classes be offered and the children be given some industrial work each day.[52] Thus while the court opened with much fanfare, it was underfunded and understaffed. Private citizens and agencies continued to meet child welfare needs with which the court was ostensibly devised to deal.

While provisions for white children were inadequate at first, they did improve over the next few years. In 1914 the juvenile court moved into an unused public school building at Fourth and Jefferson and was known informally as the "white Juvenile Court." This building had separate facilities for delinquent and dependent children, a gym, and manual training rooms. The court also housed a special school that was established and run by Mary B. West, the chief probation officer. Visitors to Memphis for the National Conference of Charities and Correction in 1914 praised the court for its excellent facilities.[53]

Conditions for black children, however, remained dismal compared to those for white children. When the juvenile court opened in January 1910, it did not have a detention home for black children, who had to be sent to the old city jail. Prompted by a delegation of black citizens headed by the pastor of a black Presbyterian church, the Juvenile Court Advisory Board held a special meeting in July 1910. Later in the year, the board suggested that an investigation be made of the Old Ladies and Orphans Home, which Julia Hooks had founded in 1894.[54] If conditions in the home were satisfactory, the Advisory Board promised to place black delinquent children there and to pay for their care. The Advisory Board asked several black churches to help care for neglected black children. By the end of 1910, after black citizens had raised enough money to pay for a separate detention home, a "Negro Probation Department" was established as part of the juvenile court. The department consisted of a separate juvenile court along with the new detention home. Julia Hooks was named matron and chief probation officer of the Negro Probation Department, and her husband became an

assistant probation officer.[55] On several occasions, Scruggs praised Hooks
for her work toward the "improvement of her race." Clearly, while Memphis women allied with Scruggs may have claimed to be working on behalf
of all children, their efforts were really aimed only at white children.

The sharp contrast in facilities for black and white children in Memphis appalled those attending the National Conference on Charities and
Corrections that, despite consisting largely of northern members, was held
in Memphis in 1914. Florence Kelley, the prominent labor and welfare activist, noted that the "colored court" was in a shabby old house and that no
city reform school, farm school, or any other educational provision existed
for black delinquent and dependent children. Black clubwomen continued
their efforts to buy a new building to service black children, but Kelley asked
pointedly why it was left up to "these Negro women of very moderate means
and many heavy burdens . . . to buy a court building, while the white children have recently been moved into admirable quarters provided at the cost
of the city?"[56] Although black children were not excluded from the new system of juvenile justice, they clearly received inferior treatment because the
court segregated its facilities by race.

The Memphis Juvenile Court reflected contemporary southern race relations in its operation and adhered to the principle of public racial separation. Memphis municipal code mandated that detention facilities and
officer duties be segregated by race.[57] In one case, when the court received
an anonymous complaint, a white officer responded but found the family
to be black and referred the case to Officer William Joy, who handled black
cases and had a higher caseload. The court had "white" days and "colored"
days for hearing cases.[58] The ideology of segregation even influenced the
court's record keeping: social files were color coded on the outside to enable
easy identification of the client's race.

Even though the establishment of a juvenile court in Memphis was part
of a national movement, child welfare advocates both inside and outside
the South acknowledged that racial considerations structured its day-to-day
operations. During the court's first years of existence, Scruggs attempted
to remove the court from police influence, find qualified personnel, and
improve its operations. In the search for qualified probation officers, Hastings Hart, director of the Department of Child-Helping at the Russell Sage
Foundation, suggested to Scruggs that the court needed southerners for the
job because someone from the North would not understand the southern
point of view. The assistant chief probation officer from the juvenile court in

Louisville, Kentucky, agreed; it was their experience that northerners could not "handle the Negro problem at all."[59]

Next to Scruggs, the most influential person involved with the juvenile court during its first decade of operation was another woman, Mary B. West, who became the chief probation officer and was also a cousin of Crump. West was instrumental in founding a juvenile court and in obtaining the passage of a nonsupport law and a mothers' pension law. She was also in charge of distributing the mothers' pension funds. In 1912 she founded the Mary B. West Special School, which would shortly become one of the strongest features of the juvenile court. The Board of Education paid the salaries of two teachers at the Special School, which served as a disciplinary school for white children in the juvenile court detention home and also for troublesome children from other city schools.[60] Even West could not escape the political machinations surrounding the court. Mayor Litty ousted her in 1917 and in her place appointed Elizabeth Brady. However, in May 1918, with Crump back in control, West was reappointed. She finally resigned in December 1918, and Alice Read Saxby took over.[61]

Dissatisfied from the start with the unprofessional and politicized operations of the juvenile court, Scruggs resigned from the Advisory Board in protest and founded the Children's Protective Union in 1911. Designed as a home-finding or child-placing agency, the Children's Protective Union complemented the juvenile court. It was made up of representatives from organizations active in child-helping work and lobbied to promote charitable assistance and better legislation for dependent children.[62] The Protective Union provided a staff of volunteer probation officers to do investigative work for dependency cases that came before the juvenile court. Scruggs argued that dependent children should not experience the juvenile court process because it was designed for delinquent children. She berated city leaders because Memphis did not properly fund children's institutions or provide monetary relief so that families could stay together. Once again, private citizens took up the cause for child welfare in the face of inadequate municipal efforts.

As part of its educational mission, the Children's Protective Union sponsored a three-day "Conference for Child Welfare" in Memphis. National leaders such as Hastings Hart of the Russell Sage Foundation and Andrew McKelway of the National Child Labor Committee attended.[63] Scruggs hoped that the national attention would prod local leaders into establishing a more comprehensive child welfare strategy. Indeed, she stressed that

Boston, New York, and Baltimore had established children's aid societies long ago and that a prosperous city such as Memphis should be able to do the same. Her comparisons to other cities showed that Memphis was slightly behind national leaders in providing child welfare services, but also that local reformers were well aware of the higher standards and were ready to try to meet them.

The Memphis Juvenile Court was also responsible for administering the mothers' pension fund. In 1915, in another example of women taking the lead in social welfare reform, the Tennessee Women's Christian Temperance Union, several women's clubs, and the Parent-Teacher Associations sponsored "A Bill for the Partial Support of Certain Poor Women." Every county that had a juvenile court could provide a maximum of four thousand dollars to support mothers and their children under sixteen years of age whose fathers were dead or mentally or physically disabled. In order to be eligible, mothers had to be residents of the county for one year and of the state for two years, and to be "a fit person, morally, physically, and mentally," to bring up their children. The grant had to enable the mother to remain at home rather than work away from the home, and to save the children from dependency. In 1917 the legislature raised the maximum appropriation for Shelby County to ten thousand dollars. The entire amount was spent on relief and supported about forty families (40 mothers and 134 children) a year at about twenty dollars per month.[64] There was always a waiting list.

The organization of the juvenile court hampered its administration of mothers' pensions. Unlike with delinquency cases, the supervision of pensioned families was not considered an emergency service. With an overburdened court staff, only immediate demands could receive attention. The court did not have the staff, let alone a person trained in household management, to pay for supervisory visits to pensioned women, keep records, get school reports on the children, or make adequate investigations.[65] The court's pension duties pulled it into the arena of social welfare provision and blurred the lines between its dependency and delinquency work, its charity and corrections functions. The court's dual role highlighted its diverse responsibilities and the central role that child welfare issues played in the development of social welfare policy in southern as in most northern cities.

After initially receiving very positive evaluations of its facilities for white children, the Memphis Juvenile Court experienced a wave of political attacks in the 1910s that greatly undermined its work. A high turnover of judges and a lack of job security for other staff made a mockery of the court's professional aspirations. Between 1910 and 1920 about ten men served as the juvenile court judge and lasted anywhere from a few months to a year or two. Many of them were lawyers and friends of Mayor Crump. For most of 1919 there was no male probation officer or stenographer, and only one woman was available for fieldwork. Not until 1920, with the appointment of Camille Kelley as chief judge and the election of the new "reform administration" of Mayor Rowlett Paine, did the court experience any stability or hire obviously qualified personnel.[66]

With the election of Mayor Paine, a new era of juvenile court administration began. According to Paine, there had been many complaints about the way the juvenile court operated because the judgeship had become a political sinecure for young lawyers. The vice-chairman of the ladies' committee for Paine, Mrs. R. Peyton Woodson, was a good friend of Camille Kelley. Kelley had made a few campaign speeches for Paine. Just after Paine was elected, Mrs. Woodson suggested that he appoint a woman as juvenile court judge. The qualifications of the job were vaguely drawn, but since Kelley was a woman and was not a lawyer, it was unclear whether she could serve. The city attorney suggested that they take a chance.[67] Coincidentally, in 1920 the final chapter of American women's suffrage was decided in the South in Nashville, Tennessee, and women got the right to vote, thus helping to assure Camille Kelley's position as chief judge.[68] In 1921 the legislature made the office of the juvenile court judge elective and guaranteed her right to serve.

Constitutional battles over the jurisdiction of the juvenile court in Memphis reached crisis proportions around 1920. Parents of children sentenced by the juvenile court filed at least three lawsuits challenging its constitutional right to commit children to the Shelby County Industrial and Training School, since the court was a county court with a city judge.[69] In applications for writs of habeas corpus, several parents also attacked the legality of Kelley's right to serve as judge (since she was initially appointed) or to take children away from them.[70] It is not clear whether these parents were genuinely troubled by the legal status of the court or simply used this claim to appeal unfavorable decisions. Nevertheless, the problem prompted Mayor Paine to request the governor to call a special session of the legislature to make the juvenile court a separate court.[71]

In 1921 the state legislature created an independent municipal juvenile court for the city of Memphis alone. The court was empowered to examine all cases of dependent and delinquent children, as well as cases of failure by separated or divorced husbands to provide for wives or children. (If the husbands pleaded not guilty, they were bound over to criminal court or a grand jury.) The court did not have jurisdiction over adoptions, illegitimacy, or adult contributory delinquency. The 1921 act did away with the previous court, which exercised jurisdiction throughout the county. To deal with cases outside city limits, a county juvenile court was established as part of probate court. In addition to county juvenile cases, probate court oversaw the distribution of mothers' pension funds, adoptions, and issues of guardianship and estates. Thus there were now two juvenile courts in Memphis; their jurisdictions and responsibilities remained separate until they were combined again in 1968.[72] The act of 1921 also made the judge of the municipal juvenile court an elective office, in an attempt to reduce the influence of politics on court appointments.[73]

CAMILLE KELLEY AND HER COURT

The Memphis Juvenile Court in the 1920s and afterward cannot be understood without examining the life and ideas of its chief judge, Camille Kelley. So much of what the juvenile court was and subsequently became was defined by her philosophy and personality. The wife of a prominent local lawyer, Kelley was previously known mainly for her part in founding the first Parent-Teacher Association in Memphis. She later served as president of the city federation of PTAS at a time when it had three thousand members. She was the secretary of the City Agricultural Commission, also known as the "Feed Memphis Committee," during World War I. In addition, she was active in the Nineteenth Century Club. Although she had no formal legal training, she had studied and worked for several years in her husband's law office.[74] Camille Kelley was the chief judge of the Memphis Juvenile Court from 1920 until she resigned in 1950.[75] She died in 1955 and is buried in Memphis.

In many ways, Camille Kelley was a typical southern woman. She was born in Trenton, Tennessee, grew up in Memphis, and although she never admitted her age, she was probably born in the early 1880s. When she was appointed, Kelley admitted to being "somewhere near the age of thirty-six."[76] Her father was the chair of surgery at Memphis Medical College. Kelley attended the State Normal School at Jackson, Tennessee, which was the precursor to the University of Memphis. While in Jackson, she decided to become a doctor and studied for two years at the Rochelle Warford Sanitarium. Just before she was ready to go to Philadelphia for medical school, her sister died and she decided to care for the children until her brother-in-law remarried. She later abandoned her medical career and instead married Thomas F. Kelley, a prominent local attorney. Before she began her public service work or made her first speech, she described herself as a "sheltered Southern woman."[77]

Kelley said that she awoke to the cause of child saving once she became a mother. She organized the Parent-Teacher Association out of concern for her own children's education. When her son was eleven years old, she realized that the walls of her house were not her boundary lines, and that she wanted to see her son's school and the streets that he walked on.[78] She believed that only women, especially those who were mothers, made truly effective child welfare advocates, and said, "I consider motherhood the greatest preparation for the work to which I have been appointed."[79] She made social service work a vital part of the PTA, whose activities enabled many children to go to school by assisting them with getting shoes, clothes, and books. She studied child psychology and became an authority on local and state laws concerning child welfare.[80] Thus, by the time she began her work for the court in 1920, she had been involved in advocacy activities long enough to have developed a philosophy of child welfare and the public relations skills to negotiate the political demands of the job of chief judge.

Camille Kelley was self-conscious and contradictory about the importance of her gender in her role as chief judge. When Mayor Paine appointed Kelley in 1920, she was the first woman in the South to hold such a position. Indeed, one article claimed she was the "only woman juvenile court judge who is a mother."[81] Her work for the PTA had introduced her to the public arena, but she emphatically stated that she was not a suffragist and that she was always a "home woman" who used cosmetics, disliked mannish clothes, and tried to make herself as attractive as possible.[82] She said that "no woman should enter public life if it makes her less a woman, for there is no height to which she may climb equal to real home making or wifehood or motherhood."[83] Although Kelley acknowledged the economic pressures for two incomes and publicly defended the right of married women to work, she blamed working mothers for neglectful family life. She felt that while children were young, "a mother in the home is of greater value to a child than money in the bank."[84] While she stressed very traditional ambitions for women, she also acknowledged the changing political climate following the suffrage amendment, expressing hope that "every woman will see her new enfranchisement as . . . a privilege toward getting better child welfare legislation."[85] Like the work of many southern women, Kelley's volunteer work transformed and politicized her. She said the PTA did a great job in "bringing women out into the public and in training them for citizenship." She also said a woman should be concerned with "the interest of rearing her children, not in reconstructing government; interested in children's welfare and getting appropriations for institutions to take care of children . . . men can not do these things; they are not the mothers of children."[86] She expanded the possibilities in public life for women of her generation by serving as a chief judge, yet she remained well within women's traditional sphere by focusing on issues of child welfare and motherhood.

Judge Kelley's beliefs about proper spheres for men and women carried over into her attitudes about differences between boys and girls who came before her in court. She thought that girls were harder to handle than boys and that it took more time and care to bring them back under control, because, as she said, "the mechanism of a girl's temperamental structure is naturally more sensitive than a boy's." One local newspaper story about the juvenile court said, "Nor does a boy have to be a 'sissy boy' to be a good boy—in fact, Judge Kelley doesn't care for 'sissy boys.' She likes boys who are manly, boys who are 'reg'ler fellers.' " The traditional sexual double standard in the treatment of girls and boys was on full display in the Memphis Juvenile Court.[87]

Importantly, Kelley never fully articulated her views about race relations in public. These views emerge through internal court documents and were often contradictory and conditioned by external factors, such as action by the city police and changing institutional options available to the court. For instance, black boys spent more time in the county jail than white boys, sometimes because of orders from Kelley but sometimes because city officials did not transfer them to detention as they were supposed to do. Black boys complained of abusive treatment from police officers, and custodial care was harsher for black than white boys, but Kelley herself did not systematically attempt to punish white and black children differently. Although some black families voluntarily sought assistance from the juvenile court, they did not do so to the same extent as did white families, and letters of thanks for court assistance almost always came from white families. Judge Kelley worked to improve conditions for black children and acknowledged that their care within the child welfare system was not always ideal.[88] For her, the condition of childhood necessitated protecting black children as well as white children. However, just as Judge Kelley upheld many traditional views on gender, she also supported contemporary conservative views on race relations. For instance, Kelley regularly upheld charges of neglect against white parents for leaving their children with black caretakers, and she used the juvenile court to enforce deferential behavior of black children toward whites.

Judge Kelley's philosophy of juvenile justice emerged in contemporary accounts of her speeches, in biographical sketches, and in her own essays. As reported in the *Memphis Chamber of Commerce Journal*, she said: "my concept of a Juvenile Court is a strong arm used to supplement home care and training, or to supply it where it does not exist, and a place where parents may go for counsel concerning the life problem of their child. It is the arm of protection that holds the child thought in correct channels until it is strong enough to stand alone."[89] She believed that an "unwholesome" home environment, divorced parents, and bad parenting were the most important causes of delinquency. Kelley believed religious training, regardless of denomination, was absolutely necessary. In the rhetoric of the famed Denver juvenile judge, Ben Lindsey, she declared that "love is the modern way to educate children." She chastised parents for spanking children because it was not "the scientific, advanced method" for discipline. She also blamed poverty, disease, ignorance, and inherited criminal tendencies for creating delinquent children.[90] Kelley believed that the best way to handle juvenile delinquents was via probation, which she defined as education through practice and teaching. It could be a quite successful method of treatment, she argued, when handled by trained professionals.[91]

Kelley outlined her reformist philosophy of juvenile justice in her book, *A Friend in Court*. She used a series of cases to illustrate that children are not inherently bad but a product of their environment. She placed substantial blame for child delinquency on selfish or neglectful parents.[92] What delinquent children and their parents needed was a friend in court, long-term, individual attention to their specific problems, and very often, material aid. She critiqued unprofessional child welfare approaches and short-term attempts to mitigate dependency and delinquency. Kelley said she preferred to put children on probation, since she did not trust the conditions of state and county institutions or the treatment that children often received in them.[93] She saw probation, and indeed the entire mission of the juvenile court, as rescue work and extolled the teamwork of laypeople and professionals in realizing the juvenile court's mission. Judge Kelley translated her philosophy into practice by operating an overtly friendly court. She created an atmosphere of informality in her courtroom and never wore a judges' robe.[94] She used her private chambers to gain a child's confidence and to establish herself as a friend. If Judge Kelley was unsatisfied with a child's statement or felt that a child was less than honest with her in the courtroom, she would take him or her into her chambers and have a private "heart to heart" conversation.

Judge Kelley also sometimes displayed remarkably idealistic views of the juvenile court's image and operation. She waxed poetic about the friendly spirit that she claimed pervaded her court, and brushed off the difficult reality of recidivism. Her discussion of dependency was riddled with heartbreakingly saccharine but somewhat unbelievable stories of desperation and comeback. She glossed over the structural roots of poverty and its link to delinquency. She also ignored the punitive power of the court: the very real intrusion of court officials into family life and the tremendous control they exerted over families. Despite Kelley's "friend in court" philosophy that emerged in newspaper accounts, the newspapers were also filled with examples of working-class parents suing to retrieve their children from juvenile court custody. One case file contained a letter of evaluation from Memphis's Child Guidance Clinic that criticized the court for "robbing" the mother of her child before court officials had tried less drastic measures for handling the case.[95] In addition, the Memphis Juvenile Court blended customary criminal procedures with juvenile ones in processing cases. Although hearings were informal and private, the court sometimes followed the rules of evidence, swore in witnesses, heard from both the prosecution and defense, and allowed attorneys. It relied on not only complaints and warrants but also petitions and summonses. Kelley overstated her use of probation and did not speak about racial issues.[96]

Certainly compared to her more famous contemporary, Judge Lindsey, Kelley avoided controversy. Lindsey was an advocate of accessible birth control and declared his intention to establish a birth control clinic in connection with his court. He traveled around the country speaking in favor of what he called "companionate marriage," defined as a marriage without children.[97] Lindsey encountered considerable opposition to his ideas from the general public, other domestic relations judges, and religious leaders who claimed that he endorsed free love. Lindsey's controversial ideas eventually cost him his position as judge, and he was also later disbarred by the Colorado State Supreme Court on suspect political charges.[98] If the kind of avant-garde Progressivism that Lindsey advocated could destroy the career of a man with his national stature, then perhaps Kelley's moderate social choices reflected honest recognition of her limited political space in Memphis as well as her personal moral judgments.

Kelley's appointment to the Memphis Juvenile Court had an immediate impact on its reputation, and she connected Memphis to national child welfare personalities and organizations. Upon her appointment, she visited numerous other juvenile courts to get a clearer impression of her job. Even during her first year as judge, she received public praise from seasoned juvenile justice experts such as Lindsey and the National Probation Association. These positive assessments continued during her tenure as judge. In 1928 the national extension secretary of the National Probation Association said that Kelley's court was "spending endless time and patience to soften the hard bumps and even leaning over backwards, so to speak, to make parents feel satisfied. But as I have analyzed your methods and compared with those of other courts, I must say honestly and sincerely that I believe you are right, for it makes the spirit of your court excellent—the atmosphere of extreme helpfulness and it gets so far away from that practice of strictly law enforcement that the results can not be anything but beneficial." Kelley belonged to the National Conference on Social Work and the National Probation Association and was chairman of the Public Welfare Committee of the National League of Women Voters and chairman of a committee in the National Association of Women Lawyers. She was also vice president of the Association of Southern Juvenile Court Judges and belonged to the Tennessee Conference on Social Work. In 1928 she was elected to the directorate of the National Probation Association at the same time George Wickersham became its president. In 1933, when the Business and Professional Women's Clubs held its meeting in Chicago, Camille Kelley discussed handling behavior problems in children with Jane Addams. The two of them also reminisced about a previous dinner at Hull House with Miriam Van Waters, Mary Bartelme, and other national juvenile court officials. By virtue of her memberships in national as well as local organizations, Kelley was well-connected to both female and child welfare networks of power.[99]

Camille Kelley used her role as judge to make urban child welfare policy. As chief judge, Kelley maintained a high public profile. She sat on numerous local committees and lobbied the state legislature on behalf of children. For example, she worked with the League of Women Voters to introduce a bill that raised the minimum age of marriage to twenty-one for men and eighteen for women and imposed a five-day waiting period for those under the age limits. By imposing a waiting period, Kelley hoped to build in some time for intervention and prevent impulsive marriages of young couples. Many of the nonsupport cases that came before her were the result of teenage marriages (one of the youngest wives to come into court was twelve years old), and she was determined to use her status as chief judge to address this problem. She received numerous national awards and also spoke many times on national radio and television about welfare provision in Memphis and juvenile justice. A local film production company also made plans for a film and television series about Kelley's work. [100]

The Memphis Juvenile Court under Camille Kelley was relatively free of political interference, largely due to her maternalist rhetoric. Kelley declared that she never took part in politics because women should not "supplant the men in public jobs they have held for hundreds of years. Women are capable, of course, but we can't spare them. We need them to concentrate on child welfare and education, work we are inherently better fitted to do than men. . . . If we will specialize in this and leave the rest to the men, the men will give us anything we ask for the children." As she was leaving office in 1950, she remarked to the mayor, "No political interference has ever touched the inside of my courtroom, so help me God." Aside from one important incident in 1937 in which a city commissioner prompted the dismissal of the chief probation officer (discussed below) and the matron, the court operated as Judge Kelley's domain. The local papers howled in protest over the commissioner's actions with headlines such as "Hands Off Judge Kelley's Court!" and "Free the Juvenile Court Of Interference," and several other experienced people left that year. [101] This show of local support along with Kelley's national reputation and her focus on children's issues no doubt protected the court from more prying.

The philosophy and operation of maternal justice under Judge Kelley had much in common with that of Miriam Van Waters in the Los Angeles Juvenile Court. Van Waters, like Kelley, assumed the role of a wise, compassionate, and professional mother. Van Waters, who had a doctoral degree in anthropology but no law degree, served as referee at the juvenile court from 1920 to 1930 and was responsible for the cases of girls and boys under age twelve. Similar to Judge Lindsey in Denver and Judge Kelley in Memphis, Van Waters played down the judicial nature of her position and tried to make the juvenile court a diagnostic center for family problems. Much of her work concerned female sexual delinquency. Van Waters argued that when parents failed to provide healthy amusement for their girls or their overprotectiveness caused the girls to rebel, the courts should intervene and act as parent.[102]

The strength of local and national female reform traditions launched and sustained both women's careers. Van Waters and Kelley both sought support from clubwomen. They drew on voluntaristic networks but also worked with other professional women within the juvenile justice bureaucracy. In her responses to juvenile delinquency, Van Waters, unlike Kelley, caused more controversy with her innovative operation of the El Retiro School for Girls. Van Waters also had a bigger national impact because of her seat on the Wickersham commission and her celebrated tenure as superintendent of the Massachusetts Reformatory for Women.[103] However, both women traveled and wrote widely, and their charismatic appeal helped raise the issues of child welfare and delinquency to national levels of concern.

Judge Kelley's child welfare work was supported by another woman reformer and important figure in the Memphis Juvenile Court. Indeed, the most well-qualified court official was the chief probation officer, Beulah Wood Fite. Born in Mississippi, Fite worked for the Red Cross during World War I and continued as a field representative afterward. She joined the court in 1922, beginning as a probation officer responsible for follow-up investigations. She became chief probation officer in 1924 and served until 1937. After becoming a probation officer, she attended night law school, was admitted to the bar in 1926, and also passed the civil service exam for federal probation workers. While she was chief probation officer, her responsibilities included a caseload of more than one hundred children and correspondence with the Juvenile Court Advisory Board, officers of local child welfare agencies, and other national social welfare organizations. Fite represented the new generation of professionally trained working women and embodied the ideal Progressive Era social worker.

Fite and Kelley enjoyed a close working relationship and shared a similar philosophy of child welfare.[104] After the death of Kelley's husband in 1928, the unmarried Fite moved into Kelley's house on Carruthers Street. Another single woman, Altye Barbour, who conducted the court's mental exams, moved in also. Like Kelley, Fite believed that women were particularly suited for child welfare and probation work. She thought that most people would talk more quickly to a woman than a man. Further, she believed that probation work was a good and expanding field for women seeking careers because it led to other social service work, including judgeships and state offices.[105] Both women received hundreds of letters from children or parents thanking them for their help. Most letters began with "Dear friend," and Fite was known colloquially as "Mamma." Their work in child welfare demonstrated the new range of professional options available to women, including women in the South.

Fite was a forceful and outspoken court officer. Her letters to other state officials were filled with remonstrations when she thought they had done something wrong. She was brusque and often scolded parents. Her willingness to speak out eventually cost her her job with the court. During a flood emergency in 1937, the Red Cross requested that the children in the juvenile court be moved to the city jail in order to make way for refugee children. When Fite refused, a city commissioner used the Juvenile Court Advisory Board to force her resignation. Kelley was strangely silent about losing one of the best-qualified members of her court. F. E. Bradley was appointed to take over her position and became the first male chief probation officer. The long reign of female officers began to change after this political shake-up.[106]

In addition to the longevity of Kelley and Fite, several other people worked at the juvenile court for many years. The longest serving officers were William Joy (1920–32), the investigating and follow-up officer for black cases; Lillian Jones (1916–32), the investigating officer for white girls who occasionally served as acting chief probation officer; and Jessie Mahan (1921–37), the follow-up officer for white girls.[107] These and other officers came to the court with a variety of experience and professional training. Charles Chute of the National Probation Association described William Joy as experienced and well-educated, and Lillian Jones as well-trained and particularly outstanding in her investigation reports. Before working at the juvenile court, Jessie Mahan was the industrial secretary for the YWCA and conducted a girls' camp. Despite their primary responsibilities, these court officers handled all types of cases.

Most court officers in Memphis gained their understanding of casework methods once they began working at the court, and while many may have attended college, they did not possess prior professional credentials. Kelley's first chief probation officer, Ada Turner, graduated from college, participated in social service clubs in Memphis, and then worked for the Red Cross in Europe. She had recently taken a special course on probation work. When Turner resigned, Margaret King took her place. King was a teacher and supervisor in public schools and served on the Memphis Board of Education. Two years later, Lula Penn replaced King as chief probation officer.

Charles Chute said that Penn had no previous training or experience in social work but that her business background and enthusiasm gave her the
makings of a good juvenile court officer. He suggested that a man would
be better for the job, although that would require paying a higher salary.[108]
Beulah Wood Fite replaced Penn later that year. Some other officers included
S. M. Williamson, who entered the work with no experience or training
and stayed only a couple of years; Belle Ogden, William Bunn, and Charles
Hood, who handled white and black nonsupport cases; and Emma Locke
and Sam Cole, who took over the cases of black boys after William Joy left.
Most of the court officers were from Memphis or other parts of the South
and worked at the juvenile court for at least five years.

Black child welfare workers clearly did not enjoy equal status within the
child welfare network. Even their fellow workers referred to them formally
by their first names (a legacy of slave tradition whereby blacks were the
property of their masters and believed by whites to have no last names).[109]
For instance, official juvenile court correspondence repeatedly referred to
Martha Franklin and Bessie Simon, directors of the Charles Wilson Home
and the Industrial Settlement Home, respectively, by their first names. The
chief probation officer referred to Emma Locke, the court's black female
probation officer, only by her first name.[110] However, the chief probation
officer, who was white, was always called "Miss Fite." In addition, the city of
Memphis paid white juvenile court probation officers more than black probation officers. In fact, in 1928 the longtime black probation officer William
Joy not only made less than all the other probation officers but also made
less than the court stenographer.[111]

The segregation of the juvenile court operations in Memphis relegated
blacks to an unequal status, even as it included them within the child welfare network. The question of whether segregation can be interpreted to
represent a margin of progress for black citizens has been troublesome for
historians. Howard Rabinowitz argues that segregation was preferable to
the outright exclusion that existed prior to segregation.[112] Black reformers
in Memphis, as we have seen, fought for and established separate facilities in
the Shelby County Industrial School, and a separate detention home as well.
They also funded the first black probation officer. Although court facilities
for black children were inferior to those for white children, they did exist
and the court attempted to improve them over the years. Despite its inherent
weaknesses, even a segregated system benefited black children in Memphis.
For the most part, it kept them out of adult jails. It also exposed them to

social services, such as probation, psychological testing, and medical care, that the juvenile court had at its disposal and that were increasingly setting a new norm for child welfare in Memphis and throughout the nation.

The founding of the juvenile court in Memphis was part of a national trend in Progressive Era juvenile justice and social reform. Juvenile courts were established in most major cities of the South by 1920. Local reformers corresponded with national leaders involved in child labor regulation, social work, and playground associations. Indeed, Memphis was the site of the National Conference of Charities and Corrections in 1914, the Southern Regional Child Welfare Conference in 1923, and the National Conference of Social Workers in 1928. Clearly Memphis had the organizations, the personnel, and the status to be viewed as a major player in national child welfare policy.

The process of reform in Memphis exemplified broader internal characteristics as well. Women's voluntary efforts on behalf of children enabled them not only to enter the public, and formerly all-male, spheres of politics and policy making but also to participate actively in the paid labor market. The work of Camille Kelley, Beulah Wood Fite, and other female court officers illustrated a local and southern example of the "female dominion" of child welfare in early-twentieth-century American social reform.[113]

While child welfare reform in Memphis provided new opportunities for white women, its effect on race relations was equally notable. Black citizens initially had to establish and fund parallel child welfare institutions on their own. As long as blacks did not challenge the rules of segregation and took on the responsibility for funding separate facilities, white reformers were willing to accept their participation in the creation of new standards of juvenile justice for all children. From its earliest stages, the juvenile justice system in Memphis was separate and unequal.

CHAPTER THREE

The Juvenile Court and the Progressive Child Welfare Network

THE FOUNDATIONS OF THE CURRENT SYSTEM of juvenile justice in Memphis began during the 1910s but achieved true elaboration in the 1920s. Child welfare workers in Memphis, like those in other American cities, combined their Progressive ideals about social justice and efficiency and transformed them into professional opportunities in social welfare service. Those committed to helping and protecting children opened special institutions, established new agencies, and developed coordinating services. This burst of activity unified disparate efforts into a tight network devoted to child welfare.

The juvenile court operated as a gateway within this network of institutions, agencies, and services by directing children from one place to another. The range of options available to the juvenile court determined many of Judge Kelley's decisions. Just as parents and other community members used the juvenile court for their own needs, so too did child welfare caseworkers. In turn, the needs of the juvenile court, as the central point in this network, also served to prod Memphis child welfare workers toward developing more sophisticated means for addressing the problems of juvenile delinquency and dependency, such as psychiatric clinics and casework training.

The components of the child welfare network specialized by both function and population served. Each of these institutions and agencies had imperatives of its own, and when children moved from one to another, they sometimes became caught up in competing institutional agendas. While much of the activity centered on children, parents were usually the more important family actors. However, in many instances caseworkers could not separate children's problems from those of their parents or vice versa. As a result, child welfare was necessarily embedded within the larger social welfare arena, which focused above all on family stability.

The particular relationship between public and private policies and services was a defining characteristic of southern child welfare. Most southern cities relied heavily on voluntary efforts well into the twentieth century.[1] This approach has been critiqued without fully understanding the organizational imperatives behind it, some of its inherent advantages, or the variety among southern cities. The focus on voluntary efforts masks the true extent of public provision. As the historian Elna Green has found in Richmond, the state has always had responsibility for social welfare. This is not to say that voluntary efforts were entirely adequate, because they definitely were not. Nevertheless, the working relationships between municipal and voluntary child welfare services need to be examined and evaluated within the southern context rather than simply compared to northern patterns.[2]

Closely related to the reliance on voluntary welfare was the child welfare network's racial segregation and imbalance of services. Except for the Shelby County Industrial and Training School (which admitted both white and blacks but kept them separate), institutions were segregated. Although fewer facilities existed for black than white children, the black working class had a long history of establishing relief societies. The denominational characteristics of Baptist and Methodist religious life stressed lay participation and community-building efforts that were less focused on institutional creation than those of Roman Catholicism or Judaism.[3] Black clubs and circles supplemented the work of those devoted predominantly to the welfare of white children. Many agencies and services in Memphis helped both white and black children, although they did so at vastly different levels of investment. Thus the child welfare network in Memphis consisted of parallel white and black networks of institutions, agencies, and services.

DEVELOPING AND ORGANIZING THE CHILD WELFARE NETWORK

An eclectic blend of private and public organizations made up child welfare services in Memphis during the Progressive Era. As was common in other southern cities at the time, volunteers from churches, businesses, and schools launched the first components of the child welfare network.[4] The first private institutions dedicated to child welfare began operating in the nineteenth century and consisted of religiously affiliated orphanages. Two state institutions for children, the School for the Blind and the School for the Deaf and Dumb, also opened in the nineteenth century. The first public child welfare agencies in Memphis were the Shelby County Industrial and Training School (1904) and the Memphis Juvenile Court (1910). Throughout the 1920s correctional institutions were publicly funded, while most of the organizations for dependent children were privately funded (although many received public subsidies).

A child welfare network based primarily on private efforts persisted in Memphis throughout the 1920s. However, during this time, many local reformers pushed for a more active state, and about a half dozen new public institutions had recently opened. Mrs. Sam Phillips, active in business and politics and a leader in the Community Fund movement, advocated a state tax for charity because she felt that charity should be provided by the government just like schools and roads. She also favored a state department of public welfare to promote social welfare just as industrial and commercial welfare were promoted.[5] Except for such general reformist ideas, however, child welfare workers did not much question the limited public role. Even during the Depression, only grudgingly did the city make a small financial contribution for relief.[6] This dependence on private welfare efforts reflected strong traditions of self-reliance born of the isolated and rural background of city residents and the powerful presence of churches. The city and the juvenile court passed on much of the responsibility for dependent and delinquent children to privately funded organizations.

The child welfare network in Memphis consisted of four broad groups. The largest and oldest group included institutions that provided shelter (either coercive or voluntary) for a specific population of children. Orphanages and industrial or training schools cared for white or black orphans, delinquent white girls, delinquent boys, and unwed white mothers. No institutions for unwed black mothers existed in Memphis or in the state, and the only institution for delinquent black girls, opened in 1923, was in Nashville. Some of these homes were denominational, some were secular, but all removed children from their families.

Agencies that offered outdoor relief or relief-in-kind (food, fuel, rent money) made up the second component of the child welfare system. Again, these agencies served specific groups of people. The Associated Charities helped white and black families, while the Federation of Jewish Welfare Agencies focused on Jewish families. The Cynthia Milk Fund, cosponsored by the Health Department and *Memphis Press-Scimitar*, gave milk to white and black families, and the Salvation Army paid for transportation. These agencies did not consider themselves committed strictly to giving relief but rather relief in combination with other services.

The third group in the Memphis child welfare network provided services such as referrals to other agencies, foster care, psychiatric evaluation, family casework, or social activities. These services brought many elements of the child welfare network together in attempts to restore family stability. The Woman's Protective Bureau cooperated with the YWCA in finding jobs for delinquent girls. Investigations made by the Associated Charities, the Children's Bureau, or the Tennessee Children's Home Society supplemented those of the juvenile court. The Child Guidance Clinic assisted all agencies by making psychiatric evaluations of white and black children and their parents. The juvenile court enlisted the aid of Big Brothers and Big Sisters to provide role models for troubled children.

Administrative functions characterized the fourth group in the child welfare network. These agencies coordinated fund-raising, facilitated communication between agencies, and managed administrative oversight. The Council of Social Agencies, the Industrial Welfare Committee, and the Community Fund all organized in the early 1920s. With them in place, a true welfare network could and did emerge in Memphis. Under the auspices of the Council of Social Agencies, committees such as Child Welfare, Girls' Welfare, and Family Social Work met regularly and formed the heart of cooperation among agencies. Although these three bodies worked with all social services, child welfare issues occupied an important place in their larger set of functions.

Some of these agencies did more than one type of work, but each had a specific role to play. For instance, the Industrial Welfare Committee was the oversight body for all black social services and the liaison to white business leaders, but it also raised and distributed money for equipment at various community centers and orphanages. The Associated Charities gave financial relief but also provided extensive family casework. The YWCA offered some shelter but mostly social activities or job-finding services.

It was not until the 1920s that these four groups of child welfare service providers formed a coherent and self-conscious network. When Judge Kelley took over the juvenile court and the Chamber of Commerce established the Central Council of Social Agencies in 1920, Memphis finally had the structural and personal elements in place to support a comprehensive system of coordinated service. Professional connections developed as social workers regularly referred cases from one agency to another and children shuttled back and forth between institutions.[7] Most social service agencies in Memphis sent representatives to the Central Council meetings. Caseworkers and agency directors served on special interest committees and, as a result, regularly came in contact with their professional cohorts.

The Memphis Chamber of Commerce made the earliest effort to coordinate social welfare services by forming the Social Agencies' Endorsement Committee around 1919. The Business Men's Club, begun in 1899, was the forerunner of the Memphis Chamber of Commerce.[8] This committee served as a financial oversight board that granted endorsements for institutions and their fund-raising drives. In order to gain the committee's approval, new institutions had to show that they did not duplicate the efforts of some existing institution. Institutions were required to have at least three businessmen on their board of directors to ensure that they operated on sound business principles. The committee also approved requests for fund-raising drives that sought money from the general public.[9] It is unclear what kind of enforcement power the committee had since these agencies, as well as the Chamber of Commerce, were private. As an arm of the Chamber of Commerce, the Endorsement Committee viewed social welfare as a philanthropic civic duty, as voluntary rather than state sponsored. This mindset helps account for the persistence of private welfare in Memphis.

The Chamber of Commerce also had an Industrial Welfare Committee made up of black businessmen that oversaw and supplemented the fund-raising efforts within the black community.[10] The head of the committee declared that its policy challenged "the colored people to get busy and raise money for their needs, when the Industrial Welfare Committee will match dollars with them."[11] He said that under no circumstances would his committee call on whites for maintenance funds. Despite these clear lines of segregation, the white and black committees cooperated and set up regular meetings. They dealt with matters of racial cooperation and promoted black institutions and agencies. In addition to addressing practical needs for communication, they also hoped that such interracial cooperation would "meet the radical propaganda now being furthered by certain misguided Northern influences." In an effort to stem the migration of blacks to the North and West and to maintain an adequate industrial labor supply, the Industrial Welfare Committee also promoted the valuable contribution of black labor to the Memphis business community. It appealed to businesses and industries to help improve living and working conditions for blacks.[12]

The next step to coordinate social services formally also came from the

Chamber of Commerce. In May 1920 the president of the Chamber of Commerce and the Social Agencies' Endorsement Committee called a meeting of representatives of all social service agencies in the city to consider forming a Council of Social Agencies. They discussed the philosophy and desirability of a central council. Anxious that Memphis not be "left behind other cities in providing the way for social service organizations to develop through cooperative efforts," the group drew up a constitution and elected temporary officers. The Council of Social Agencies held its first regular meeting in July and spent the next several months adding organizations as members. [13]

Once the Council of Social Agencies was formed, it began to deal with practical matters. At its first meeting, the members discussed the relationship between the Council of Social Agencies and black social service workers. While everyone agreed that including black agencies was crucial, opinions ranged from letting black agencies have membership on the same footing as white agencies to having all black agencies represented by a single at-large delegate. The council postponed the matter of black representation, but the subject was a continuing source of concern until it created a Committee on Negro Welfare in 1923. This Council of Social Agencies committee worked with the Industrial Welfare Committee of the Chamber of Commerce.

By the end of 1920 the administration of the social welfare network in Memphis consisted of the Social Agencies' Endorsement Committee of the Chamber of Commerce, the Council of Social Agencies (along with its Executive Committee), and the Industrial Welfare Committee. These three bodies formed the umbrella under which individual organizations fell. The Endorsement Committee continued its financial oversight. The Industrial Welfare Committee coordinated welfare efforts for the black population of the city. The Council of Social Agencies took over the Confidential Exchange started by the Associated Charities around 1916 and expanded it to include names of all people who had any contact with or assistance from any social service agency. The meetings of the council and its subcommittees essentially set welfare policies in Memphis. This coordination and centralization at the highest levels of decision making gave organizations cohesion, turning them into a network.

Later that year, the president of the newly formed Council of Social Agencies announced that it was time to consider a plan for financial federation of social agencies in Memphis. [14] Similar to developments in other southern cities, the Memphis community chest plan would consolidate the budgets of all charitable organizations and raise funds in a single citywide campaign. The plan was designed to promote cooperation between agencies and improve efficiency and economy of administration of social service by eliminating duplication of fund-raising efforts.[15] Two years later, the Memphis Community Fund was established, and in April 1923 the city held its first campaign. Fund organizers hoped to raise $450,000 for the maintenance of twenty social service agencies and institutions.[16] The campaign was successful, raising almost $480,000.[17]

Despite its rousing start, after the first year the Community Fund operated with a deficit and continually failed to meet its goals. More important, the extent to which social welfare was the province of private initiative was reinforced in 1927 when the Community Fund appealed to the county for emergency appropriations. In asking for government money (begging, really), the treasurer of the fund stressed that all money taken in was spent on relief and that the fund was as "systematized as any business in Memphis." Fund administrators pointed out that they had checks in place to prevent fraud by clients and worked on behalf of children. At first the county refused to give money, declaring it illegal (for some unspecified reason). The city and county eventually worked out a plan whereby each would make a one-time emergency appropriation of forty-five thousand dollars to pay for food, fuel, and clothes for ten Community Fund institutions.[18] The *Memphis Press-Scimitar* editor cautioned, however, that "friends of the Community Fund should realize this is only an emergency contribution and that they should see that the Community Fund continues its usefulness and does not pile up another deficit. Individuals must still make the Community Fund successful."[19]

After this close call with disaster, in 1928 newspaper editors announced "that there must not be a repetition of the failures of the last two years" and urged the public to take their responsibility seriously because "other cities are watching us . . . we must not let them think that Memphis, the convention city, the Heart of Dixie, does not care for her own."[20] As fund-raising conditions worsened, however, the Community Fund reduced allocations, and agencies retrenched by refusing to take new cases. Fund administrators asked Ralph Blanchard of the National Association of Community Chests to survey the situation. He declared the fund sound and recommended against dropping any agencies such as character-building organizations because the Community Fund needed to present the public with a unified message about the worthiness of all its work.[21] These disappointing results in a time of relative economic prosperity highlighted the inadequacy of relying solely on voluntary welfare measures and foreshadowed the difficulties of the Great Depression.

The most obvious, and perhaps complicated, dividing line in Memphis social welfare as in many other southern cities was, of course, race. The Council of Social Agencies left all matters concerning blacks up to the Industrial Welfare Committee.[22] Regular meetings between white and black social welfare workers coordinated overall efforts, but black contributions paid for black welfare institutions and services.[23] In the 1925 Community Fund drive, a total of $20,000 was allocated specifically toward black welfare, all of it for the Charles Wilson Home. The Community Fund hoped to raise $550,000 that year to be split among twenty-eight organizations. Despite this imbalance of private funding, blacks at least got back what they contributed, and this may have had a positive meaning at the time (compared, for example, to some public services, such as schools, which received black tax money but denied them adequate services).[24] Further, it is not clear whether the Community Fund budgets were really so separate as the meetings and newspapers made them sound. Agencies such as the Associated Charities, the Cynthia Milk Fund, and the Child Guidance Clinic primarily aided whites, but they also assisted some black families and therefore, to some extent, subsidized efforts aimed strictly at black social welfare.

The emerging child welfare network in Memphis was dominated by women, confirming that what the historian Robyn Muncy calls the "female dominion" in national social policy began on the local level. The high-profile roles that women played in the Memphis Juvenile Court made Memphis unique among the national network of child welfare agencies. Many court officials from other cities assumed that the people they corresponded with in Memphis were men and addressed their letters to "Mr. M. G. King" or "Mr. Fite."[25] In fact, it was not until 1937 that the court had a male chief probation officer, and from 1920 until 1965 a woman served as chief judge.

Not only did women dominate the court but they also ran the entire child welfare network and, indeed, the more general social welfare network of Memphis. Women directed the Tennessee Children's Home Society (Miss Georgia Tann), Children's Bureau (Miss Clara Kummer, Mrs. Marie Riddick), Division of Child Hygiene of the City Board of Health (Dr. Marie Long), Women's Protective Bureau (Mrs. Anna Whitmore), Public Health Nursing Association (Miss Marie Peterson), Industrial Settlement Home for black children (Bessie Simon), Associated Charities (Miss Mary Russell),

Federation of Jewish Welfare Agencies (Miss Stella Lowenstein), and numerous orphanages and maternity homes.[26] They were heads of Council of Social Agencies committees such as the Child Welfare Committee, Committee on Handicapped, Legislative Committee, Membership Committee, and Family Welfare Committee.[27] Women representatives of the participating agencies formed the majority of those who attended the monthly meetings. Men, however, generally served at the highest level of board membership. The Executive Committee of the Council of Social Agencies and the Community Fund Board of Directors were run by men.[28]

At the council meetings, representatives of the member agencies continually voiced three main concerns that reflected national trends: efficiency, standardization, and professional development. They were concerned with efficiency in the administration of the agencies themselves but also in the provision of services to clients. They sought to standardize intake procedures at orphanages and make sure that all agencies used the Confidential Exchange client registry to prevent duplication of services. The special interest committees in the Council of Social Agencies conducted numerous studies of the individual agencies in Memphis and also evaluated how well the clusters of organizations were serving their constituents.

Council members and social service caseworkers in Memphis also identified with other cities' contemporary efforts toward professional accreditation and affiliation. The president of the Council of Social Agencies commented on the need for and difficulty of getting trained social workers.[29] The council formed a committee called "Training of Social Workers" in June 1924. Social service agencies did make progress on this issue, because in 1927 Memphis social workers organized a branch of the American Association of Social Workers whose membership was restricted to professional social workers. The city of Memphis also hosted the National Social Workers' Convention in 1928.[30]

Although many of these women got their start in club work, they were not gradually pushed out of social service work by professional women (as happened in some other cities) but rather embraced professional development themselves. As a result, there was much continuity, and the individual players in the child welfare network stayed virtually the same throughout the 1920s. One explanation for this persistence of female power can be traced to the community-based and voluntary nature of welfare work in the South. Traditional southern expectations for women, which emphasized moral guardianship well into the early twentieth century, also legitimized and enabled their work to protect the interests of children, women, and the poor. For women in Tennessee, unique in the South for its support of women's suffrage, these formal positions of public power represented continuity of women's reform work and political activity.[31] For instance, Marie Riddick was president of the Junior League and on the board of the Porter Home and Leath Orphanage, but she also trained at the New York School of Social Work and the University of Chicago. She, along with Bessie Simon, Stella Lowenstein, and Mary Russell, served her organization for more than a decade.

New professional opportunities for white and black women expanded as council members identified the need for new agencies. With the creation of the Charles Wilson Home in 1923, the Aid Division of the Tennessee Children's Home Society in 1924, and the Children's Bureau in 1926, as well as the growing caseloads of the juvenile court and the Associated Charities, new director and caseworker positions emerged. Therefore, increasing professionalism along with new opportunities merged with existing personal relationships and laid the basis for the creation of a well-integrated child welfare network in Memphis. In other parts of the South, the fundamental tension of southern Progressivism was between the new professional and the long-standing personal, between reform and tradition. In Memphis, at least, this dichotomy was not so important.[32]

The Council of Social Agencies established a variety of client-oriented committees such as Girls' Welfare, Negro Welfare, Transient and Homeless, Working Girl, and Child Welfare—all of which served three main functions. First, they demonstrated that welfare workers had goals, such as efficient use of resources and racial cooperation, which went beyond immediately rendering services to clients. These larger citywide goals required coordination. Second, these committees showed that the creation of welfare policy was often client driven. That is, the needs of individuals shaped the development of policies, rather than policies existing apart from or simply trying to control the behavior of welfare's intended recipients. Third, regular committee meetings reinforced the personal and professional connections of caseworkers and turned child welfare in Memphis into a "network" rather than simply a collection of organizations that happened to have a common agenda.

This elaboration of the child welfare network in 1920s Memphis demonstrates that those active in welfare work believed in the need for coordinated efforts and an official forum in which representatives from different agencies could meet. The emergence of such a system in Memphis is important for interpreting regional variations in the historiography of social welfare. To outsiders (and historians), the continued reliance on a mix of mostly voluntary efforts combined with key public institutions seemed to indicate a stunted system of social welfare. In fact, the organization of welfare was an issue of style more than substance because the network was functional in its local milieu and connected to national developments. While a well-established social welfare system did not necessarily meet the full needs of its clients (no city did, for that matter), the Memphis example suggests that the South was not isolated from broader child welfare trends during the Progressive Era.

THE JUVENILE COURT AS A GATEWAY TO JUSTICE

The juvenile court served as a principal gateway to the child welfare network in Memphis. It linked the myriad public and private agencies and institutions that dealt with the problems of juvenile poverty and delinquency. Beyond its legally specialized functions, the juvenile court took on many other responsibilities, often with a vengeance. Court officers sought control over areas of clear-cut juvenile justice work, such as insufficient guardianship on the part of parents or the delinquent behavior of boys and girls. In addition, community members drew the juvenile court deeply into other areas of family and community welfare, such as incest, race relations, household budgeting, and the search for employment. The juvenile court operated as a social welfare agency and cooperated with others involved in family casework.[33]

The court was the gateway for three reasons: all varieties of people initiated cases, it handled both dependency and delinquency cases, and it sent children to both public and private agencies, correctional as well as charitable institutions (reform schools as well as orphanages). As will be shown in subsequent chapters, the juvenile court released most children to their families on their first appearance. However, 30 percent of the children appeared before court again, and the network became most apparent in these long-term cases. Although the orphanages and reform schools accepted commitments directly from parents, the vast majority of juveniles who were eventually sent to custodial institutions passed through the juvenile court. Thus the juvenile court unified the structure of Memphis child welfare.[34]

The juvenile court controlled the route to and from public custodial institutions and many public and private noncustodial charitable agencies.

The State Training and Agricultural School, the Tennessee Industrial School, and the Vocational School for Girls accepted only court commitments. Most of the boys at the Shelby County Industrial and Training School and most of the girls at the Convent of the Good Shepherd were placed there by the juvenile court. At the time of one study of children's institutions, the juvenile court made 87 percent of the commitments to the Shelby County Industrial and Training School.[35] In turn, the sisters at the convent and the superintendent of the Industrial School consulted Judge Kelley before they released children. Home-finding agencies that coordinated care for dependent children also received cases from the juvenile court. While child welfare workers did not object to the juvenile court as the gateway for delinquents, they continually expressed concern about the high number of dependent children who experienced the court process. A study of the Tennessee Children's Home Society in 1920 found that about half of its children came from the juvenile court. As late as 1938 the Children's Bureau, a foster care agency, still received 50 percent of its cases from the juvenile court. The directors of these two agencies felt that court officers were hampered in dealing with truly delinquent youth because of having to process so many children who simply needed foster care.[36] The juvenile court, then, was the gateway to justice and placement for both dependent and delinquent children in Memphis.

Juvenile court was a gateway to the child welfare system in ways that went beyond its formal functions and paid duties. Judge Kelley's forceful personality made the court highly visible in Memphis. Kelley was a well-known public figure, describing herself as "a friend in court" to all in Memphis. Consequently, parents appealed directly to her as a helper, woman, or mother because she personalized the court. In almost every type of juvenile case, family members were the largest category of complainants. Since the court was not mysterious but often a place of first resort, parents and children sought out individual court officers personally.

Judge Kelley herself envisioned the juvenile court as a gateway. She argued that the juvenile court had broad and diversified powers and operated as a social clinic for children. The juvenile court had at its disposal a wide range of treatment options for children, much wider than criminal courts had for their offenders. Kelley said, "the juvenile court of the future will develop into a kind of clearing house, co-ordinating all social interests pertaining to children, and co-operating with all welfare agencies and relatives responsible for their well being."[37] This attempt to transform the Memphis Juvenile Court into a "clearing house" began during the 1920s.

The juvenile court also unified the network of social relations underlying child welfare administration in Memphis. In addition to Kelley's long tenure as judge, other court officers worked for many years at the juvenile court. They built personal and professional relationships with other child welfare agencies and within the community. This longevity of careers along with the personal element served to minimize distinctions between court officials who represented public authority and other child welfare workers in private agencies and institutions. The long-term service of child welfare workers, both in court and other agencies, fostered cohesive personal relationships because everyone knew each other.

COMPONENTS AND CHARACTERISTICS OF THE NETWORK

Several representative case histories illustrate how child welfare agencies operated together as a network and how the juvenile court served as the central node in that network. While these cases highlight the workings of the child welfare network and the gateway function of the juvenile court, chapters 4 and 5 more systematically address the social and operational systems in which these cases fit. For example, patterns of family and class background, ways in which cases were initiated, the nature of crimes, and placement decisions for dependent and delinquent children are all discussed in the next two chapters. The four cases to be discussed here, two white and two black, activated different clusters of child welfare services. The first case, a white girl, progressed through the two broad areas of court jurisdiction, dependency and delinquency. Most typical of the court's caseload, the second case illustrates how the network dealt with the delinquency of black boys. The third case, also black, illustrates some of the limitations of resources for dependent black children. Finally, the fourth case, a white family with pressing financial and health problems, reveals the range of resources that child welfare officials potentially had available to assist white children and parents in urgent need.[38]

Case One (White): The Patterson Family

The Patterson family had a long history of encounters with the Memphis child welfare network. The case initially came to the attention of relief agencies, but it eventually turned into a female delinquency case. The Patterson family's first contact with child welfare workers came in 1924, when the juvenile court received an anonymous complaint that a woman with several children was begging and selling flowers on the street. When interviewed by a probation officer, the mother said that her husband was "making a corn crop" in Arkansas and that they lived in a houseboat on the Arkansas side of the river. She sold flowers to make extra money so that she could buy clothes and shoes. In their first conference at the juvenile court, Judge Kelley took no formal action but said that if the mother found it necessary to sell the flowers, she must get a permit and leave the children at a day nursery.

One year later, a downtown businessman alerted juvenile court authorities that a woman was selling flowers, and the probation officer recognized the woman as Mrs. Patterson. The mother told much the same story as before, that she needed extra money. This time the probation officer put her and the children on a bus back to the family farm in Arkansas. The Patterson family came to the attention of the juvenile court for a third time in 1926 when an attendance officer of the Board of Education complained that Inez, the oldest daughter, was neglected. Since the family's last stay in Memphis (Mrs. Patterson's parents lived in the city), the Associated Charities had given them groceries and the mother had placed Inez in the Preservation Class (for dependent girls) of the Convent of the Good Shepherd after she claimed that her stepfather had raped her. The juvenile court took no action other than an investigation until a caseworker from the Associated Charities complained that Inez was neglected and that the stepfather who raped her was out of jail and apparently residing in the home. Thus far, four different sources had brought the family to the juvenile court, and the family had benefited from financial assistance and institutional protection.

The case of the Patterson family shifted to one of delinquency and became quite complicated as Inez got older. Inez was in and out of the convent in order to protect her from her stepfather. In 1929, when she was fourteen, the police brought her to the juvenile court for being drunk and disorderly. She told the probation officer that she had married two years ago (at age twelve) and that her husband mistreated her. Later that year, the Church Mission of Help informed the juvenile court that Inez was pregnant and in the Bethany Training Home. After the birth of Inez's baby (a stillbirth), Judge Kelley transferred her to the Convent of the Good Shepherd so that she could be treated for syphilis. At the same time Inez was in the convent, Judge Kelley sent two of her younger brothers to the Tennessee Industrial School in Nashville. Georgia Tann of the Tennessee Children's Home Society and Clara Kummer of the Children's Bureau, although not involved in the case, gave advice at the juvenile court hearing for the brothers.[39]

This family experienced almost all that the Memphis child welfare network had to offer in the way of care for dependent children. A wide array of people brought family members to the attention of the court. Institutions and agencies cooperated with each other and with the juvenile court. The court case file, for example, shows that "Record read by Mrs. Crim, A.C. worker" and "Record read by Miss Tayler, St. Peter's worker." The family members received half-rate train tickets for their trips back and forth to Arkansas. Various institutions provided shelter and financial assistance. Further, the case brought the juvenile court into delinquent behavioral problems (drinking) as well as serious family instability (begging and incest).

The Patterson case also demonstrated that a cluster of institutions was available to care for white unwed mothers and delinquent girls (there were no such institutions in Memphis for black girls). Girls such as Inez stayed at the Bethany Training Home until they had their baby, at which time they were transferred to Memphis General Hospital. Memphis had two girls' rescue homes: Bethany Training Home and Ella Oliver Refuge.[40] The Girls' Welfare Committee of the Council of Social Agencies discussed ways to formalize cooperation between the Ella Oliver Refuge, making it a maternity home, and the Bethany Training Home, which provided job training and follow-up casework. Over time, the role of maternity homes diminished as girls "in trouble" were less inclined to withdraw to a refuge, and the Ella Oliver Refuge closed its doors in the mid-1930s.[41] The Convent of the Good Shepherd had a division for dependent girls and one for delinquent girls. It did not accept feebleminded girls or pregnant girls, but it had medical facilities for girls with venereal diseases.

In cases like that of the Pattersons that dragged on for years, Judge Kelley usually used progressively harsher levels of punishment. Her final resort was generally the state institutions that were located in other parts of Tennessee. Judge Kelley never sent Inez to the Tennessee Vocational School for Girls, but she did send another girl named Vera. Kelley publicly stated that she did not always consider the care at the state institutions to be adequate, and Vera's experience confirmed her suspicions. The Tennessee Vocational School evidently handcuffed and beat girls. The school returned Vera to the Memphis Juvenile Court with bruises on her wrists and ankles. She told of night watchmen and guards hitting girls with mop handles, and also said that girls were chained together and made to work on the farm cutting bushes. Her stories were corroborated by representatives of two social service organizations in Memphis who saw the guards with handcuffs and attested to the girl's bruises. This experience in the Vocational School left Vera deeply antagonistic toward all social workers.[42]

The problems of the Patterson family also highlight several imperatives of Memphis social service agencies. Agencies continually tried to define their turf and delineate their clientele, even as the needs of clients exerted their own force on the agencies. The delineation of clientele served to limit each agency's caseload, a goal the agencies achieved also by enforcing residency requirements and returning children to their proper jurisdiction. At an early point in the Patterson case, the chief probation officer said that since the family lived in Arkansas, jurisdiction belonged to Arkansas rather than Tennessee. As we saw, however, the Pattersons returned to Memphis repeatedly, and court officers did not turn their backs on the family. Efforts to enforce residency were a continuing concern among child-caring institutions and agencies in Memphis because many of their clients were recent migrants. In fact, the Council of Social Agencies had a Non-Residence Committee, and the Associated Charities advocated returning nonresidents as soon as possible.[43]

These policies had very real implications for institutions that provided shelter and for agencies that provided outdoor relief, since bed space and resources were limited. In reality, Memphis agencies took responsibility for many nonresident children. This was true partly because Memphis had resources and extensive facilities that the surrounding trade area did not. The Convent of the Good Shepherd, for instance, cared for many girls who did not live in Memphis or Shelby County. For some at the convent, the concept of religious service transcended geographical lines or financial responsibilities. However, maintaining an institution such as the convent was expensive.[44] The need for shelter and financial assistance were acute because many of the families who appeared in the juvenile court had migrated to the city in search of employment and subsequently lacked systems of support. Thus the immediate needs of dependent clients defined and tested the resources of the child welfare network in Memphis.

Case Two (Black): The Browns

In contrast to a white dependency case such as that of the Pattersons, which involved the entire family, a black delinquency case, that of the Brown brothers, triggered somewhat different components of the child welfare network. Despite the rhetoric of therapeutic intervention, the juvenile court had few

treatment options other than commitment to a custodial institution or as-
signment to an overworked probation officer. Jasper and Curtis Brown had
long juvenile court histories.[45] The brothers first came before Judge Kelley
in 1928 when they were eleven and twelve years old, respectively, and their
cases continued for the next five years. Jasper was first brought to the juvenile court by the police for stealing a can of cooking oil from a grocery
store; the police initially brought in Curtis for prowling. Judge Kelley sent
Jasper to the Shelby County Industrial and Training School and placed Curtis on probation to Officer Joy. One month later, Curtis was charged with
breaking into a store and stealing some candy and money. For this offense,
Judge Kelley committed him to the Industrial School. The next year, 1929,
Curtis's father brought him to court for running away from home, and he
declared the boy incorrigible. By seeking assistance from Judge Kelley, Mr.
Brown reinforced the court's role as a gateway to justice. Judge Kelley sent
Curtis to the Industrial School for a second time. Jasper was also returned to
the Industrial School for trying to sell some stolen cigarettes. Over the next
couple of years, each boy went back to the Industrial School a third time
(their average stay was around six months) and made several more appearances in the juvenile court, usually for stealing or prowling. Curtis's father
told Officer Joy that he wished the court would commit his sons to the state
reform school because the boys were constantly giving him trouble. Finally,
in 1932, Judge Kelley sentenced them to the State Training and Agricultural
School in Pikeville for one year.

After their release from the state school, the boys got into trouble again
and were resentenced to the Shelby County Industrial School. Soon after
his release from the Industrial School, the police brought Curtis back to the
juvenile court for housebreaking, larceny, and reckless driving, and Kelley
sent him to the state reform school for a second time. While awaiting transfer to the reform school, Curtis was placed in the county jail because the
detention home was not strong enough to hold him (he had run away in the
past). While in jail, Curtis, along with a buddy, wrote to Judge Kelley, making many promises and begging her not to send him to the reform school.
Kelley had her secretary write back to Curtis at the county jail. The letter
said, "Judge Kelley has tried repeatedly to give you both another chance
without sending you to the Reform School, and this time she thinks that
sending you is giving you another chance. She asks me to say she hopes you
will both make good records and that she will be interested to help you when
you come back, and she wants you to try very hard to do what is right from

now on. She is sorry you have gotten yourselves into so much distress, but you are young and can change if you really want to do so." Communications like these were not uncommon in the Memphis Juvenile Court. Despite her authority, Judge Kelley and her clients often had very personal exchanges.

Judge Kelley regularly sent delinquent and dependent boys, black and white, to the Shelby County Industrial and Training School. It was the only local correctional institution for boys, and the juvenile court was the main route to the Industrial School. In 1920 Sara Brown investigated children's institutions for the National Child Labor Committee report on child welfare in Tennessee. At the time of her visit, she found that the juvenile court had committed all the black boys and 87 percent of the white boys. Parents had committed the other 13 percent of the white boys without formal court intervention.[46] The case of the Brown brothers also shows that the county jail was part of the child welfare network for some delinquent black boys (less so for black girls).

The only other institutional option for delinquent boys, the State Training and Agricultural School in Nashville, was beset with the traditional problems of state institutions, such as overcrowding, poor management, lack of rehabilitative programs, and unqualified staff. In 1918 the school was divided into white and black departments, and the black department moved to Pikeville, Tennessee. A 1938 investigation of juvenile correctional institutions commented bitterly on the unfortunate location of the black department in the far eastern end of the state, where few blacks lived, making family visits almost impossible. The report also criticized the school for using farming and mining as vocational training, since most boys came from a city and would return to one.[47]

Although the Brown brothers never benefited from psychological evaluations, many other boys and girls, white and black, did. For about two years, one of the treatment options for delinquents included consultation with the Memphis Child Guidance Clinic. Child welfare workers in the early twentieth century, concerned that existing juvenile court procedures did not further understanding of delinquency nor seem to reduce delinquency, turned to scientific research for help. Elaborating on the juvenile court's emphasis on individual treatment, some cities established psychiatric clinics. With prodding from Julia Lathrop of Hull House, the Chicago Juvenile Psychopathic Institute opened in 1909, and in 1917 the Judge Baker Guidance Center opened in Boston. These clinics formalized the role of psychiatrists in delinquency prevention. The clinics operated as research and diagnostic centers, not as treatment facilities. Their scientific and medical approach formed the basis for the development of new preventive strategies for juvenile delinquency.[48]

As part of the scientific philanthropy movement of the Progressive Era, the Commonwealth Fund set out to "do something for the welfare of mankind."[49] Founded in 1918 by Anna Harkness, the widow of Stephen Harkness (who had made a fortune investing with John D. Rockefeller in Standard Oil), the Commonwealth Fund concluded that juvenile delinquency was one of the most pressing social problems of the day. The Commonwealth Fund seized on the issue of delinquency prevention and from 1922 until 1945 was the primary donor to child guidance. The fund decided that a psychiatric rather than an environmental approach to treatment, research, and fieldwork was the best course to follow in delinquency prevention. Its original "Program for the Prevention of Juvenile Delinquency" provided seed money to open and staff child guidance clinics across the country.

As early as 1921 welfare workers in Memphis talked about the need for a psychological clinic. At a meeting of the Council of Social Agencies, the chairman of the Committee on Family Social Work recommended the establishment of a "psychopathic" clinic.[50] In 1924 the Commonwealth Fund of New York visited Memphis and approved the city as a site for one of its child guidance clinics. The National Committee for Mental Hygiene chose Memphis from among twenty-six other cities with a population under five hundred thousand. The National Committee felt that child welfare service agencies in Memphis were sufficiently developed to support a psychological clinic. With much fanfare, visits from national officers, and grand expectations, the clinic opened with some initial funding from the Rockefeller Foundation and the understanding that it would eventually be supported locally by the Community Fund of Memphis.[51] The clinic's staff included a psychiatrist, a psychologist, and a caseworker. The clinic was to assist the juvenile court, schools, and other agencies in psychological evaluations aimed at preventing juvenile delinquency.[52]

Two years later, in 1926, the fate of the Child Guidance Clinic looked grim. The director, R. R. Williams, resigned his position in Memphis to take a similar one in New York at a substantially higher salary.[53] The Community Fund had a serious deficit and considered eliminating the clinic from its budget. Since its establishment it had cost sixty thousand dollars.[54] Representatives from social agencies, the public schools, the juvenile court, and the Shelby County Industrial School came forth praising the clinic's work and said that its closure would devastate child welfare work in Memphis.[55] However, Mary Russell of the Associated Charities said that Memphis had not been ready for the clinic when it was established. She also said that many agencies were unwilling or unable to carry out the clinic's recommendations, which had limited its effectiveness. Ultimately, the directors of the Community Fund declined to fund it, although they adopted a resolution declaring the clinic a worthy cause that should be supported by public taxes.[56] By April 1927, however, it had gone out of existence.[57] Although Memphis self-consciously sought to embrace national attempts at therapeutic solutions to delinquency, the city's voluntary welfare network was not strong enough to sustain the child guidance clinic concept on its own.

Case Three (Black): The Taylors

Another black family, a dependency case, highlights both the inclusion of black children within the Memphis child welfare network and some limitations in the levels of assistance the network could offer to blacks. The Taylor case began in 1922 when police officers brought the family's three children to the black detention home because the police claimed their mother lived an indecent life.[58] Judge Kelley sent the children to the Industrial Settlement Home until the mother "prepared a proper home" for them. Three years later, in 1925, one of the children went on his own to the juvenile court and told Judge Kelley that he had been whipped unmercifully by Bessie Simon, director of the Industrial Settlement Home (although an investigation later showed that he had not been mistreated). The next year, Judge Kelley received a series of anonymous letters alleging cruelty in the Settlement Home and asking for the release of the Taylor children. Kelley felt compelled to investigate the complaints and asked for an evaluation of the oldest girl by the Memphis Child Guidance Clinic. The clinic director said in his evaluation,

> regarding her placement: As to whether her present environment be proper, I cannot definitely advise. Clara seems satisfied and quite happy. She wishes to remain there. She has there opportunity for education and is being protected during the adolescent period. Perhaps you could leave it to Clara to make her choice of plans, home and school. Relative to the Settlement House, its desirability as a home and training place for children I cannot state. I have merely heard adverse criticism: it was not supported by Clara's

statement. I talked with Bessie Simon; she is very convincing. If her methods are questioned, investigations should be made: but I question if I should make an issue of this case.

In addition to the clinic's observations, the juvenile court hearing included testimony from Emma Brown, president of the City Federation of Colored Women's Clubs, who said she visited the Settlement Home often and thought it was a good place for children. The wife of the president of the black bank in Memphis, who was a board member of the Settlement Home, also testified that it was a good place for children. Because their grandmother had a good home, the children were ultimately placed with her since Judge Kelley preferred to keep families together whenever possible.

The Taylor case reveals the court as both the gateway and the coordination link among various components of the child welfare network. Anonymous citizens initially alerted Judge Kelley personally to possible abuses in the Settlement Home; after his first appearance in court, one of the Taylor children chose to report to Kelley rather than a family member and asked her for help on his own. By using the Guidance Clinic to try and elicit information about Bessie Simon's treatment, Kelley used the juvenile court to bring those two organizations in contact. Finally, the presence of black clubwomen and other community members linked the juvenile court to the larger social context of child welfare.

The Taylor case also indicates that despite recent improvements in institutional treatment, physical abuse of children persisted inside custodial institutions. As early as 1921 the Council of Social Agencies discussed whether "vicious conditions" existed in the Industrial Settlement Home run by Bessie Simon. The chairman of a committee that investigated the Settlement Home because it was operating without a license decided that the committee did not need to take steps toward closing the institution.[59] Over the years, however, numerous case files indicated that Bessie Simon illegally detained children and did, in all probability, abuse them.[60] Child welfare personnel ignored these cases, and indeed, Judge Kelley praised Simon: "in my opinion, you are a most unusual social worker and understand children and organization. You must love your work or you would not devote your life to it and I appreciate the results already felt by your help with the colored children."[61] The Industrial Settlement Home continued to play an important part in the network of black agencies. Physical abuse of children was not limited to those in black institutions, however. As discussed earlier, Vera's experience at the Tennessee Vocational School for Girls revealed clear-cut abuse.

The operation of the Industrial Settlement Home finally came to a dramatic end in 1929 after a fire burned the facility, killing eight children. In a series of sensational revelations, the true conditions inside the home came to light. The home was overcrowded, delinquent and dependent children were mixed together, the building had been declared a fire hazard, and children told graphic stories of cruelty. In fact, one young girl admitted that she started the fire in order to escape the home because she did not want to be beaten.[62] During the ensuing investigation, children told bizarre tales of torture, while child welfare workers, including Judge Kelley and Georgia Tann, defended Bessie Simon. However, when a black doctor examined the children, he found that many of them were underfed and some had scars and bruises that indicated severe beatings. Bessie Simon stood trial and eventually served a ninety-day workhouse sentence on charges of mayhem, assault and battery, and disfiguring children. The girl who confessed to setting the fire, Rosebud Ankton, age fifteen, pleaded guilty to arson and two counts of second-degree murder. She was sentenced to fifteen years in prison. She was to be sent to the Tennessee Vocational School until she reached twenty-one and then transferred to the state penitentiary.[63] In the meantime, the public rallied around the homeless children and quickly raised fifteen hundred dollars toward their care.

After the Industrial Settlement Home closed, the Charles Wilson Home took over much of the responsibility for housing dependent black children. Inspired by the dedication of Charles Wilson, a custodian at the federal building who raised the initial four thousand dollars for the institution, an interracial board came together and founded the home in 1924. It was built with an additional twenty-five thousand dollars from the Community Fund.[64] Martha Franklin, who had worked previously for the Associated Charities and had ten years of experience in child welfare services, ran the home. She did investigations and placed children in boarding homes, adoption homes, free foster homes, and the orphanage. The Charles Wilson Home accepted children from the juvenile court, the county probate court, and individual families. During a survey of the home, Franklin's record-keeping procedures were found to be inadequate. Since she had no case committee, she pleaded lack of time rather than lack of knowledge about the condition of her records.[65] Although Memphis had fewer institutional options for black children, and black welfare agencies survived on fewer resources since they received little money from the Community Fund, a parallel network for black children existed and occasionally overlapped with that of white children.

Case Four (White): The Franklins

In contrast to the limited range of options for dependent black children such as the Taylor children, the Franklin children, white and similarly dependent, were the concern of half a dozen welfare agencies plus the juvenile court.[66] A school attendance officer complained to the court that one of the Franklin daughters missed school because she was at home nursing her tubercular mother and that two other children were neglected. When the probation officer showed up at the home for the investigation, the mother said that she was grateful for help because she had tried to hold the family together but had recently become desperate. Although she had sought help from her relatives, they could not care for her, so she returned to Memphis. The husband apparently drank and did not provide financially, so she relied on the two oldest children for money. One worked at a candy company and the other drove a taxi. The officer told the mother to have the father come to the juvenile court; if he did not come, the officer would put the mother into a hospital and find shelter for the children.

Three days later, the court officer returned to find that the mother had given up their room, had packed and dressed and was ready to go with the officer to the hospital. The Associated Charities took over the mother's case and tried to get her into Oakville Sanitarium. One girl was sent to the YWCA, two boys to Cheerfield Farms, and Lance Forsdick of the YMCA made boarding arrangements for the two older boys. One of the boys, Sammie, was released to his father, who showed up about a month later. The father's employment was irregular, however, and when the mother died of tuberculosis, the boy came before the court again and was sent to the Shelby County Industrial and Training School as a dependent. Sammie finally ended up in the Porter Home and Leath Orphanage for the next ten years. The number of contacts with the child welfare network for this family reflected, in part, the range of problems they faced. The Franklin family experienced the full range of options available, all coordinated by the juvenile court: financial relief from the Associated Charities; shelter from an orphanage, industrial school, and tuberculosis hospitals; and casework service from the Public Health Nursing Association, juvenile court, YMCA, YWCA, and Associated Charities.

Orphanages constituted a key component of the child welfare network in Memphis, although they played different roles within white and black communities. As Sammie Franklin's case shows, orphanages did not always house children without living immediate family members. Contemporary child welfare workers and numerous historical studies have demonstrated that orphanages cared for few true orphans.[67] Instead orphanages mostly provided temporary or emergency care for white and black children until they returned to their families.[68] In the South, the development of white and black orphanages was slightly different. Orphanages for white children were generally part of the hierarchical and institutionalized Roman Catholic and Episcopal churches. Black orphanages originated from a combination of women's secular club activity and church fund-raising networks. In many cases, the black population lacked sufficient resources to support separate homes for the aged, sick, or orphaned children, and many communities, including Memphis, offered more than one service at the same institution. The more democratic forms of worship and structure of black Baptist and Methodist churches also served to downplay institutional solutions for dependent black children.[69]

Instead of keeping Sammie Franklin in Memphis, Judge Kelley could have placed him in the Tennessee Industrial School in Nashville, which operated as a state-run orphanage (although for most of its existence it accepted both dependents and delinquents). Originally the Randall Cole Industrial School for "Orphan, Helpless, and Wayward Children," it was taken over by the state in 1887 and became the Tennessee Industrial School. Parents themselves could place their children in the school until around 1918, when it began accepting only court commitments. The school originally cared mostly for white boys, some white girls, a few black boys, and even fewer black girls. As mandated by law, it maintained separate departments for boys and girls and whites and blacks.[70] Although the school was primarily an educational institution for dependent children, the superintendent had to battle public perceptions that his institution was a reform school for delinquents, because investigations noted its "prison-like repression," severe overcrowding, and lack of vocational opportunities. By the 1920s the school evidently no longer had a black division.[71] This transformation may have resulted from deteriorating race relations in the South around the turn of the century. Restrictive

Jim Crow legislation and race riots in other cities aggravated racial animosity in Memphis. Since each county had only a limited allotment of spaces, the hardening of race relations served to limit public responsibility for dependent black children.

Rather than institutionalization, another possible solution to the cases of Inez Patterson, the Taylor children, or Sammie Franklin would have been foster care.[72] Two agencies in Memphis arranged adoptions, placements in boarding homes, and foster care for both white and black children. The Tennessee Children's Home Society, headquartered in Nashville, opened a branch office in Memphis in 1913. The society initially arranged adoptions only for orphaned children under the age of seven. In 1924 the Council of Social Agencies recommended that its work expand to include an Aid Division. This new division placed children of all ages who were not eligible for adoption in private homes. The state of Tennessee paid for the adoption work while the Community Fund of Memphis and Shelby County paid for the work with dependent children.[73] The Children's Bureau, created by the Council of Social Agencies in 1926 and supported by the Community Fund, complemented the work of the Tennessee Children's Home Society by housing dependent children. Since the Children's Bureau's ultimate goal in each case was family reunification, it did not handle adoptions but placed children temporarily in private homes. At the time of its founding, the Children's Bureau was envisioned as the premier child-caring organization for dependent children in Memphis, and it attempted to relieve the juvenile court of some of its welfare responsibilities.[74] Although child care workers had grand hopes for the Children's Bureau, it never surpassed the juvenile court as a gateway into the child welfare network in terms of the number of children helped or the scope of services offered.

The so-called scientific charity movement emerged in Memphis about the same time as in other southern cities. Proponents of scientific charity believed, according to the historian Michael Katz, that "laws governing charity [were] as fixed as those which underlie any other department of social or political economy, and that Organized Charity [was] the way, and the only way to discover and apply them."[75] Founded in 1911 by a coalition of Protestant churches, the Associated Charities in Memphis was the first citywide charity organization society. During its early years, it partly financed the Visiting Nurse Association, a dispensary, a special milk fund, a black home for the elderly and orphans, a medical social worker in the city hospital, and a Summer Baby Hospital, which evolved into the Municipal

Children's Hospital. It also set up a black auxiliary called the "Colored Federated Charities." Around 1916 the Associated Charities began the first Confidential Exchange, a central registry of clients who received assistance from social agencies in the city. The Associated Charities slowly distanced itself from simply providing relief and focused its mission explicitly on preventive family casework.[76] An internal report declared that its work "is never investigating for relief. It is laying a basis of history of a family upon which to build a plan which has the most possibilities for abating the difficulties which are ship-wrecking both families and members of families. Relief may or may not be part of any given plan."[77] Thus, the Associated Charities used investigative casework methods to counsel unstable white and black families on their underlying problems. Of the fifty-four hundred people it helped in 1923, nineteen hundred were children under fourteen years old.[78]

These charity society developments in Memphis were similar to those in other southern cities. The Associated Charities' budget grew rapidly, but it spent nearly three times as much money for whites as for blacks in 1921, and in 1923 it proudly declared that it had spent one-fifth of its money on black families. The size of its staff also expanded from three caseworkers to fourteen by 1922. As it grew, it not only assisted more people but expanded opportunities for professional social work. Although it moved slowly away from emphasizing moral behavior, the society did have rules for granting relief. In the case of the Franklin family, at one point the Associated Charities refused to "come back in on the case" because it felt the family was trying to "shuffle" its responsibilities. Inez Patterson's mother told a probation officer that the charity had refused relief on the grounds that the whole family was begging.[79]

Even though the Associated Charities assisted black families, most charity and family casework for black children in Memphis, as we have seen, was organized by a parallel network of black social service agencies and clubs. In 1925 the Inter Racial League prepared a list of "Institutions and Organizations Engaged In Welfare Work Among Negroes In Memphis and Shelby County" for the Council of Social Agencies. Along with the three children's homes, it listed more than twenty clubs that contributed to charity. It also included churches, three colleges, and the Rosenwald Fund.[80] Institutional approaches, or those that cared for children apart from their family or neighborhood, played a smaller role in the black child welfare network than they did for whites and reflected both more limited resources and the less hierarchical organization of black churches.

In addition to the local network in Memphis, juvenile courts and other child welfare organizations across the country cooperated with each other and participated in a nationwide network. They shared information about clients, did investigative work for each other in their own locales, and regularly returned runaway children to their legal jurisdictions. The Memphis Juvenile Court contacted regional child welfare agencies in Mississippi and Arkansas as well as those farther away. Red Cross officials in another town helped the juvenile court and the Tennessee Children's Home Society with the adoption of an illegitimate child.[81] Memphis participated in this nationwide network of juvenile courts, particularly with those located along the Mississippi River. Memphis and Chicago juvenile courts corresponded regularly. One case contained an evaluation done by the famous Institute for Juvenile Research connected with the Chicago Juvenile Court, and another contained a detailed statement from a Memphis child while she was held in Chicago.[82] Probation officers in St. Louis and Kansas City also did investigations at Judge Kelley's request. This pattern of communication exemplified the common Progressive child welfare tradition in southern urban areas as in cities throughout the country in the early twentieth century.

Throughout the 1920s, a decade of uneven prosperity, child welfare workers in Memphis were keenly aware of the adverse economic situations of numerous urban families, white and black, and of the limited ability of privately funded agencies to provide assistance to them. They perceived a correlation between the local economy and their caseloads. When the price of cotton fell after World War I, resulting in a regional depression, the Social Agencies' Endorsement Committee felt that "no new or extension work should be undertaken at the present time, in view of the fact that the present charity resources of the city are needed for maintenance of the home agencies already established."[83] The Associated Charities noted in 1925 that Memphis was faced with an influx of unskilled white and black migrants seeking industrial employment. Since wages for unskilled labor were too low for subsistence, many migrants came to the attention of the agency sooner or later.[84] At a meeting of the Council of Social Agencies in 1927, the members decided, after considerable discussion of the "unemployment situation," to appeal to the community to report all odd jobs to them in order to provide temporary work for those who most needed it. Mary Russell (of the Associated Charities) reported "that there was a thirty-three percent increase in unemployment in January over December."[85] By mid-1930 many social service agencies began to feel severe economic pressure. In June 1930 the

Associated Charities declared that it could no longer afford to take new cases.

Despite numerous improvements during the 1920s, child welfare workers acknowledged that much more needed to be done. The Child Welfare Committee of the Council of Social Agencies, headed by Judge Kelley, conducted a survey in 1930 to assess conditions of care for children. The survey recommended better temporary and long-term provisions for dependent children, especially black children. It also said that the city needed a psychiatric clinic along with more caseworkers for black families.[86]

The 1920s saw dramatic growth and elaboration of the child welfare network in Memphis. Emerging professional opportunities for women in social work contributed to the founding of new institutions and agencies that served specific populations of children and facilitated the longevity of their social service careers. Camille Kelley's appointment as chief judge of the juvenile court brought stability and professionalism to court operations and transformed the court into an efficient gateway into the city's growing child welfare network. She established long-term relationships with child welfare caseworkers, hired new probation officers, and steadily expanded the investigative duties of the court, thereby enabling it to play the role of a gateway into the child welfare network. The Council of Social Agencies and the Community Fund brought a new level of efficiency and regularity to the myriad organizations involved in child welfare activities.

CHAPTER FOUR

Juvenile Justice and the Treatment of Dependent Children

HISTORIANS OF JUVENILE JUSTICE and child welfare have much to gain by examining the role that the juvenile court played in handling dependent, neglected, and abused children.[1] Although the juvenile court was created primarily to remove children from adult criminal courts and jails, it served a much broader set of roles within the child welfare system than simply responding to delinquent behavior. Dependent as well as delinquent children formed a major part of the court's clientele. Their appearance in court compelled juvenile justice authorities to deal directly with long-term family struggles and dramatically expanded the social welfare duties of the juvenile court. In dependency cases, the juvenile court officers investigated the entire family situation and explicitly scrutinized the parents' behavior and lifestyle. A picture of the children's lives emerged mainly through critical assessments of the activities of their parents. As we shall see, the court's power to monitor families of dependent children vastly outweighed its ability to solve their fundamental problems. The intractable domestic disputes and chronic economic insecurity that many of these families faced lay well beyond the rehabilitative reach of the juvenile court and of the child welfare network more generally.

Child savers in Progressive Era Memphis attempted to combat the hazards of urban life for children by legally classifying some of them as dependent. To be sure, orphans, waifs, and child beggars had long existed, but labeling them as "dependent" transformed their conditions of life into a social problem. The growing public discussion of dependent children in the Progressive Era elevated their status to a national concern and further legitimated the concept of childhood as a distinct phase of life in need of special monitoring and protection. In making a public issue of child dependency, child welfare workers alerted the citizenry to how vulnerable some people were to the urban wage economy and how inadequate traditional family economic strategies often were to the realities of modern urban life. Since the juvenile court was the only public agency in Memphis with jurisdiction over dependent children, its welfare work was considered essential to civic well-being. To understand the operations of juvenile courts in the Progressive Era, we need to examine their welfare work with dependent children as fully as their work with delinquent children.

More vague than delinquency, dependency was broadly defined by the dialectic between child protection and parental rights. Among the middle-class citizens who led the campaign for child welfare reform in the urban South, family ideals were shifting from the disciplined, hierarchical family of the nineteenth century to the affectionate, democratic, child-conscious family of the twentieth century.[2] With the passage of juvenile court, child labor, and compulsory attendance laws at the turn of the century and the creation of the United States Children's Bureau in 1912, local and national governmental agencies began for the first time to take systematic responsibility for children's overall well-being and to hold parents to certain standards of care.

A new relationship between private and public life began to emerge in the early twentieth century as the juvenile court, with its broad array of powers and personnel, attempted to define more concretely than ever before new standards of parental responsibility, proper child rearing, and home upkeep. This new level of intrusion by the state into private family life created some conflict within families, but it also made room for new types of involvement by nonfamily private citizens in the court's day-to-day affairs. For all of the considerable power that it exercised on its own, the juvenile court was not an autonomous institution. Community members, particularly parents, requested help from the juvenile court in times of distress and thereby helped legitimate its social welfare role. Families brought their private disputes into the public arena when they sought the juvenile court's jurisdiction. Neighbors and strangers also turned to the court to enforce standards of behavior. Since most dependent children were quite young and not likely to be (or at least not recognized as) independent actors, the fray of activity took place mainly above them. This mediation of public and private, juvenile and adult rights took place in the juvenile court.

EVERYDAY MEANINGS OF DEPENDENCY IN THE
JUVENILE COURT

The state of Tennessee began dealing with problems of dependency in the eighteenth century with narrow concepts of both who constituted a vulnerable child and state responsibility for vulnerable children. Care for abandoned or orphaned children included apprenticing them (or binding them out) to a local bidder or committing them to private orphanages. In the early 1820s the state passed legislation that allowed county courts to bind out illegitimate children if their mothers were unfit, or other children whose fathers abandoned or refused to support them.[3] County courts also appointed guardians for orphans and were supposed to hold orphans' court once a year to register all orphans and ascertain the quality of their care.[4] Rather than addressing the internal dynamics of families, orphanages and apprenticeships dealt with the problem of dependency mainly by dissolving families.

Informal and community efforts to care for war orphans and other dependent children predominated during the nineteenth century. Families and neighbors simply took orphaned children into their homes. Among blacks, this voluntary individual and familial care far surpassed institutional care, although ex-slaves contributed to orphanages established before the Civil War and opened new ones during Reconstruction.[5] Black orphanages often struggled to provide basic necessities and could not offer elaborate educational programs. Orphanages for white children also continued as a community solution for dependent children. While some orphanages were supported by states or cities, most were private, with Catholics establishing the largest number. During the 1880s many white child-caring institutions developed model industrial education programs that were later adopted by public schools.[6]

After the Civil War, however, the state played a larger (and sometimes contradictory) role in policies toward dependent children, especially blacks. Apprenticing (binding out) came to represent efforts by white landowners in the South to regain control over the labor of newly freed black children and their parents. The Freedmen's Bureau, in trying to protect the rights of former slaves, became involved in apprentice disputes because of its responsibility to supervise contracts. In North Carolina, from which Tennessee drew many of its own welfare laws, legal authority to indenture orphaned and fatherless children resided with county courts and with the

Freedmen's Bureau's federal mandate, which included a parental consent clause. White landowners used these categories ("orphan," "illegitimate," "abandoned") against black families as grounds for apprenticeship.[7] Black parents and relatives, in turn, used the Freedmen's Bureau (and higher state courts) to counter attempts by whites to reimpose forced labor on their children by appealing to the bureau to break indentures. Many of the disputes revolved around conflicting understandings of kin relationships. Although black families knew which children belonged to which families, bureau agents and landowners disputed the parentage of some black children and considered them to be "orphaned" or "abandoned" when their families did not.[8] The state attempted to mediate between white landowners and black parents as newly freed black slaves struggled to keep their families together.

As Progressive Era reformers and the public became disillusioned with drawbacks of institutional care, such as overcrowding, regimentation, and lack of proper socialization, the ideology of national child welfare reform shifted from family dissolution to family preservation. Foster care, or placement in homes of nonrelatives, had gradually gained favor in the midnineteenth century and complemented the new emphasis on keeping children in homes with families.[9] Beginning around the turn of the twentieth century, the provision of monetary support in the form of mothers' pensions was inaugurated to help children to stay in their own homes. Along with other southern states, Tennessee enacted a Mothers' Pension Law in 1915, one of the state's first attempts at outdoor relief.[10] During the Progressive Era, child welfare reformers in Memphis began to emphasize keeping families intact whenever possible. The founding of the juvenile court, with its legal mandate and staff of probation officers, not only expanded the role of government in child welfare but created novel machinery to give new operational meaning to traditional ways of addressing dependency.[11]

As a condition rather than a specific act, dependency took many forms. The legal definition of dependency used vague language such as "without proper and sufficient guardianship" and included conditions such as being "neglected and living in bad environment."[12] Legal definitions aside, community members and court officials actively interpreted how "proper guardianship" translated into everyday life. The range of perceptions of what constituted dependency reflected the worldview of those who made the charges. As we shall see, parents and court officers tended to focus on different types of behaviors and situations. Some behaviors and situations, such as physical abuse or hunger, were fairly widely accepted as providing legal grounds for dependency charges. Alcohol abuse and begging were less clear-cut indicators of dependency, and some adverse child-rearing conditions, such as crowded living and poor housekeeping, became highly contested issues between court officials and parents.

Some of the most obvious signs of dependency included poverty and material deprivation. Despite national economic prosperity in the 1920s, many clients of the Memphis Juvenile Court, both white and black, remained particularly vulnerable to the low wages maintained by the South's racial system. In addition to its stagnant industrial base, Memphis absorbed many rural families displaced by the boll weevil invasion and the end of the coal-mining boom.[13] With only one-third of the fathers in the juvenile court working full-time and about half working irregular hours, many families lacked basic physical necessities. Many clients lived in poor neighborhoods where sanitary conditions were sometimes appalling. Some lived in shacks, while many had no running water and could not afford to buy food or clothes. In one case, probation officers found a single white mother and her three children living in a tent. When another mother, who was single and black, was questioned as to whether her son was fed regularly and whether the food was wholesome and substantial, she responded that she did the very best she could on the five dollars a week she earned doing laundry. Out of that amount she had to feed her mother, two children, and herself.[14]

Chronic economic insecurity took a high toll on family members, forcing separations from children and tensions between parents. One single white father left his children in St. Peter's Orphanage for more than a year and did not pay board during that time. His place of employment in Memphis had shut down and he had moved to Los Angeles while looking for work in cities along the way. He had intended to send for his children once he found a steady position, but so far had been unsuccessful. A probation officer in the Los Angeles Juvenile Court communicated that "most of the plants in this city have been working on part time, or half time scale [and] laborer and tradesmen work . . . have been rather scarce in this city for sometime. . . . He [the father] apparently has worried much over this problem he had been facing as he could not control himself while talking with me and broke down."[15] Financial problems exacerbated distrustful or shaky marriages and caused parents to quarrel. Many dependent children, at some point in their lives, lived temporarily in a local institution or orphanage even though one or both parents were living. These temporary placements were common and suggest that in Memphis, as elsewhere, orphanages were not viewed simply as an alternative to the family, but rather as a broader community response to assist families in acute need. [16]

However, some contemporaries who came in contact with the juvenile court questioned whether poverty itself provided sufficient grounds for declaring children dependent. These critics also felt that poor parents were judged more harshly for otherwise common adult behaviors. For instance, an attorney retained by the father of two white children wrote to Judge Kelley that "there is not a home in the land where there is not 'a problem.' In the home of the millionaire and mendicant alike, there is a problem. . . . There is in my judgment more real religion, morality, sympathy and love in the hovel than in the mansion. It is said that the aged father of Mr. Thomas Anderson [the father in court], uses alcoholic liquors. The rich use alcoholic liquors. The debutantes of elite society, it is said, drink alcoholic liquors and smoke cigarettes. . . . This is called fashion." Although the attorney may have exaggerated for effect, his arguments about double standards of behavior, and whether financial poverty per se indicated physical or emotional neglect, highlighted the extent to which operational definitions of dependency could be arbitrary and/or class driven. [17]

Indeed, neglectful child-rearing conditions were not always a result of financial instability but also reflected troubled marriages, complicated dynamics between parents and other adults, and prejudiced race relations. Not all poor children were considered dependent, and not all parents charged with neglect were poor. Almost one-fifth of the dependent children in court came from families in which the father worked in a clerical, proprietary, or professional occupation. In some financially stable families, parents fought continuously, were separated, or accused each other of impropriety. Mr. and Mrs. Green were a good example of a white couple who had no financial troubles but argued incessantly about their relationship. Mr. Green, a foreman who earned $135 a month (a very good salary at the time), wanted the children removed from his wife and accused her of being cross and immoral and of neglecting the children. He signed a warrant alleging that the children were neglected. A few days later the wife came to court and signed a nonsupport warrant against the husband, claiming that Mr. Green was jealous and had left home. She also said that family relations were unpleasant because her husband's family disliked her Irish Catholic background. The husband soon returned home, but two years later he came to court again and claimed that his wife had deserted the family, although the family reconciled soon after. The next year the wife threatened the husband with a gun, and the children were removed to St. Peter's Orphanage. This case did not revolve around money or food but rather a dissolving marriage.[18]

Community members also used the legal power of the juvenile court and the ambiguity of dependency statutes to reinforce racial segregation. The case of Elsie Jones began when a neighbor complained "that a white baby 5 or 6 years of age [Elsie] stayed with a colored family all day." The probation officer spoke to the black woman, "who admitted that a little white child named Elsie Jones played in the yard and sidewalk with the little colored children in her family, that her niece worked for this child's mother and that the child would come home with her but that she wouldn't keep her now that she was notified not to do so." The woman said she rented rooms and took in washing, and the officer noted that the rooms were decently furnished and fairly clean. The officer then spoke to Elsie's mother and found that she too rented rooms and had been in her house only two months. The rooms were "dirty and the entire atmosphere of the place unfavorable. Neighborhood questionable." The officer "explained that Elsie could not play all day in the negro house and [the mother] promised to keep her at home. Denied that Elsie stayed there all day, but admitted that she stayed on sidewalk in front of their house occasionally, however promised to keep her at home. Elsie was neatly dressed and clean." The neighbor who initiated the complaint could have been unhappy with the racial implications of the child care arrangements, the apparent lack of supervision (since Elsie played on the front sidewalk), or even the fact that the white mother's former husband rented one of the black woman's rooms. The home of the black woman appeared to be better than Elsie's own home, but the issue of improper race relations transcended the quality of the physical environment.

Elsie's case continued later in the year when her mother and her new husband were arrested for bigamy, providing yet more grounds to charge that the mother neglected her children. The police sent Elsie to the juvenile court, as they always did with children when their parents were arrested. The mother said that she did not know her husband already had a wife and blamed her troubles on "a Mrs. Owens, who was angry with her and it was a case of spite." This "case of spite" had serious consequences: neither the mother nor her new in-laws were able to regain custody of Elsie. Upon questioning by a probation officer, the mother said that she had been married four times; the first two husbands had died, the third she divorced, and the fourth had just been arrested for bigamy. Several days after the court hearing, the child's parents returned (the husband having obtained a divorce) and were anxious to take Elsie and move to Georgia to live with the father's parents. Judge Kelley refused to let them have Elsie, and in 1921 the judge committed her to Leath Orphanage, where she stayed for the next nine years. The mother tried several times over the years to regain custody of Elsie, but caseworkers told Kelley that the home conditions were unfavorable. Elsie was not allowed to live with her mother again until 1930.[19] Questions of adulterous behavior and fights between jealous men and women sometimes rendered the child almost incidental to the situation. Dependency cases, then, were often made up of many interacting problems.

Charges of dependency focused the court's attention on the entire family, not simply the children. To be sure, parents of delinquent children (as we will see in the next chapter) sometimes endured humiliating and intrusive home investigations by court officials. However, unlike delinquency cases, which often consisted of a relatively isolated incident in a child's life and short durations of punishment, dependency cases usually involved families with several long-term problems. Parents of neglected children often faced systematic, dogged, almost inevitably judgmental oversight. As family problems emerged in full light, the scope of a case usually expanded rapidly; more than half of the dependent girls and boys had their siblings in the juvenile court on the same charge.

For children, the effects of being dependent varied, although the multiple formal and informal meanings of dependency complicate any objective attempt to assess a child's true situation. In an effort to discredit each other, parents often gave conflicting reports about the treatment of their children. Agency caseworkers, court officers, and police officers each had their own biases and agendas. Thus the situations of dependent children could vary widely. They usually moved frequently, lived in an orphanage, or were even homeless. They might be sick, not have enough food or clothes, or be physically abused. Many were not in school and instead hustled for themselves by begging, stealing, or selling newspapers. Dependent children were also caught in the middle of vicious disputes between their parents and exposed to their verbal and physical fighting or left with questionable caretakers.

While many dependent children suffered in conditions of abject poverty, some simply lived in home environments or engaged in street behaviors that did not fit with middle-class family ideals that probation officers embraced. Out of economic necessity, many children lived in crowded housing arrangements with several people, sharing not only the same room but also the same bed. In their home investigations, probation officers disliked the casual mingling of women and men. Most particularly, they were upset that people dressed and undressed in front of each other. Further, they viewed the cleanliness and furnishings of living quarters as a means to gauge the adequacy of attention given the children. Court officials were frustrated by children who habitually sold newspapers or begged despite repeated warnings in and out of court, and by mothers who left their children with hired help during the day while they worked. The parents sometimes did not see anything wrong with their or their children's behavior and ignored the court's negative comments and orders.[20]

Court officials and social services agencies in Memphis espoused policies based on the ideal of the two-parent, male-headed household; both mothers and fathers were judged on how well they performed their respective familial responsibilities. The juvenile court functioned quite openly to reinforce patriarchy in family relations.[21] Court officers routinely made judgmental observations about a mother's attention to the cleanliness of her home and children and about a father's provision for his family. For example, the chief probation officer wrote to a white father: "I wish to state to you that this is an outrage . . . and it is imperative that you come to Memphis at once and take your children home with you. If you do not do this it will be our duty to come to Brownsville and instigate non-support proceedings against you. Your wife has not behaved in the way she should at all times, but you certainly neglect your children shamefully. There is no reason I can see why society should have to support your children."[22] These harsh words echoed frequently in the juvenile court as probation officers tried to cajole parents to fulfill their prescribed gender roles.

In addition, mothers bore a disproportionate moral burden: their sexual behavior was evaluated in ways that fathers' sexual behavior was not. Consider the different descriptions of two so-called immoral parents, one white mother and one white father. The mother ran a rooming house, but her husband said that she was too friendly with male boarders. He therefore had the occupants of the house arrested for disorderly conduct and reported her for neglect. She claimed that her husband hit her and did not support the family and that she had no parents to help her. The children were released to the mother, and the father was ordered to pay fifteen dollars every two weeks. When the court officer visited about two weeks later, the mother said that she had advertised for married boarders but could not get any and could not let the current male boarders go until she had replacements. The officer replied that if men continued to live with her, the court would be forced to take away the children until she had carried out the judge's orders.

In contrast to the close scrutiny given this mother's behavior, court records described a father in another case as follows: "man has had repeated affairs with women since first known to Juvenile Court in 1921. These women, however, were all older and in no sense could man be accused of 'ruining' them as all of them were women of as much or more experience than man himself. . . . Has very little moral sense in regard to sex. Lives first with one woman then another. . . . This would seem to indicate that women play a large part in his conduct." He had quite "evidently little moral stamina. Seems rather more un-moral than im-moral." This father repeatedly deserted his family, could not keep a job, had been divorced, and had a criminal record. However, he was described as coming from good, plain country farming stock. Abandoned once again by the father, the mother finally took the children and moved in with her brother. No one mentioned the possibility of taking away this man's children because of his promiscuity.[23]

Unlike delinquency cases in which the burgeoning sexuality of girls played an important part in their juvenile court appearance, sex rarely figured in girls' dependency cases, and when it did, the girl's sexual behavior was more ambiguous in determining the disposition. Only 11 percent of the dependent girls, compared to 50 percent of the delinquent girls, had engaged in some kind of sexual activity. The younger ages of the dependent girls accounted for much of this difference, since most accusations of sexual activity involved older girls. Some dependency cases, such as those that involved a girl running away or living with a man, might have easily been classified as delinquency cases. For instance, the Women's Protection Bureau brought in Rose, age sixteen, for vagrancy and lacking proper guardianship. She had gone riding with some boys who held her and a girlfriend as prisoners in a hotel room. She later escaped but could not give a clear description of the boys. She admitted "immorality" about a year before but refused to give the boy's name. Although her grandmother offered her a home, everyone agreed that the Tennessee Industrial School was best for Rose. Despite her classification as a dependent child, Rose's case was in fact typical of female delinquents in that she was older, was employed, had engaged in consensual sex, went out with boys, and in the end was institutionalized by the court.

Other cases involving sexual behavior by dependent girls consisted mainly of incest or forced prostitution, and these usually evolved out of a larger set of confusing circumstances involving parents and other adults.

Effie May, age sixteen, suffered from numerous abuses. She came to the attention of the juvenile court because a neighbor complained that the people she lived with were part of a prostitution operation. Her father had been sentenced to the Missouri penitentiary for two years, so she and her mother had moved from the family's Missouri farm to live in Memphis with an aunt. Since the aunt and Effie May did not get along, Effie May was living temporarily with a Mr. and Mrs. Tipper (their relation to the family is unclear) at the time of her appearance in court. The Tippers said that they wanted to adopt the girl because her mother was unfit. Once in the juvenile court, Effie May said that her father had used her for immoral purposes between the ages of ten and twelve and that her grandfather had tried also. She also charged that her father was cruel to her mother, that her mother lived the life of a prostitute, and that she, with the mother's knowledge, had been a prostitute.[24] Unlike Rose in the previous case, Effie May experienced long-term abuse at the hands of family members and close acquaintances. The context of Effie May's sexual activity was quite different from Rose's, even though they were both formally adjudged dependent. Again, a broad operational definition of dependency captured a wide variety of circumstances.

In both theory and practice, then, the concept of dependency was ambiguous and inclusive. The growth of state power, as embodied in the form of juvenile court, lent new force to middle-class standards of child rearing. Some dependent children suffered from material deprivation such as poor housing and inadequate food, which resulted from their family's poverty. Dependent children also came from families whose parents' behavior included physical abuse, continual quarreling, sexual impropriety, or staying out late. However, common working-class family strategies such as living in boarding houses, leaving children with nonrelative caretakers so that mothers could work, and having children sell newspapers were grounds for alleging that a child was dependent. Dependency cases focused attention primarily on adults; the resolution of such cases often rested on how well other family members, neighbors, or the parents themselves fulfilled their prescribed gender roles.

CHARACTERISTICS OF DEPENDENT CHILDREN AND THEIR FAMILIES

Perhaps the most salient feature of the dependency caseload in the Memphis Juvenile Court was race; 85 percent of the dependent children were white (as contrasted with 44 percent of the delinquents). This tremendous imbalance highlights the competing social functions of the juvenile court in Memphis. White children both benefited from the court's attempts to alleviate their dire circumstances and chafed under its intrusion, whereas black children primarily experienced the juvenile court coercively as delinquents. Why this severe racial imbalance occurred in the dependency caseload is not entirely clear. The large white social service agencies clearly channeled few black children to the juvenile court. Equally important, though, may be that whereas white families initiated many complaints of neglect (as we shall see shortly), black families may have intentionally avoided the juvenile court. Historians have shown that in southern cities, churches, along with neighborhood and family networks, formed the bedrock of black mutual support.[25] Mabel Brown Ellis, who surveyed juvenile courts in 1920 for the National Child Labor Committee's report, *Child Welfare in Tennessee*, attributed the racial imbalance in public welfare to the custom among blacks of taking orphaned or stray children into other families.[26]

The low portion of black children among dependency cases in Memphis was consistent with patterns in other southern juvenile courts. In North Carolina, a state considered by some historians to have been quite active in black child welfare, an investigation conducted by the North Carolina State Board of Charities and Public Welfare and the University of North Carolina found a similar pattern of underrepresentation among black children.[27] Based on 23,443 cases handled between 1919 and 1929 by North Carolina's system of county juvenile courts (ninety-four in all), only 22 percent of dependency cases were black. The study concluded, as did Mabel Brown Ellis, that relatives and neighbors more readily took in neglected children among blacks than whites.[28]

Nevertheless, as Howard Rabinowitz has demonstrated more generally, dependent black children in Memphis were not entirely excluded from the protection of the juvenile court.[29] The few black families who did appear in court had both good and bad experiences that closely resembled those of white families. Court officials did not make simplistic assumptions that black parents were inherently neglectful. Instead, as in white cases, they generally attributed neglect to a variety of internal family dynamics and external pressures that sometimes overwhelmed otherwise "good" parents. Some black families in troubled circumstances came in contact with a wide array of social service agencies, and probation officers were not reluctant to remove children from abusive caretakers. Thus black children in Memphis derived some benefits from the juvenile court's attempts to enforce higher standards of parental responsibility.

The basic characteristics of dependent children differed from delinquent children in two important areas: sex and age. Unlike delinquency cases, which were predominately boys, almost the same number of girls and boys appeared before the court as dependents. Dependent children were also much younger than delinquent children. The average age of girls was 7.9 years and of boys 7.2 years, about half that of delinquent children. The largest age group, 14 percent, was one-year-olds; overall, 35 percent were too young to be in school.

Families of dependent children were much more unstable than those of delinquent children. Consequently, dependent children, although much younger, appear to have experienced considerably more stress in their family lives than delinquent children. Marriage patterns show that families of neglected children had higher rates of separation than families of delinquent children.[30] Only 20 percent of the children's parents in dependency cases claimed to be married. Forty-seven percent of the parents said they were divorced, separated, or had been deserted. Thirty percent of the children had experienced the death of one or both parents. The parents of the youngest children (ages one to five) were the most likely to be separated, while parents of the oldest children (ages twelve and over) were the mostly likely to have died. The truth about these marital arrangements is very complicated: sometimes clients lied to protect themselves or boost their claims, did not bother or could not afford to get divorced, or lived together as spouses without being formally married. Very clear, however, is that parents were continually separating and reuniting and that their relationships were constantly in flux.

Examination of the child's primary caretaker sheds further light on the household structures of dependent children (see table 1). More than one-third (37 percent) of dependent girls and boys lived with their mother alone, whereas only 17 percent lived with both parents.[31] In about 12 percent of the families, children lived with a natural parent and a stepparent, and 6 percent lived with a relative. The rest of the dependent children lived with foster parents, in orphanages, or in some temporary placement. Almost half of the youngest children (ages one to five) lived with their mother only, but older children lived in a wider range of households. These figures suggest

TABLE 1. Primary Caretaker for Dependent Children (N = 186)

	GIRLS		BOYS		TOTAL	
	N	%	N	%	N	%
Parents	15	15.8	17	18.7	32	17.2
Mother and stepfather	10	10.5	7	7.7	17	9.1
Father and stepmother	4	4.2	1	1.1	5	2.7
Mother	35	36.8	33	36.3	68	36.6
Father	9	9.5	10	11.0	19	10.2
Relative, no parents	5	5.3	6	6.6	11	5.9
Adoptive parents	5	5.3	5	5.5	10	5.4
Public institution	1	1.1	1	1.1	2	1.1
Private institution	7	7.4	7	7.7	14	7.5
Temporary placement	3	3.2	1	1.1	4	2.2
No regular residence	1	1.1	3	3.3	4	2.2
Total	95		91		186	
	SUMMARY					
Parents	15	15.8	17	18.7	32	17.2
Parent and stepparent	14	14.7	8	8.8	22	11.8
Single parent	44	46.3	43	47.3	87	46.8
Other	22	23.2	23	25.3	45	24.2
Total	95		91		186	

that the historical incidence of single motherhood was quite high and not limited to one race.[32] They also suggest that the youngest children in court came from the least stable households.

The reasons for the high incidence of male-absent households in dependency cases were complicated. As a rule, female-headed households were most common among the economically disadvantaged. For white women, lack of nearby relatives, high rates of desertion, and death of a spouse accounted most often for single motherhood. Among blacks, high male mortality, the tendency of rural women to migrate to the city after the death of a husband, out-of-wedlock births, and greater opportunity for female wage labor in the city were the principal causes of single motherhood.[33] Incarceration also sometimes explained parental absence. At least one-fifth of the children had guardians who had committed a crime.[34] Several fathers, similar to Effie May's (discussed above), were in the state penitentiary for selling drugs or murder.

Parents, particularly mothers, often had ambiguous living arrangements or relationships. Many families lived in rooming houses or light-housekeeping rooms, and quite a few women ran their own rooming houses. This common arrangement raised potential problems in the eyes of court officials. Male "boarders" were often indeed boarders, but some were also lovers or longtime companions who contributed financial support to the mother's household. One young single mother said that the man who lived with her and her child had been kind to them and that she had just drifted into a sexual relationship. When the court officer, appalled by this arrangement, threatened to take away the daughter unless the mother and boarder either lived apart or got married, the mother was genuinely surprised. The probation officer noted that the "mother did not seem to realize her conduct would not warrant keeping the baby." In this case, the officer viewed the lack of legal marriage as equivalent to child neglect. The presence of boarders in a home often reflected badly on mothers, especially single mothers who most needed the extra income. In another case, the court noted that the "status of the boarder is questionable since at the time of officers' visit, he was half undressed in the room with [the mother]." This mother was told to straighten up her home. These personal relationships, which usually began out of economic necessity, flouted the court's ideal of proper moral guardianship for children.[35]

In addition to the instability resulting from the absence of one or both parents, dependent children experienced a variety of other serious problems. At least 8 percent of the children experienced sexual or physical abuse, and another 11 percent experienced other family violence, particularly the abuse of their mother by their father.[36] In at least 15 percent of the cases, either the mother or the father had a discernible alcohol problem. Dependent children were twice as likely as delinquent children to experience abuse, family violence, and alcoholism at home. The families of dependent girls were slightly worse off, because more girls than boys experienced sexual abuse, family violence, and criminality, and more of their mothers worked away from home.

The Allen family highlights numerous characteristics of a typical dependency case because of the need to focus on the issues in the adult world rather than the needs of the children. The paternal grandfather complained to the juvenile court that his two granddaughters, nine and five years old, had been deserted by their parents. The parents were separated and the current whereabouts of the mother were unknown. When court officers contacted the father at work (Buick Motor Car Company, where he was a mechanic earning twenty dollars a week), he said that if the juvenile court "wanted him, they had his permission to send a patrol wagon and bring him in and that was the only way they could get him." When the mother finally appeared at the juvenile court, having learned from her husband where the children were, she stated that their marriage had been very troubled from the start, that they had separated many times, that the husband was abusive and failed to support the family, and that he refused to let the American Legion give her money when the children were hungry. Her relatives were in North Carolina and were disgusted with her. Moreover, because Mr. Allen had threatened her entire family, they were afraid of him. She asked for some short-term arrangements for the girls until she could get a job and could keep them with her. The mother also claimed, contrary to the grandfather's interpretation, that she had purposely sent the children to their grandparents' house rather than abandoning them there without notice.

During court testimony, Mrs. Allen admitted that she was afraid of her husband. She described his physical abuse, his refusal to buy food when he was angry, and how he ordered her out of the house. In turn, the husband testified that he had tried for ten years to make a home and that he did everything he possibly could. He promised that he would care for the children as long as the mother was forbidden from moving them. The children were released to the Children's Bureau for boarding, to be paid by the father. Shortly after the court hearing, the mother entered the hospital, where she stayed for about two months. She expressed appreciation to the court for its assistance because she felt that the court would not allow her husband to take the children without another hearing. Later the husband came to the juvenile court to claim that his wife was in a very bad state of mind. She would poison the children if the court attempted to remove them from her, he claimed. He also stated that his wife felt very unkindly toward the court, although he felt that the court was his best friend.

After the parents met with Judge Kelley several times, the director of the Children's Bureau conceded that the parents should be given a month to work things out and that she would not charge them board during that time. The parents agreed to reconcile, and the children were released to the parents under court supervision. Two weeks later, however, the situation deteriorated again. The landlady called the juvenile court to complain that the parents quarreled so much that she had asked them to leave. The probation officer noted that "Mrs. Allen's face and head were terribly bruised and swollen, and her front tooth was loose. The children were neatly dressed and clean." The case continued in this manner with several more court appearances in which the parents accused each other of sexual perversity, infidelity, and insanity. Shortly afterward, Mr. Allen stabbed his wife, which led Judge Kelley and other caseworkers to resolve not to return the children to the parents. The Allens' long-term and ultimately unsolvable marital troubles had drawn in a large number of relevant actors—all the family members, neighbors, friends, doctors. In an involved, long-term dependency case such as this one, parents usually spent far more time in the juvenile court than did the children. In fact, the cases generally did not revolve around the behavior of children at all.[37]

Many of the court's clients were also physically unhealthy. Indeed, due to climate and poverty, southerners were more likely to be unhealthy than other Americans.[38] Poor diet, inadequate housing, and lack of simple preventive public health and sanitation measures led to the widespread incidence of malaria, hookworm, and pellagra.[39] Families of dependent children reported chronic illness at almost twice the rate as families of delinquent children. In 28 percent of the families, at least one family member had a discernible illness. Of those cases, more than half were mothers. Chronic or even sudden illness of either the breadwinner or caretaker could upset the delicate balance that these families maintained. Poor nutrition resulted in difficult childbirth and underweight children, many of whom later contracted tuberculosis. During this time period, Tennessee had the highest resident death rate from tuberculosis of any state in the country. It also ranked lowest in state aid and facilities for the treatment of the "white plague."[40] The death rate from tuberculosis among blacks was much higher than for whites.[41] Since the court fed and bathed children who stayed in the detention home, the care they received there may have been better than in their own homes.

Case files reveal that many of the families also had someone with a discernible mental illness. They were described as "unstable," "neurotic," or "feeble-minded." Those with the most serious symptoms spent time in Western State Hospital in Bolivar, Tennessee. Probation officers and neighbors occasionally recognized some of the worst cases. A probation officer wrote that "it could readily be seen that there was some mental trouble." Since mothers bore the primary burden of child care, managing the household, and keeping the family intact (in addition to working outside the home), it is not surprising that mothers comprised half of those with some kind of an illness. Many mothers had clear symptoms of depression, such as lack of interest in their children or in cleaning house and unresponsiveness to outside help. The director of the Children's Bureau complained in 1929 that one mother was "completely satisfied with the idea that someone else is taking care of her children and allowing her to see them. Her husband is paying her board and she has nothing to do but sit by the fire and walk up and down Main street. She says she does not love her husband . . . and gives no material evidence of her love for her children."[42] Factors such as being victims of abuse, living in poverty, and fulfilling multiple social roles may have contributed to depression and more serious mental illness among the mothers of dependent children in the Memphis Juvenile Court.

The working-class occupations of parents of dependent children were similar to those of delinquent children. Most fathers were working class, with 80 percent listing an unskilled, a semiskilled, or a skilled occupation. Although fathers of dependent children were more likely to be unemployed than those of delinquent children, the majority did work either full-time or indeterminate hours. Around half of the white mothers and three-quarters of the black mothers were in the paid labor force. White mothers predominated in less skilled occupations while black mothers worked mainly in domestic and personal service.

Although they lived publicly segregated lives, the private lives of white and black women were intertwined. White mothers, and sometimes fathers, coped with domestic chores by hiring black women. For instance, Mrs. Rogers, a white woman, worked in her husband's bakery and hired a black woman, Betty Rollins, to cook and care for her three children while she worked. The Rogers children also stayed at Rollins's home for several days while the family moved.[43] White families hired black women to do laundry and provide child care without giving much thought to the lives of their helpers. These black women earned as little as $1.50 a week, although they usually averaged $4 to $5 a week. The relationship was not completely one sided, however; black women brought their own children with them when they did laundry, or they took the laundry or sewing into their own homes. Black women themselves also hired black neighbors to care for their children.[44]

Families of dependent children were highly transient between Memphis and nearby small towns and farms but also within the city. White and black families moved in search of work as they drifted between farming and other work and were reduced to day labor.[45] In Memphis, they moved frequently from one boarding house to another, usually paying rent by the week. Case files show that few families had formal church affiliations. Not surprisingly, families without community and familial support systems were more likely to seek assistance from the formal social service network.

In times of crisis, white and black poor families turned to a variety of sources for help. Kinship networks were usually the first recourse in times of crisis.[46] Relatives provided child care, lodging, and financial support in times of need. However, since many families in Memphis had migrated from surrounding farms, they lacked nearby kin and had to call on outside agencies for help. More than half of the families in the Memphis Juvenile Court were already known to another social service agency. For instance, Thelma Day's father had recently deserted her mother. Since no family members could take them at that time, Mrs. Day (who was white) came to Memphis from a nearby farm to put the four children in Leath Orphanage. To pay board at the orphanage, she got a job but soon lost it. Fearing that her children would be given away, she appealed to the juvenile court for help. She soon got another job at the Iten Biscuit Company, which she preferred to working in the cotton fields. About one month later, Mrs. Day and her children went to live with a sister in Florida.[47] As this case illustrates, while families were the preferred source of support, the services that the Memphis child welfare network (including the juvenile court) had to offer could fill vital short-term needs.

In sum, families of dependent children who came before the juvenile court faced many long-term problems, such as violent domestic disputes and never-ending economic insecurity. Although the families were overwhelmingly white, they had much in common with the black families in the court and, indeed, with the larger black population of Memphis. Dependent children generally came from single-parent households. Mothers of dependent children were likely to be single, to work outside the home, and to be ill. Vagaries in employment (a husband's underemployment or unemployment, or a mother with very young children who had to work outside the home) all pushed families to the brink of solvency. Illness of either the breadwinner or the caretaker also created financial hardship. Alcohol abuse, physical abuse, unsupervised children, or parents refusing to fulfill child-caring responsibilities, also left children highly vulnerable to neglect. Dependent children were quite young and experienced various kinds of mistreatment and misfortune. Compared to the families of delinquent children, the families of dependent children were more structurally and emotionally unstable.

ADJUDICATING DEPENDENT CHILDREN

Dependent children came to the attention of the juvenile court in a variety of ways (see table 2). Court personnel initiated hardly any cases. Unlike some juvenile courts or child-caring agencies elsewhere, the Memphis Juvenile Court did not go out and seek clients.[48] Rather, for girls and boys of all ages, family members (parents and relatives) made up one-third of the complainants in dependency cases. A few children even sought help for themselves from the juvenile court. The virtual absence of court-initiated dependency cases complements the findings about an overburdened probation staff in the next chapter. If probation officers could barely handle cases that came to them, they were unlikely to spend much energy looking for cases. In light of these referral patterns, it is essential to analyze what parents thought they were gaining when they invoked the authority of the juvenile court on their own behalf, as well as to evaluate how much unregulated power the juvenile court actually exercised over their private domestic affairs.

Many of the reasons parents turned to the juvenile court involved marital disputes and arguments about domestic responsibilities. Husbands blamed wives for poor housekeeping or unwise budgeting. As demonstrated earlier in the cases of Mr. Green and Mr. Allen, husbands also complained about their wives' sexual indiscretions, both real and imagined.[49] Wives most often blamed husbands for inadequate financial support of the family because of desertion or drinking. Husbands and wives tended to have different perceptions of their commitment to the children, because one or the other was continually deserting the family and then returning home. Parents regularly accused each other of neglecting the children when they lived together. When the parents did not live together, it was common for them to accuse the absent parent of not fulfilling his or her role.

Even though women had to endure the prying of court officials into their sexual lives while men did not, wives potentially had a powerful rejoinder against their husbands. They could sign dependency warrants and initiate the intervention of the juvenile court to challenge their husband's authority in the family. Women, both separated and married, used the court to achieve this goal in two ways: on the one hand, to counter their husband's

TABLE 2. Complainant against Dependent Children (*N* = 188)

	GIRLS		BOYS		TOTAL	
	N	%	*N*	%	*N*	%
Probation officer	3	3.2	5	5.4	8	4.3
Police	17	17.9	12	12.9	29	15.4
Women's Protection Bureau	8	8.4	3	3.2	11	5.9
School	2	2.1	8	8.6	10	5.3
Social service agency	13	13.7	18	19.4	31	16.5
Parents	25	26.3	22	23.7	47	25.0
Relative	9	9.5	6	6.5	15	8.0
Foster parents	2	2.1	7	7.5	9	4.8
Neighbor	9	9.5	3	3.2	12	6.4
Private citizen	5	5.3	3	3.2	8	4.3
Juvenile	1	1.1	2	2.2	3	1.6
Anonymous	1	1.1	4	4.3	5	2.7
Total	95		93		188	
	SUMMARY					
Law	28	29.5	20	21.5	48	25.5
School/social services	15	15.8	26	28.0	41	21.8
Parents/relative	34	35.8	28	30.1	62	33.0
Other	18	18.9	19	20.4	37	19.7
Total	95		93		188	

power in their family or, on the other hand, to reinforce his role as family breadwinner. Some dependency cases clearly highlighted economic relations between the sexes. Wives complained about the unemployment of a husband, his problem with alcohol, or the fact that he worked but for some reason refused to give money to his wife for rent or food. In other instances, mothers clearly used the juvenile court to help escape useless, drunk, or violent husbands.

The juvenile court proved to be more effective following up on accusations of sexual indiscretion by mothers than at remedying the financial negligence of fathers. It was easier to remove children from mothers than to force fathers to pay household expenses. For all of the charisma and professional respect that she commanded, Judge Kelley maintained a traditional view of family life and gender roles. She did much to perpetuate the sexual double standard in court. For example, when a husband had deserted his wife twice and had given her a venereal disease, Kelley ordered the man to pay $10 every two weeks and to deed the house to his wife. The wife came in several months later and said that her husband had not paid as ordered, nor had he taken care of the deed. In a conference with the chief probation officer, he was ordered to make up the back pay. Later, however, the husband accused his wife of being pregnant, even though they were not living together. Judge Kelley thereupon ordered the payments suspended until an investigation of the wife was made (not that the husband was paying regularly). However, in the absence of any "corroborative proof," payments were later ordered resumed. Several months later, the wife complained that her husband was behind on payments and had not given her the proper deed.[50] This case suggests the power that an accusation of sexual misconduct could have over women involved in domestic disputes in the juvenile court, and the corresponding latitude that men experienced even when directly defying the court's orders.[51]

Next to family members, law enforcement (probation officers, city police, and the Women's Protection Bureau) made up the second largest category of complainant. Overall, 26 percent of dependent children came to the juvenile court via a law enforcement complaint. Law enforcement complaints often resulted because one or both of the parents were arrested (as demonstrated earlier in Elsie Jones's family). Parents were arrested variously for drunkenness, bootlegging, disorderly conduct, vagrancy, or adultery ("open and notorious lewdness").[52] Police also picked up children on the streets and sent them to the juvenile court for temporary shelter. Sometimes children and their parents used the police as a first resort, such as a fourteen-year-old white boy who went to the police station asking for a place to sleep after leaving his father's house to look for work.[53]

Families who appealed to social service agencies or charities for aid could also wind up in the juvenile court on dependency complaints. Social welfare agencies in Memphis reported a fairly even mix of girls and boys but hardly any black children. This gender and racial breakdown reflected the overall dependency caseload of the juvenile court. One possible reason for the absence of complaints by social service agencies on behalf of black children was the small black caseload of the citywide agencies. It is not clear how agencies chose which cases to report and whether the parents had any input into the decision. Agency "experts" who identified a need in a family sometimes felt that the family needed a more intrusive kind of help that only the juvenile court could provide. The Associated Charities, which gave groceries and coal or paid rent for destitute families, was in a strategic position to provide court referrals. Agencies for unwed mothers such as the Bethany Training Home sometimes reported newborns as dependents. The Children's Bureau, a foster care agency, reported that a fifteen-year-old girl needed supervision because her mother was about to go to the tuberculosis hospital and there were no relatives in the city because the family had just moved to Memphis.[54]

School officials also reported dependent children to the juvenile court. Truancy in early-twentieth-century Memphis was more systematically enforced for boys than girls, and truant officers in Memphis mostly reported boys. In some cases, the city's truant officers knew that a child was supposed to be in school and went looking for him or her; in other cases, children were picked up wandering the streets by the police and adjudged homeless or deserted by their parents. Truancy often indicated a variety of neglectful conditions in a child's home background. For instance, Lester Thomas, a fourteen-year-old black boy, came to the juvenile court as a dependent child, but when the court referred him to the Child Guidance Clinic for evaluation, the "problem as referred" was listed as truancy and untruthfulness. The larger problems in Lester's life emerged during his evaluation at the clinic:

> His mother died in 1916 and his father is serving a 10-year sentence in the state penitentiary for killing a woman, having been convicted in 1923. He is said to have some sort of "nervous spells." He set Lester an example of drinking, swearing, gambling and living with various women. He did live for some time with a woman named Willie, whom Lester calls his stepmother. . . . The parents were separated before the mother's death and Lester came to Memphis with his father. He moved about considerably. When the father was sent to the penitentiary he was left with the stepmother. On 1-1-25 a white neighbor complained at the boy's request, that the stepmother had been beating him. Conditions were found to be "deplorable" and the boy was removed and placed in the care of the Charles Wilson Children's Home. He has since been placed in five boarding homes, each in turn refusing to keep him because of his behavior, while he in turn complained of them.[55]

In addition to the reasons that Lester reported for not going to school (absence of caretakers, household instability, and physical abuse), some children lived in economic situations in which they had no shoes or money for lunch or books. Sometimes a family needed extra income and even the youngest children were compelled to work. One black mother said she forced her fourteen-year-old son Max to work because she had no other source of income. Max had not been in school for some time because he did not have clothes or shoes to wear. Billie, a white boy, was not in school "because the father did not make enough money to support him and keep him in school." [56] Rather than be shamed at school, extremely poor children often chose not to attend.

Anonymous complaints about parental neglect regularly came to the court's attention. Although they often proved unreliable, the court repeatedly followed up on these reports without insisting on much proof of accuracy. One time the court received an anonymous phone call claiming that the parents of some children were drug addicts and drunks and that the family was supported by the Associated Charities. Upon investigation, none of these accusations turned out to be true. While the true circumstances of the case were indeed grave, they bore no resemblance to the initial complaint. [57] Anonymous complainants usually turned out to be a neighbor who did not wish to become directly involved with the family or its problems. Thus community members sometimes tried to use the juvenile court to mediate standards of private and public behavior in their neighborhood.

Lizzie May Williams's case illustrates how a group of black neighbors and family members used the juvenile court's authority to condemn the behavior of some abusive foster parents in the neighborhood. A neighbor complained that Lizzie May, age five, had been beaten and asked that the probation officers come at once. Two white probation officers responded immediately and found that the "neighborhood was greatly excited." The neighbor said that in the morning the foster mother had whipped the girl "unmercifully and that the neighborhood became so enraged and called the baby [i.e. Lizzie May] to her home where they [the neighbors] talked to her and that her foot was bleeding profusely and she [the neighbor] called the City Hopt. The ambulance arrived and Carrie Lee, the foster mother, refused to let the child go. She then called the J.C. Mattie Bryant, Celeste Brooks and E.D. Lewis all close neighbors, also stated that they were prepared to prove in Court that the child had been abused." The two probation officers took Lizzie May to the hospital. When Officer Joy investigated the home, his report noted that it "was very dirty, house looked as though hogs had been occupants of it, instead of people. All neighbors seen stated that this family has a very bad reputation. That the reason they have to move so often is that

THE TREATMENT OF DEPENDENT CHILDREN 115

they never pay their rent. The neighbors also stated that the child was not only cruelly treated but did not have enough to eat nor to wear." Two more neighbors agreed to testify in court.

When the foster parents came to the juvenile court, they denied that they were abusive and disputed the testimony given by the neighbors. The child had been given to the foster father when she was a baby, and the birth mother's address was unknown. Sentiment ran so high against the couple, however, that the attorney they retained decided to withdraw from the case. Judge Kelley gave the couple a "severe lecture" and placed the girl on probation to her aunt. During the six weeks that the court deliberated on the case, Lizzie May was cared for at both a hospital and the black detention home. Taking one last swipe at the situation, the mother of the foster mother called the juvenile court about three months later to say that she had heard Lizzie May was being mistreated. Upon investigation, however, Officer Joy visited Lizzie May and found her happy and attending school regularly.[58] As this case suggests, black community members sometimes saw to it that the juvenile court took action to protect black children and to censure abusive caretakers within their own neighborhood. This case also shows that while few blacks benefited from public child welfare services, the juvenile court did occasionally take the needs of dependent black children seriously. In dire emergencies, black children could receive the range of care available to white children.

Neighborhood gossip was at the heart of many complaints to the juvenile court and had very serious implications for some families. A white father who was distressed that his children were in the juvenile court blamed the "gossip" of the women in his rooming house. In another instance, a white woman with a young male boarder was "advised that she let [him] move as neighbors were gossiping." Based on a rumor spread by her husband, a mother was arrested on charges of living with another man, and her son was brought into the juvenile court as a dependent. The man in question turned out to be her cousin. In response to one query about a white family, the chief probation officer received the following observation from the local postmaster: "it is impossible for any one to judge as to how he would take care of his family—you might say he is a perfect stranger here."[59] Court officials not only relied on informal testimonials but also actively sought opinions of community members who knew something or other about a potential court client.

Once the court received a formal complaint, probation officers did a home investigation. The case files often revealed condescending observations by the probation officers about a client's lifestyle, appearance, or demeanor. One probation officer noted that a white family had a fixed salary, with a regular job and nice furniture, and that the "family appears to be above average poor client class."[60] Another probation officer described a white mother as a "most ignorant woman, she does not know the ages or birth day of her children, nor can she name them in the order born."[61] The Memphis Juvenile Court was a bastion of tradition regarding home life. The lifestyle the court officials considered appropriate and respectable for their clients was often at odds with economic realities. One probation officer noted that "Annie [the child] works and takes care of the home, so she states," and then went on to say that the home was not well-furnished or well-kept.[62] Caseworkers for social service agencies sometimes displayed remarkable lack of empathy. For instance, in one case the children were ragged and dirty, the house was not clean, and all the furniture had just been repossessed. While Martha Franklin of the Charles Wilson Home noted that the mother made only five dollars a week, all she could say was that the mother did "not put this money to good use."[63]

Using information obtained in home investigations in combination with testimony from diverse parties, Judge Kelley adjudicated each case (see table 3). More than one-third of dependent children (31 percent of girls and 41 percent of boys) were released outright to the care of their parents, relatives, or foster parents. The largest group of children so released were of primary school age (six to eleven), probably because they were too old to be placed easily for adoption and too young to contribute to their boarding expenses. Judge Kelley tried to keep families together and pressed relatives to help as much as possible. In 1921 the Associated Charities advised Judge Kelley that it was too risky to send a family of white children back to Missouri with their father because of the condition in which they were found. They had been living in a tent by the river. The judge replied that in spite of the risks, she preferred to keep the family intact because the state could offer only institutional care in Memphis.[64] Similar to the pattern that the historian David Tanenhaus has found in Chicago, Judge Kelley's placement decisions reflected contemporary beliefs in the superiority of noninstitutional care for dependent children.

In addition to releasing children outright, Judge Kelley could order different levels of supervision upon the children's release. She could place children on probation, place them in free foster care or paid boarding homes,

TABLE 3. Disposition for Dependent Children ($N = 205$)

	GIRLS		BOYS		TOTAL	
	N	%	N	%	N	%
Probation to parents	1	1.0	3	3.0	4	2.0
Probation to relative	11	10.5	8	8.0	19	9.3
Probation to other	5	4.8	8	8.0	13	6.3
Probation to officer	8	7.6	10	10.0	18	8.8
Tennessee Industrial School	10	9.5	2	2.0	12	5.9
Convent of the Good Shepherd	4	3.8	0	0.0	4	2.0
Shelby Co. Industrial School	0	0.0	6	6.0	6	2.9
Old Ladies and Orphans Home	0	0.0	1	1.0	1	0.5
Charles Wilson Home	0	0.0	5	5.0	5	2.4
St. Peter's Orphanage	3	2.9	4	4.0	7	3.4
Porter Home, Leath Orphanage	5	4.8	3	3.0	8	3.9
The Church Home	4	3.8	0	0.0	4	2.0
Cheerfield Farms	4	3.8	1	1.0	5	2.4
St. Agnes Academy	1	1.0	0	0.0	1	0.5
Tenn. Children's Home Society	11	10.5	8	8.0	19	9.3
Children's Bureau	5	4.8	0	0.0	5	2.4
Dismissed, no proof	5	4.8	5	5.0	10	4.9
Dismissed, first offense	0	0.0	1	1.0	1	0.5
Dismissed at request	1	1.0	0	0.0	1	0.5
Released	27	25.7	35	35.0	62	30.2
Total	105		100		205	
	SUMMARY					
Probation	25	23.8	29	29.0	54	26.3
Institutionalized	31	29.5	22	22.0	53	25.9
Foster care	16	15.2	8	8.0	24	11.7
Dismissed/released	33	31.4	41	41.0	74	36.1
Total	105		100		205	

or commit them to an institution. About 26 percent of dependent children (more boys than girls) were placed on probation. More girls than boys were placed in foster care or boarding homes. Overwhelmingly, it was the youngest children (ages one to five) who were placed with foster families, presumably because of the intensity of care that they needed but also because their young age made them good candidates for adoption. The court maintained the most intense level of contact with the youngest children. Overall, more girls than boys were committed to institutions (30 percent versus 22 percent). The court may have devoted more resources to supervising girls than boys in new settings to protect them from potential sexual danger or because, as we saw earlier, they had previously experienced higher rates of sexual abuse and family violence and criminality.

Despite the large portion of children who were released back to their families either outright or under probation, the potential loss of child custody was implicit in every dependency hearing. Parents regularly voiced their fears that their family would be split up and their children placed for adoption. Therefore, some families hired attorneys and used testimonials to their advantage whenever possible. One black grandfather wrote a heartfelt two-page letter to Judge Kelley saying that he owned his house, paid his taxes and water bill, had a stable life, and would gladly care for the children if he had custody. Dr. T. O. Fuller, an important black leader in Memphis who was president of Howe Junior College and pastor at the First Baptist Church, wrote to Judge Kelley on behalf of a boy who was his chauffeur. In another case, a white neighbor said to Judge Kelley, "I am writing you as to recommend Mr. & Mrs. C.W. Miles. I have been living by them two years. They are a fine family of people. They go to church, Sunday school and believe in raising their children right in every way."[65]

Fear of losing their children was well-founded and contributed to the endemic tension between the juvenile court and parents. Sometimes Judge Kelley appeared to overstep her authority and contradict her philosophy of keeping families together. One mother accused the court of holding her child illegally and was "quite ugly in attitude and remarks," refusing to give her new address to the probation officer. Another mother went a step further when her daughters were adjudged dependent and committed to the Tennessee Industrial School. She hired an attorney, who filed a petition in a higher court for a writ of certiorari and an order supersedeas against the juvenile court. Before long the juvenile court was compelled to release her daughters.[66] In another difficult case, after a mother took her child out of the Charles Wilson Home, Judge Kelley ordered the mother to cooperate with the Associated Charities and the Charles Wilson Home. The social worker, Martha Franklin, complained to the juvenile court that the mother would not cooperate. Instead she clung to the children and refused to go to the hospital on the days she was told.[67]

Some parents refused to give information, were highly indignant at the court's intrusion, and often expressed contradictory feelings toward court personnel. For example, Mrs. Allen (introduced earlier), who could be quite emotional, "held herself with great poise, and said she did not blame the Judge for her position" upon finding out that Judge Kelley refused to release her children. One month later, however, she "spoke very uncomplimentary of the Juvenile Court and Judge Kelley and stated that she was prepared to commit murder herself before she would allow her children to be taken permanently away from her."[68] Toward the end of another case, a volunteer worker from the court called on a young white mother. She was very resentful that the juvenile court kept "dogging her footsteps" and checking up on her so often on the suspicion that she was not taking care of her child. The court, she felt, did not give her a chance to succeed. The volunteer tried to assuage the mother by saying that the court only had a friendly interest in her family and liked to see cases turn out happily.

Court officials expected children and their parents to be compliant with the court's decisions. Letters from children and parents show that they understood the importance of placating court officials. One fifteen-year-old white boy wrote from the Tennessee Industrial School, "I would like to see all my friends and, And dear Mrs. Kelley I hope you let me come home soon and I will be a good boy if you let me come home. . . . Sincerely, Henry Smith (one of your boys)."[69] In another case of a white family, a neighbor complained that Harriet Lindsey, age four, stayed in a black woman's house during the night while the mother held parties. Later the mother wrote, "please pardon my delay in letting you hear from me. . . . First I wanted to be able to give you the kind of report that I knew you wanted to receive which would at the same time, substantiate my position in the matter." She stated that she now rented rooms to two older women (rather than men). She went on: "I wish to take this opportunity to thank you for your kind and courteous treatment and while the matter was very unpleasant to me. . . . still, it seems to have been made a little brighter on account of your nice and kind treatment. Just had to make mention of same, as it was so noticeable. Again thanking you and assuring you, that a visit from you at any time, will be most welcome."[70]

As in the Allen case but with more success, court officials sometimes devoted enormous effort to help families work through their problems. The case of the Bartons, a white family, lasted six years, and for periods at a time, probation officers visited the home every day. The family consisted of nine children, whom the mother had difficulty managing. Although her husband made a decent salary, he worked for the railroad and was away much of the time. Even though the wife used bad language, was away from the home frequently, and quarreled regularly with her husband, the chief probation officer was clearly sympathetic and scolded the husband for not taking more responsibility. At one point, probation officers essentially took over the family, visiting the home every day for six months and then every two or three days thereafter. They took the children to school, ordered groceries and coal, bought clothes, took the mother to the hospital, and delivered checks. They visited the family's creditors and informed them of the plans to "re-establish the family and manage their affairs on a business basis." Until the family's many debts were paid, all living expenses and accounts were paid through the court. The case file gives no indication that the parents protested such intervention; obviously, the probation officers could not have carried out such intrusive plans without significant cooperation of the parents. Numerous other parents sent thank-you notes and expressed appreciation for the court's interest and courteous treatment.[71]

As many of the cases discussed in this chapter make clear, the needs of community members pulled the juvenile court directly into the province of social welfare. The juvenile court often provided diverse kinds of assistance apart from ongoing cases under its official jurisdiction. Parents came in voluntarily seeking advice about family matters years after formal hearings were over. One of the court's most important and immediate welfare functions was the provision of temporary shelter for children. Two sisters went to the juvenile court and spent the night there because their father threw them out of the house. One mother used the juvenile court as a temporary day nursery while she searched for work. Judge Kelley's great personal appeal encouraged community members to identify the court as much more than a place of punishment. Many struggling families clearly regarded it as a place to seek advice and refuge.

Even though mothers sought the help of the juvenile court, the probation officers were largely unable to prevent violence against them and their children.[72] The Allen case shows that despite providing boarding care and indigent hospital care, as well as arresting Mrs. Allen's husband, Judge Kelley could only do for her as much as she allowed. Other cases highlight the lack of options for women or children who were abused by men. One woman admitted to knowing that her husband sexually abused their daughter, but she chose to stay with him because she had small children for whom she could not otherwise care. Still another woman went back to her husband at the suggestion of Judge Kelley, even though the woman had tried to commit suicide on account of her husband's cruelty.[73] In many cases, the juvenile court could provide only emergency assistance unless women chose to leave their abusive spouses. Similar to other social welfare institutions, the juvenile court could not exert its authority if its clientele pursued independent, personal agendas.

In adjudicating the cases of dependent children, the juvenile court embodied and responded to the concerns of the broader Memphis community. Its actions rarely revealed unmitigated imposition of its will on a totally recalcitrant clientele. As did much of early-twentieth-century American society, the juvenile court reinforced a sexual double standard with regard to domestic responsibilities for women and men. Families preferred to keep their children with them, even under desperate circumstances; the court could not always be guided by the wishes of family members if it was objectively to safeguard the best interests of children. Judge Kelley and court officers were almost always ambivalent about breaking up families and generally tried to keep them together, despite clear indications of stress.[74] The juvenile court's most useful service to families and children in distress may well have been to provide short-term emergency assistance so that the families did not experience irreversible disintegration.

The Memphis Juvenile Court operated in a social welfare system that largely ignored the needs of black families. Southern racial ideology rendered the poverty of black children almost invisible to the public; black families were compelled to seek aid primarily from private sources within their community. However, the appeal of childhood itself sometimes transcended race relations, and the Memphis Juvenile Court occasionally provided important assistance for black dependent, abused, and neglected children.

CHAPTER FIVE

Juvenile Justice and the Treatment of Delinquent Children

THE MEMPHIS JUVENILE COURT spent most of its resources handling delinquent rather than dependent children. Chief Judge Camille Kelley even claimed in her book *A Friend in Court* that "delinquent children are my specialty." Children became the subject of juvenile court authority and were adjudged delinquent for two broad categories of behavior: status offenses and criminal offenses. Status offenses applied only to juveniles; their conduct was illegal only because they were minors (i.e., under age eighteen). Status offenses included refusing to attend school (truancy), running away from home, refusing to obey parents (incorrigibility), violating curfew, and engaging in consensual sexual activity. Criminal offenses, by contrast, included any activity that would result in criminal prosecution if committed by an adult. Disorderly conduct, alcohol use, gambling, trespassing, and traffic violations were among the less serious criminal activities that juveniles were accused of, whereas larceny, housebreaking (burglary), car theft, and assault constituted the bulk of their more serious crimes. Girls and boys had distinctive patterns of status and criminal offenses.[1]

In Memphis, juvenile justice officials and parents interpreted delinquency differently for white and black females. For white girls, it was mainly sexual rather than criminal activity that concerned both juvenile justice officials and parents. For black girls, the court's main concern was their criminal activity, whereas the black parents' main concern was their daughters' precocious sexual behavior (although they too struggled with their daughters' petty thefts). These differences, in turn, affected the court's processing and disposition of girls' cases. Although the court handled far fewer delinquent girls than delinquent boys, the girls' cases caused the court greater consternation and delay because of the perceived moral and public health threat represented by their behavior.

If female delinquency was more troubling to families and court officials, male delinquency was much more common, and the juvenile court spent most of its time on male delinquents. The overwhelming majority of delinquency cases (80 percent) in the Memphis Juvenile Court involved boys, a distribution similar to other courts in the South and the rest of the country.[2] Interestingly, however, the crimes of delinquent boys have not been as extensively analyzed by historians as those of delinquent girls.[3]

In Memphis, neither the boys' crimes nor the court's punishment of them was particularly serious. An appearance in the juvenile court was, therefore, usually not an invasive or prolonged experience for delinquent boys or their families. The boys' delinquencies were not generally perceived as posing fundamental challenges to parental or societal authority. One-time incidents of petty theft (particularly of coal), vandalism, or neighborhood fights made up most of the boys' offenses. The majority of boys were simply released following admission of guilt, or the charges against them were dismissed; the court did not have an adequate probation staff to monitor the boys' subsequent behavior. Although the Memphis Juvenile Court, like most juvenile courts, focused as much attention on the circumstances of the boys' lives as on their actual crimes, its overall day-to-day operations were often a mix of a compassionate adult system and a purely juvenile one.

FEMALE JUVENILE DELINQUENCY

Changing attitudes toward female sexuality and sexual behavior in the 1920s embodied important generational and social conflicts. As many young white and black women took jobs and attended public schools, they moved beyond their home spheres and, with less family supervision, experienced new leisure and independence among their peers. Increased mobility and the privacy of the automobile enabled women to assert their autonomy and experiment more easily with premarital sex. Adolescent females who rejected Victorian morality went to public dance halls and embraced heterosexual romance; they viewed these opportunities as self-assertion and relief from rigid social conventions and frustrations in their everyday lives. Most adults, however, expressed fear about the girls' new social and sexual freedom. They emphasized the girls' moral depravity, the crisis in the family that their behavior symbolized, and of course, the spread of venereal disease. As young women asserted new autonomy, they encountered resistance and attempts at repression from their families and from state officials, who continued to view their behaviors as aberrant and labeled them as delinquent.[4]

Although middle-class young women also engaged in rebellious behavior, it was primarily young women from working-class families who experienced formal censure by the state, which often acted explicitly on behalf of the girls' parents. Newly arrived to the city, white and black working-class families in Memphis faced adjustments that were fairly similar to those of European or Mexican immigrants in other cities.[5] While white working-class families tried to maintain a hierarchical family structure, the city had school attendance requirements and offered liberal work opportunities that facilitated opportunities for young women to meet strangers in unsupervised settings and engage in sexual activity. In somewhat different ways, black parents also struggled to protect their daughters from the attractions of street life and the sexual opportunities it offered. The distinctly precarious economic status of working-class black families may have rendered them particularly sensitive to internal threats to their emotional stability. White and black working-class parents alike were more willing than middle-class parents to bring family disputes with their daughters into the public arena, because the public and private dimensions of working-class families were less clearly defined.[6]

Municipal efforts to address the problems of female delinquents in Memphis were typical of those in other urban communities in the early part of the twentieth century. In 1921 the head of the Police and Fire Commission established the Women's Protective Bureau. Headed by Mrs. Anna Whitmore, the bureau had three ostensible purposes: to aid women or girls on the police docket to "become good and useful women"; to offer protective and preventive work for girls who showed delinquent tendencies so that they would not become offenders; and to protect the citizenry from the "evil effects" of the actions of offenders. The bureau investigated cases brought to the police department and made recommendations to the city court and juvenile court judges. It helped locate runaway girls, assisted parents with incorrigible and delinquent girls, and found the girls jobs or places to live. The bureau chief also visited dance halls, hotels, and rooming houses to keep girls away from "evil" influences.[7]

The Women's Protective Bureau's concern with "protecting the citizenship" reflected the concerns of the national social hygiene and eugenics movements during the Progressive Era.[8] Venereal disease reached epidemic levels, and infections were disproportionately high among blacks, the poor, and the young. New medical knowledge about the devastating effects of syphilis and gonorrhea, such as sterility, blindness, deformity, and insanity, fueled grave concerns about preserving the sanctity of the family unit and prompted physicians to enlarge their sphere of public health responsibility to protect marriages from the introduction of disease. Allying with the early eugenics movement, Progressive Era physicians argued that their expertise was necessary to help ensure a healthy race. They advocated major new educational efforts to stem venereal disease that emphasized the need for sexual control, especially among the working class.[9] During the 1920s public health officials continued their attempts to control the spread of venereal disease through education and moral suasion rather than prophylactic medical treatment.[10]

The nationwide changes in adolescent sexual behavior in the early twentieth century affected white and black families in Memphis, albeit in different ways. The Women's Protective Bureau and other public officials (such as the city police) tended, by and large, to ignore the sexual activities of young black girls. However, black parents were very much interested in regulating the sexuality of their daughters; they expressed the same concerns as white parents about their daughters' increasing autonomy, sexual experimentation, and disobedience.[11] Nonetheless, the city of Memphis did not accept responsibility for policing the sexuality of black girls, as it did that of white girls, except when black girls became involved with white men.[12] Rather, city officials used the juvenile court primarily as a place in which to punish black girls (but not white girls) for petty criminal activity, such as shoplifting. Delinquent black girls were overrepresented in the juvenile court, and especially overrepresented among criminal cases. They made up more than half of the female delinquency cases. However, blacks were only one-third of the overall female population in Memphis under age nineteen.[13] Thus race strongly influenced the definitions of, and the processing of, female delinquents in Memphis.

Significant racial differences were evident in the offenses with which girls were charged and in the circumstances surrounding the offenses (see table 4). Twice as many black girls as white girls were charged with criminal offenses (54 percent versus 27 percent). The girls' criminal offenses included mainly petty theft (primarily shoplifting from department stores), disorderly conduct, and gambling (shooting dice and playing card games

TABLE 4. Charges against Delinquent Girls (N = 65)

	WHITE		BLACK		TOTAL	
	N	%	N	%	N	%
Incorrigible	9	30.0	11	31.4	20	30.8
Runaway	10	33.3	5	14.3	15	23.1
Immoral conduct	3	10.0	0	0.0	3	4.6
Disorderly	3	10.0	4	11.4	7	10.8
Gaming	0	0.0	1	2.9	1	1.5
Larceny	5	16.7	14	40.0	19	29.2
Total	30		35		65	
	SUMMARY					
Status offense	22	73.3	16	45.7	38	58.5
Criminal offense	8	26.7	19	54.3	27	41.5
Total	30		35		65	

on the street). Their status offenses consisted mainly of incorrigibility, running away from home, and sexual activity. Although white and black parents were both clearly engaged in a struggle to control their daughters' social and sexual freedom, public and private authorities employed different criteria for determining which behaviors warranted formal intervention for black versus white girls.

Both white and black working-class families often initiated status offense charges against their own children. In these cases, parents and relatives overtly used the juvenile court to reinforce their authority in the home; they readily admitted that their daughters were beyond their control. Parents complained that their daughters regularly disobeyed or quarreled with them, stole money, stayed out late, went to picture shows and dance halls, or worst of all, ran around with boys. One white uncle said that he tried to coax his niece to accept the discipline of the home but that she insisted on coming and going as she pleased.[14] After exhausting intrafamilial disciplinary options, exasperated parents and relatives turned to the court and requested that the judge or probation officer give their daughter a "good scare" or even institutionalize her. Parents often appealed directly to Judge Kelley via a phone call or letter. To these desperate parents, Judge Kelley personalized the juvenile court in Memphis, and they identified with her as a parent. She clearly empathized with the parents of delinquent girls, especially girls who were sexually active. According to Judge Kelley, "it takes more time and care to bring a girl back to the standard of right-thinking" because a "girl's conscience is not as 'flexible' as a boy's."[15]

The girls, in turn, often complained that their parents scolded and "picked on" them or made them work too hard at domestic chores. They also felt that their parents refused to let them go out with friends or have fun. In many cases, the girls singled out a stepparent with whom they could not get along. The niece referred to above complained that her aunt and uncle simply wanted to use her as a servant. One girl gave no reason for running away other than being tired of washing dishes. Mildred, a white girl who was charged with running away, used bad language, was very tough, and refused at first to give her name. In detention she cursed the matron, tried to set fire to the building, and attempted to choke another girl. The matron intercepted a letter that she tried to sneak out to her sister. In it she referred to the "old huzzies" in the detention center. Mildred behaved so badly in detention that the court transferred her to the Convent of the Good Shepherd before her hearing and kept her there until she was released to her father six days later.[16] Girls, in short, often rebelled against strict supervision and limitations on their associations with friends. Their parents and court officials believed that they could not be controlled. The girls were old enough to make decisions deemed highly inappropriate. Delinquent girls were clearly actors in the juvenile justice system, and the patterns of their behavior decisively shaped the juvenile court's operations.

In contrast to the emotional exasperation associated with status offenses, female criminal cases caused considerable shame for parents and their daughters. White and black parents usually expressed surprise that their daughters would get into trouble or steal. One white mother was so upset that she burst into tears when she attempted to talk to a probation officer about her daughter's conduct. Finding out what she wanted to know, the probation officer assured the mother that she would not do a school investigation so that the family would not be embarrassed. Parents often pleaded with the officers to "temper their justice with mercy" and assured them that their daughters would never again be delinquent. Girls who were charged with criminal offenses reacted in a variety of ways to their court experience. Many thieves, for example, were immediately contrite and promised not to steal again, saying that they had never stolen before and had not really planned to take the merchandise. For example, Francis, a black girl, said that she "must have been out of her head." Some girls, however, were impudent or indifferent to their court appearance, could give no reason for their behavior, or claimed it was not their fault; some even gave false names.[17]

Girls' criminal offenses consisted primarily of petty larceny or shoplifting (see table 4). Both white and black girls stole hosiery, jewelry, clothes, perfume, or other small items from large department stores such as Bry-Block Merchant Company, Goldsmith's, and Kress. In these cases, special agents hired by the Memphis Retailers' Association usually caught the girls. Some girls also stole from neighbors or unsuspecting passersby. For instance, the neighbor of a black girl, Louise, complained that the girl had stolen a pair of socks from off her back porch. In another case, Callie, a nine-year-old black girl, and some family members lured a white man into their home and stole his wallet.[18] Young girls' embrace of the growing consumer culture may have prompted these thefts (advertisers, of course, specifically targeted women). Participation in the latest fads and fashions was particularly tempting for working-class girls because the necessary accessories were too expensive for their families.[19]

In addition to petty theft, the other major category of criminal charges against girls was disorderly conduct, which included a variety of activities. For example, one sixteen-year-old white girl was charged with drunkenness. In another instance, when a neighbor complained to the police about a loud party, a fourteen-year-old white girl and her two older sisters were charged with disorderly conduct. Since the older sisters were not juveniles, their cases were handled in criminal court. Another case of disorderly conduct involved two black girls who were fighting with a razor. Race relations were central in several disorderly conduct cases involving black girls. The juvenile court clearly helped enforce rules of public racial segregation and deferential behavior by blacks in the South.[20] Under the generic charge of disorderly conduct, one black girl was brought before the court for "using disrespectful language to a white woman." In another case, the police stopped a car with a group of black adolescents on their way home from a party. The mother of one girl said that she thought the "trouble came up from officers thinking the girls were white girls with colored boys. The girls [were] so near white that the mistake [was] quite natural."[21]

When girls were charged with status offenses, court officials and parents often used legal terminology to obscure the true reason why the girls were in court.[22] This discrepancy is evident from comparison of the official court docket with information contained in the social files of individual cases.

Generally, a charge of "runaway" meant that a white girl was sexually active; a charge of "incorrigibility" meant that a white or black girl was sexually active.[23] Of the white girls who were formally charged with status offenses (incorrigibility, running away, or immoral conduct), 82 percent had engaged in sexual or morally suspect activity. The majority (62 percent) of black girls charged with status offenses were also sexually delinquent. It was rare (4.6 percent) for girls to be formally charged with sexual activity (i.e., "immoral conduct" or "lewd and lascivious associates"), and these charges usually indicated prostitution. Instances of prostitution, however, were sometimes buried within charges of "runaway" or "incorrigibility." Public officials generally did not report the sexual activity of black girls to the juvenile court unless it involved solicitation.

Families were very active in trying to police their daughters' sexual inclinations. They considered a wide range of behaviors to be inappropriate and precursors of sexual activity. Such behaviors included writing letters to boys; dressing in a flashy manner; visiting dance halls, theaters, or cafés; riding in a car with boys; staying out late; and of course, masturbation, kissing, and petting. For many families, even the suspicion of sexual intercourse was as much a cause for court intervention as proof of intercourse itself. Parents and court officials always demanded a full list of boys with whom a girl had been intimate. Interestingly, court officials never used specific clinical terms to describe the girls' sexual activities, but rather general ones that cast moral judgment. They usually called sexual intercourse "immorality," as in, "she stated the she had been immoral with perhaps 6 boys," or "she also admitted that she had been immoral." When girls confessed to masturbating, it was referred to as "misusing themselves."[24]

Contemporary observers of the juvenile justice process noted the larger implications of this coded language and the discomfort and fear that adolescent female sexuality caused the court and parents alike. Mabel Brown Ellis, a member of the board of directors of the National Probation Association who investigated the Memphis Juvenile Court for the Tennessee Child Welfare Commission in 1919, observed, "as everyone familiar with juvenile courts knows, girls are rarely brought before the judge for any other cause than some sort of sex offense. But immoral conduct with regard to sex matters is not a felony, although the girl arrested for grand larceny is usually far less a menace to society than the girl who is a potential source of venereal infection or the possible mother of illegitimate children."[25] While acknowledging the dubious legality of criminalizing female sexual activity,

Ellis could not completely escape her cultural milieu. She clearly echoed the concerns of the Progressive Era social hygiene movement and its sexual double standard.

Some notable racial differences were apparent in the ages of delinquent girls in the Memphis Juvenile Court. These age differences partly reflected differences in offense patterns. The average white girl was nearly a year and a half older than the average black girl (14.7 versus 13.4). Most black girls were fourteen or younger, whereas most white girls were fifteen or older. Not surprisingly, issues of sexual misconduct were likely to emerge as girls got older.[26] Black girls charged with sexual misconduct appear to have been younger and exposed to sexual exploitation. For example, Ruby, an eleven-year-old black girl, claimed that she had sex for pay, although a hospital exam showed no signs of intercourse. A black garage owner saw Ruby get into an ice wagon with a white man, and she said that she had consented to his sexual requests two or three times and was paid each time. She also said that her mother forced her to have sex with a black boy who paid the mother. Officer Joy said that Ruby's family lived in the worst part of Memphis, where white and black men went for "immoral purposes." After spending about two weeks in detention, Ruby was released to her mother. Ruby's experience in the juvenile court must not have been completely negative, because in 1930, when she was twenty, she returned to the juvenile court seeking protection from her mother, who (she claimed) wanted her to be a prostitute. Judge Kelley advised her to stay with a cousin.

It is difficult to determine the degree to which delinquent girls' sexual activity may have been encouraged or facilitated by the freedom they gained as wage earners.[27] Most (63 percent) of the girls were in school, almost a quarter of them worked for wages full-time, and the rest were not in school and did not work. White girls made up almost the entire working population and were mostly fifteen and sixteen years old. They worked in dime stores or department stores, cafés or restaurants, large factories, and the telephone company.[28] More white families than black families relied on the wages of their daughters. With few employment opportunities beyond domestic service, many black girls in Memphis may have stayed in school longer than white girls.[29] Of the white girls who worked, almost 70 percent were sexually active, but a substantial portion (50 percent) of the delinquent girls who were still in school were also sexually active. It is not clear how much working per se increased the girls' autonomy within their family or contributed to their family's perception of their ungovernability.

Similar to those in other juvenile courts, female delinquents in Memphis were overwhelmingly from working-class families; their parents' occupations conformed to racial patterns in other southern cities. White girls' fathers worked primarily in semiskilled or skilled occupations and were employed full-time. The fathers of black girls, by contrast, predominated in the unskilled occupations (most were also employed full-time). Occupational differences applied to the mothers also. The great majority of white mothers were housewives; only one-quarter indicated either full- or part-time employment. By contrast, 75 percent of black mothers listed a paid occupation (half in domestic service).

The structures of the girls' households reflected regional migration, marriage, and mortality patterns. Many families moved back and forth between Memphis and surrounding farms. Poor economic circumstances forced many of the girls to leave a family farm and move to Memphis to live with a relative.[30] The move often meant the breakdown of family cohesion. Parents and children were often separated, and responsibility was sometimes placed in the hands of an older sibling or aunt who lacked authority.[31] The migration from farms to the city of Memphis also presented new social and employment opportunities for white girls and, consequently, disrupted familiar parental and familial authority. Many of the white girls who were accused of sexual delinquency had moved to Memphis very recently before being brought to court. Complaints about their behavior usually began almost immediately after their arrival in Memphis. About half of the delinquent girls, both black and white, lived in two-parent households (which included both natural parents or one stepparent). Kinship networks were very important for white girls; one-third of them lived with a relative instead of a parent, probably due to recent farm-to-city migration. One-third of the black girls lived with their mother only, which resulted mainly from the high rates of mortality and desertion of black men and from the frequent migration of black women to the city for wage labor (as evidenced in the case files). Interestingly, more of the black girls than white girls lived with their natural mothers.[32]

In early-twentieth-century Memphis, traditional family restrictions on female adolescent sexual behavior sometimes broke down in the face of new consumer and leisure opportunities and changing urban household structures. As Mary Odem argues for early-twentieth-century Los Angeles, adolescent girls in Memphis had many new opportunities and incentives for engaging in consensual premarital sex.[33] White and black parents increasingly responded to intrafamilial turmoil by seeking the assistance of the juvenile court in maintaining control over their daughters' sexual behaviors. Many of these families consisted of single mothers or those with limited kin resources in the city. Female delinquency, defined primarily as sexual activity outside of marriage, challenged working-class families with new middle-class norms of adolescent pleasure seeking and peer-group behavior.[34]

ADJUDICATING FEMALE DELINQUENTS

Girls came to the juvenile court in a variety of ways (see table 5). Dividing complainants between private and public sources highlights the distinctive patterns for white and black girls. Parents, relatives, neighbors, and private citizens made up the private complainants. Public sources included probation officers, police, store owners/store police, and social service agencies. For white girls, the complainants were about evenly divided between public and private sources. However, private sources accounted for two-thirds of the complainants against black girls. The single largest category of complainant for white girls was the police; for black girls, it was their own parents. The second largest group of complainants against black girls was private citizens. The importance of private networks in initiating the juvenile court's intervention for black girls, and the corresponding lack of interest in black children by public authorities, reflected more general patterns of social welfare provision in Memphis.

For white girls, informal appearances and consultations with probation officers often preceded a formal charge or appearance in the juvenile court. Indeed, the court handled a substantial number of unofficial cases each year.[35] By the time of a formal appearance, family relations had often deteriorated to the point that parents refused to make bond or fetch their daughter from detention. Fourteen-year-old Sarah, for example, had tried the patience of her mother and stepfather for several years. She stole money, cursed her mother, stayed out late at picture shows, and refused to go to school. Her mother finally complained informally to the juvenile court (without filing a complaint) that she was incorrigible. During the home investigation, the probation officer convinced Sarah to stay home and help care for the smaller children. The next week the probation officer called on the family, who reported that Sarah's behavior was not good. Three months later, the Women's Protection Bureau brought Sarah in on a charge of runaway that was filed by her older married sister. This time she was detained at the juvenile court, but her parents refused to get her. One week later,

TABLE 5. Complainant against Delinquent Girls ($N = 60$)

	WHITE		BLACK		TOTAL	
	N	%	N	%	N	%
Probation officer	1	3.4	0	0.0	1	1.7
Police	8	27.6	5	16.1	13	21.7
Store police/owner	5	17.2	5	16.1	10	16.7
Social service agency	2	6.9	0	0.0	2	3.3
Parents	7	24.1	12	38.7	19	31.7
Relative	4	13.8	2	6.5	6	10.0
Neighbor	1	3.4	1	3.2	2	3.3
Private citizen	0	0.0	6	19.4	6	10.0
Other	1	3.4	0	0.0	1	1.7
Total	29		31		60	
	SUMMARY					
Law	14	48.3	10	32.3	24	40.0
Social services	2	6.9	0	0.0	2	3.3
Parents/relative	11	37.9	14	45.2	25	41.7
Other	2	6.9	7	22.6	9	15.0
Total	29		31		60	

Sarah was examined by a doctor and found to have gonorrhea. After a long informal process, she finally appeared before Judge Kelley, who placed her on probation to her sister and brother-in-law.[36]

Unlike white girls, black girls and their families usually had no prior contact with the juvenile court before a formal hearing. Court officials were far more willing to intercede on behalf of white girls and attempt informal, preventive social work. While court officials may have been relatively indifferent toward the problems of black girls due to racial bias, the absence of informal intervention may also have reflected racial differences in the nature of the charges. Petty theft (in which black girls predominated) in department stores was a one-time event, whereas sexual delinquency (in which white girls predominated) was an ongoing behavioral problem. Black girls, it should be reemphasized, displayed similar kinds of sexual behavior as white girls, but black parents did not use the court as a place of first resort in the same way that white parents did. The court also lacked a probation staff that could carry out extensive preventive social work with black children.

In difficult cases of female delinquency, the juvenile court regularly sought the advice of the Memphis Child Guidance Clinic during the years of its operation (1924–26).[37] Although the clinic's director, Dr. R. R. Williams, stated that he did not "believe in the inheritance of criminalistic traits," he did seem to believe in inherited mental abilities. He displayed little hope for many of the girls who passed through the clinic. In his view, many of the girls would not be able to do more than unskilled or low-skilled work, such as manual or factory labor. For example, the clinic's report on Sarah (introduced earlier), age sixteen, said:

> Psychiatric Summary: A Jewish girl with markedly developed secondary physical sexual characteristics, low inferior intelligence (low moron grade); suggestible, weak inhibitions, lethargic and unambitious; weakly evasive, and untruthful with defective reasoning and judgment. Incapable of scholastic training beyond the 3rd grade; scholastic training served to accentuate a feeling of inferiority. The intellectual inferiority apparently has not been recognized; proper provision for scholastic training fitted to capacities not made.
>
> Her home training indicates a lack of instruction relative to sexual matters; outlets for interests not provided; as a result of an inadequate supervision and innate suggestibility due to her inferiority she developed a venereal infection and became pregnant. Upon her return home, home life more restricted; her marriage encouraged; her stepfather was critical of her idleness; again she yielded to her sex urges desire and for excitement went on an escapade had sexual intercourse and was left in a house of ill repute.
>
> Outlook: The inferior intelligence of the girl will make constant supervision and guidance necessary: with industrial training and supervision over a number of years she may become partially self supporting and able to adjust in the outside world: in all probability she will need supervision: her inhibitions will be always weak.

In his evaluation of Nellie, charged with larceny, Williams wrote:

> Psychiatric: She is a 14-year old girl, rouged, quite of the flapper type. In appearance and general reactions, she is quite sophisticated and self-contained. She is agreeable, always agreeing; she is suggestible. She seems not antagonistic in any way. She is contradictory, and with many quite absurd discrepancies showing up, and these she seldom sees. She appears to be defective.
>
> She shows very superficial reaction regarding the minor theft; comparatively superficial reactions to the existing disturbed, broken home situation.

She does not seem greatly worried over it. She sees the instability of her mother, but is rather indifferent to that. . . . But she has not become greatly rebellious as yet. The theft of the 49¢ ring seems to have been to satisfy a childish wish. Other girls in the crowd in which she was had rings; she has a practically superficial reaction to this.

Despite the routinely pessimistic assessments of most children's mental capacity, the clinic did attempt to offer professional psychological help and to coordinate rehabilitative plans for children. For Sarah, Dr. Williams recommended a long-term institutional placement under continuous supervision so that she could get industrial training and medical treatment. He also consulted with the Federation of Jewish Welfare Agencies to see if Sarah could eventually be placed with relatives. In Nellie's case, he recommended that she stay in her present home but go away to a summer camp and then later get a job as a dime store clerk. He suggested that she take swimming and dancing classes at the YWCA and that her friend Fanny go along with her.[38]

Although much of the clinic's caseload was composed of white children (boys mostly), it did examine black girls also. Dr. Williams said of Mary:

On the basis of norms for her race, Mary has an I.Q. of 108 which places her as a high average. She would rate as of low average intelligence according to norms for the white race. . . . She has the mentality to succeed in High School and with good application in a college for her people. . . . In view of Mary's relatively good intelligence and her interest in school work, I would advise that Mary have the opportunity to continue through High School. A modification of her school program perhaps should be arranged: either a domestic science or business course [could] be chosen.

Williams could not escape contemporary racial stereotypes of the black girl's mental capabilities.[39] However, the inclusion of black girls within the network of citywide treatment agencies is noteworthy.

The court's medical services included a doctor who was paid by the Board of Health. He worked at the court every day and, among other duties, conducted pelvic exams on the girls at the detention home.[40] The doctor attempted a clinical determination of whether a girl had engaged in sexual intercourse and took specimens for analysis of venereal diseases. The court examined most white delinquent girls routinely, regardless of the charge filed against them, although the examinations were not as systematic as in some other juvenile courts.[41]

Once the girls formally appeared before Judge Kelley, the juvenile court
had three broad options for dealing with them: release or dismissal, probation, or institutional placement. Again, racial differences were evident in
treatment plans. For white girls, 40 percent were committed to an institution and 40 percent were placed on probation. Only 20 percent of the white
girls were released outright. For black girls, only 9 percent were committed
to an institution and 31 percent were placed on probation. The majority of
black girls, 60 percent, were released outright or had the charges against
them dismissed. Clearly, the sexually active and older white girls received
far greater supervision, treatment, and punishment than the younger black
girls who, though often sexually active themselves, had been brought into
court for criminal rather than status offenses.

The pattern of dispositions in the Memphis Juvenile Court was closely
linked to the available treatment options for white and black girls (see table
6). The relatively low frequency of probation (40 percent for white girls and
31 percent for black girls) is somewhat surprising, considering that Judge
Kelley often extolled the benefits of probation and stated that it was her
preferred method of dealing with delinquent children. Clearly, the actual
use of probation was much lower than Kelley implied. In the first half of
the 1920s, the Memphis Juvenile Court simply did not have an adequate
staff of probation officers. One officer, Beulah Wood Fite, handled follow-
up work for all white girls and young boys and had a caseload of well over
two hundred. Until the late 1920s the court had only one black probation
officer, William Joy, who handled both girls and boys.

Despite Progressive Era reform ideology, which emphasized probation
as more effective for rehabilitation than institutionalization, the Memphis
Juvenile Court relied heavily on custodial institutions to address the problems of white delinquent girls.[42] In his survey of the Memphis Juvenile Court
in 1924, Charles Chute, general secretary of the National Probation Association, noted that "the proportion sent to institutions is larger than most
courts, due, I believe, to inadequate probation." Lack of probation staff,
then, meant that juvenile court regularly used custodial institutions as a first
recourse.[43]

The Memphis Juvenile Court relied on traditional private institutions
for delinquent white girls. The Convent of the Good Shepherd, run by the
Sisters of the Good Shepherd and opened in 1875, had facilities for up to
two hundred girls and provided medical treatment for venereal diseases.
The convent aimed to effect a permanent moral change and inculcate girls
with the principles of right living. Despite its strong religious foundation,

TABLE 6. Disposition for Delinquent Girls ($N = 65$)

	WHITE		BLACK		TOTAL	
	N	%	N	%	N	%
Probation to parents	1	3.3	1	2.9	2	3.1
Probation to relative	1	3.3	2	5.7	3	4.6
Probation to other	0	0.0	5	14.3	5	7.7
Probation to officer	10	33.3	3	8.6	13	20.0
Tennessee Industrial School	1	3.3	0	0.0	1	1.5
Convent of the Good Shepherd	7	23.3	0	0.0	7	10.8
Tenn. Voc. School (Nashville)	0	0.0	2	5.7	2	3.1
Tenn. Voc. School (Tullahoma)	4	13.3	0	0.0	4	6.2
Industrial Settlement Home	0	0.0	1	2.9	1	1.5
Dismissed, no proof	0	0.0	2	5.7	2	3.1
Dismissed, first offense	1	3.3	5	14.3	6	9.2
Released	5	16.7	14	40.0	19	29.2
Total	30		35		65	
	SUMMARY					
Probation	12	40.0	11	31.4	23	35.4
Institutionalized	12	40.0	3	8.6	15	23.1
Dismissed/released	6	20.0	21	60.0	27	41.5
Total	30		35		65	

the convent claimed that it did not attempt to induce girls to become members of the Catholic faith and that it accepted girls of all faiths. Girls received academic instruction, industrial training, and religious education.[44] The convent cared for dependent as well as delinquent girls. While the Sisters claimed to keep the two groups of girls separate, the atmosphere at the convent was decidedly punitive.

As the only custodial facility for girls in Memphis, the Convent of the Good Shepherd played a crucial and expansive role in the treatment of white female delinquents. Many of the girls were sent in and out of the convent regularly. Judge Kelley usually sent white girls to the convent for an indeterminate sentence, to be released when the Sisters felt the girl was ready. Family members also committed girls to the convent without court intervention. The absence in Memphis of nondenominational custodial institutions created some problems for delinquent girls and their families. One mother said that the family "did not want to put Inez in the Convent again as they were making a Catholic out of her."[45] Since the convent fully exercised its coercive powers, cooperative behavior on the part of family members was a must. The convent reported back to the juvenile court that one girl's sister had visited and was "very impudent" toward the nuns. The convent said that the girl could not have visitors if they showed no respect for the sisters in charge.[46]

The high rate at which the juvenile court dismissed outright cases of black delinquent girls reflected mainly the lack of institutional options, inadequate probation services, and perceived pettiness of the girls' offenses. The city of Memphis had no institution for delinquent black girls. About 10 percent of white girls and 14 percent of black girls were released outright after a stay in detention. Rather than long-term institutional placement, short-term detention at the juvenile court was the most common serious punishment for black girls. The Tennessee Vocational School for Colored Girls, in Nashville, did not open until 1923. The Industrial Settlement Home, a private black industrial school in Memphis, could handle only sixty children, and many of them were dependents. The chief probation officer wrote to the Tennessee commissioner of institutions in 1926 that "there is no provision made in Shelby County for the care of delinquent colored girls and the only thing we can possibly do with Mary is to turn her loose unless the Vocational School can take her . . . it looks like rather a shame to turn a bright girl like Mary loose to go straight to destruction."[47]

Since the juvenile court had only one black probation officer, probation for black girls was largely an ad hoc affair and fell to private black women or family members. Follow-up options for black girls included visits by black women who were private or volunteer social workers. Although these women had social work experience, it is not clear whether they had professional training. One of them eventually became the director of a black orphanage that opened in 1925, and another ran the Industrial Settlement Home. In one case, Judge Kelley placed a girl on probation to an unnamed black "social club." One of the first black female physicians in Memphis, Francis Kneeland, also supervised delinquent girls.

During the late 1920s probation services improved when the court hired a black female probation officer and two other white male probation officers. Charles Chute's survey recommended hiring more and better-trained probation officers. He did say that the court had splendid women workers but needed more men. Two years later, Judge Kelley credited Chute's survey for many improvements in the juvenile court's operations. The city increased probation officers' salaries, hired a new officer, replaced three others with better-trained workers, and secured time off for a summer course at the New York School of Social Work for one of the officers. Judge Kelley herself pointed out that before the employment of the new follow-up workers, it was sometimes necessary to send delinquent children to an institution or release them. With the additional officers, first-time offenders could more readily be placed on probation.[48]

The juvenile court officials dealt more consistently with sexually delinquent white girls than with sexually delinquent black girls. White girls who committed some kind of sexual delinquency were either placed on probation to a court officer or placed in a custodial institution. None of the girls who were sexually active was simply released. By contrast, the court handled sexually delinquent black girls in myriad ways. They were placed on probation to a variety of individuals (usually private citizens), held in detention, sent to a local industrial home, or released. Again, court officials did not demonstrate nearly the amount of concern for, or a readiness to invest resources in, addressing the precocious sexual behavior of black girls compared to white girls. Benign rather than aggressive racial prejudice characterized the differences in treatment decisions for white and black girls in the Memphis Juvenile Court.

It is evident that the Memphis Juvenile Court had uneven success in attempting to bring about changes in the behavior of delinquent girls. In some cases, the experience in court appeared to have the desired effect, and family relations seemed to stabilize after the first court appearance. Parents often expressed their gratitude for the court's interest, and the girls wrote affectionate letters to Judge Kelley and other officers. Most girls charged with criminal offenses appeared to be sufficiently frightened and humiliated, or at least their parents were, that they did not formally appear in court again. Incorrigible or sexually delinquent girls, however, often made repeat appearances before the juvenile court.[49] Their circumstances changed very little with each court appearance. With an air of resignation, court officials and parents braced themselves for a continuing struggle with the girl's intransigent sexual behavior, probably until the time she was old enough to move out of her parents' household and establish a residence of her own.

MALE JUVENILE DELINQUENCY

Juvenile court ideology and operations were rooted in theories that attributed the causes of adolescent male delinquency to working-class lifestyles as well as to inherent male characteristics. In the late nineteenth century, Darwinian ideas shaped the emerging disciplines of child and educational psychology, and especially of G. Stanley Hall's theories of mental evolution and adolescence. Hall also incorporated the concepts of psychic arrest and inherited biological defect from the Italian criminologist Cesare Lombroso to explain juvenile delinquency.[50] These hereditarian explanations for crime derived more from social prejudices than scientific knowledge, and they meshed easily with the eugenics movement and its fear of the rising tide of new immigrants to America. Because these theories logically pointed to the futility of preventing delinquency, they were increasingly challenged by child welfare reformers around the turn of the century.[51]

As interest in naturalistic theories of delinquency began to wane, familial and environmentalist explanations of, and psychiatric responses to, delinquency began to emerge to prominence. The diagnostic approach of William Healy emphasized the interplay between the individual, his family, and his broader social environment. Leading child welfare reformers in Chicago, New York, Boston, and elsewhere began to emphasize the environmental basis of delinquency: the changeable external factors that were amenable to treatment and prevention. These approaches looked to probation, social investigation, and individualized treatment to modify a delinquent's surroundings and correct bad habits and attitudes. The Chicago School of Sociology, using an ecological approach, extended the environmentalist perspective on delinquency as a social problem and a group activity. Male gangs especially came to symbolize urban disintegration, slum life, and the pressures of urban life on immigrant family structure.[52] By World War I, most experts accepted multicausal explanations for male delinquency (theories of female delinquency, however, continued to emphasize sexuality). Especially with regard to gangs, delinquency in the interwar period was increasingly interpreted as an extension of masculinity itself. For purposes of public discussion, the "delinquent" came to be identified almost exclusively as a male.[53]

Judge Kelley, like her contemporaries in Chicago and elsewhere, identified the delinquent as a boy. In terms of causation, she stressed family problems and, to a lesser degree, blamed inheritance. When asked by an interviewer, "What is a delinquent child?" Kelley responded: "Delinquency is often mistaken for misplaced energy and misdirected ability.... The boy who goes about performing mischievous pranks often grows to manhood strong of character, with his energy directed in constructive channels.... It isn't the child so much that's delinquent, but the parents or unwholesome environment back of the child. . . . The cure is in making home life so attractive for that child that his stealing habit is curbed. The sooner he is brought to us with a petty crime on his hands the better for him and his parents." She went on to say that, "of course, there comes the child who has inherited criminal tendencies. He is indeed a problem. He will ignore the chance the court gives him and go right on pursuing his petty crime career. He is the child we finally send to the reform school. . . . No amount of teaching will save him." Kelley placed great faith in probation. "Any child brought to my court goes on probation," she said. "And probation, according to my definition, means the education thru practicing and teaching of the younger generation, to stabilize it against crime." Although Kelley's actual use of probation for delinquent girls and boys did not match her rhetoric, her philosophy wholeheartedly embraced the therapeutic ideal, reluctantly acknowledged some aspects of determinism (which had fallen out of widespread favor in the 1920s), and held parents responsible for their son's social environment.[54]

During the 1920s the public in Memphis as well as the rest of the nation perceived a growing "boy problem" and an explosion of crime in America. Many commentators, including the president of a local Rotary Club, attributed the crime wave to a loss of religious bearings and the failure of modern middle-class families to maintain the nineteenth-century work ethic and ascetic morality. From this perspective, materialistic, pleasure-oriented middle-class homes and permissive child rearing inspired criminal behavior.[55] Judge Kelley echoed this thought when she blamed "gallivanting" parents for juvenile delinquency. Highly visible crimes among young boys were especially alarming and were associated with newsboys, street and alley life, and youth gangs. Thus the same concerns that were widely raised about girls who tested parental authority, and the larger crisis in family life, came to bear on boys. A critique of modern society, aggravated by circumstances associated with working-class life such as poverty, lack of schooling, and child labor, underpinned popular understanding of the "problem of American boyhood" in the interwar period.[56]

That delinquent boys in the Memphis Juvenile Court came from working-class families is evident from both occupational and employment data on their parents. White fathers predominated in skilled and semiskilled occupations, whereas black fathers mostly worked in unskilled and semiskilled occupations. Most white mothers were housewives, whereas most black mothers worked in a domestic or personal service occupation. In addition, obvious racial patterns appear in employment among the boys' mothers. Twenty-six percent of the white mothers said they worked full-time, and another 8 percent worked an indeterminate number of hours. The rest of the white mothers (64 percent) were housewives who did not work. However, 43 percent of the black mothers worked full-time, and an additional 24 percent worked indeterminate hours. Only 26 percent of the black mothers said they were housewives.

The household structure in which the delinquent boys lived also differed by race. Black boys lived in a wider variety of household situations. Fifty-five percent of the white parents said they were married, compared to only 35 percent of the black parents. Eighteen percent of the black parents said they were separated compared to only 3 percent of the white parents. Many white and black boys experienced the death of a parent (33 percent and 39 percent). As for living arrangements, 52 percent of the white boys but only 30 percent of the black boys lived in two-parent households. Thirty percent of the black boys lived with only their mother, compared to less than 20 percent of the white boys. Twice as many black boys as white boys lived with relatives. Similar to the families of delinquent girls, these household patterns reflected regional migration patterns, family networks between the city and surrounding countryside, and high mortality rates among white and black parents.

Despite alarmist characterizations of the families of delinquent youth that were common in the early twentieth century, the families of delinquent boys in Memphis maintained fairly strong ties to the labor force and to conventional society. They married, had children, sent their children to school, and worked. Three-fourths of the fathers, both white and black, were employed full-time, and another 10 percent worked an indeterminate number of hours. A quarter of the fathers performed skilled labor, and about another 10 percent had middle-class occupations. Most families of delinquent boys, from an economic standpoint, functioned on more than a subsistence level.

Similar to the black delinquent girls, black delinquent boys were over-represented in the juvenile court. More than half of the male delinquents in the juvenile court were black, but blacks comprised only one-third of the total male population under the age of nineteen in Memphis. The Memphis Juvenile Court was not noticeably aggressive in seeking out delinquent boys to supervise: it had barely enough probation officers to manage investigation and probation duties, and it had little control over who came before it.

The forces that brought disproportionately more black delinquents into the justice system appear to have been largely external to the juvenile court.

Delinquency charges against boys can be classified into four broad categories: status offenses, nonproperty and nonviolent crimes (minor criminal offenses), personal attacks, and property crimes (see table 7). Status offenses consisted mainly of incorrigibility, curfew violation, prowling, truancy, running away from home, and immoral conduct. Nonproperty, nonviolent offenses included disorderly conduct, gambling, trespassing, traffic violations, and hanging on a streetcar. Highway robbery, rape, assault, and assault with a weapon made up the bulk of personal attacks. Finally, property crimes generally consisted of petty larceny, car theft, housebreaking, and breaking and entering.

Overall, despite the ostensible mission of the juvenile court to intervene into the lives of predelinquents, the great majority of boys (82 percent) were brought into court for criminal rather than status offenses. The boys were overwhelmingly accused of minor property offenses, especially petty larceny, rather than personal offenses. (Serious violent offenses did not occupy much of the juvenile court's time; criminal courts handled those cases.) Nearly half of the delinquent boys committed their offenses with companions; criminal offenses especially tended to be joint rather than solo ventures. Only 3 percent of the delinquents appeared to belong to a gang. Unlike the case in Chicago, there does not appear to have been much formal gang activity in 1920s Memphis.

Unlike most of the delinquent girls' cases, which involved complicated behavioral issues that went to the heart of family relations and the girls' emerging sexual identity, the boys' cases consisted of fairly straightforward incidents of theft. Whereas status offenses dominated girls' cases and, as such, focused on the girls' developmental paths as "adolescents," criminal offenses dominated boys' cases. Only 18 percent of the delinquent boys were charged with status offenses. Delinquent girls mainly challenged familial authority, whereas delinquent boys challenged the formal authority of the state, especially its role in safeguarding the rights of property.

Charges against the delinquent boys differed significantly by race (see table 7). Not only were black males disproportionately overrepresented among delinquents, but they were also charged with serious offenses more often than white males. Twenty-three percent of the white boys were charged with a status offense compared to only about 15 percent of the black boys. Fifty-five percent of the black boys were charged with property crimes,

TABLE 7. Charges against Delinquent Boys (N = 315)

	WHITE		BLACK		TOTAL	
	N	%	N	%	N	%
Incorrigible	11	8.0	6	3.4	17	5.4
Curfew violation	1	0.7	1	0.6	2	0.6
Truancy	10	7.3	12	6.7	22	7.0
Runaway	10	7.3	3	1.7	13	4.1
Immoral conduct	0	0.0	4	2.2	4	1.3
Disorderly	25	18.2	21	11.8	46	14.6
Gaming	6	4.4	5	2.8	11	3.5
Trespassing	1	0.7	8	4.5	9	2.9
Traffic violation	6	4.4	4	2.2	10	3.2
Hanging on streetcar	3	2.2	3	1.7	6	1.9
Highway robbery	1	0.7	2	1.1	3	1.0
Rape	0	0.0	2	1.1	2	0.6
Assault	1	0.7	5	2.8	6	1.9
Assault with weapon	0	0.0	5	2.8	5	1.6
Larceny	44	32.1	70	39.3	114	36.2
Car theft	5	3.6	6	3.4	11	3.5
Housebreaking and larceny	5	3.6	8	4.5	13	4.1
Breaking, entering, larceny	8	5.8	13	7.3	21	6.7
Total	137		178		315	
	SUMMARY					
Status offense	32	23.4	26	14.6	58	18.4
Minor criminal	41	29.9	41	23.0	82	26.0
Attacks/property	64	46.7	111	62.4	175	55.6
Total	137		178		315	

compared to 45 percent of the white boys. Although the overall rate of personal attacks was quite low, black boys were charged more frequently (8 percent versus 1 percent). While the formal charges against many of the male delinquents often sounded very serious, the actual crimes were less intimidating than the labels attached to them. For example, cases of highway robbery could easily be relabeled as petty larceny; they involved stealing food from a pushcart or helping to steal eggs, not using overt force or a weapon. In contrast to white males, black males were charged with personal attacks and property crimes at a higher rate than they were charged with status and minor criminal offenses.

The single most common charge against delinquent boys, both white and black, was petty larceny. This minor theft reflected two types of behavior: one, impulsive pilfering of miscellaneous things from a variety of people and places; and two, systematic gathering of coal from railroad and coal yards. Black boys stole coal in addition to other things, but white boys generally did not steal coal. This difference in behavior may account for the slightly higher incidence of larceny among black boys. Also, most trespassing charges actually involved theft of coal from coal yards and could easily have been reclassified as larceny. The other major type of stealing by delinquent boys in Memphis involved forcible entry into a house or business, usually classified as housebreaking or breaking and entering. These crimes also sounded more serious than they often were, as is suggested by the descriptions below.

Much of the boys' theft was impulsive mischief that resulted in no great financial or personal gain. As occasion presented itself, they stole small items such as clothes and food from department and grocery stores, neighbors, street vendors, and classmates. They took milk bottles, car tires, or newspapers to resell and bicycles or roller skates to keep for themselves. They broke into gumball machines and took the money or they grabbed toys off a store shelf. The boys mainly took opportunities that came their way: a dropped wallet or purse, an unattended bicycle or lunch stand, or an unsuspecting person. Given the economic instability of many families, some of the stealing was probably motivated by hunger or other need, but much of it reflected sheer opportunism.

Stealing coal, however, was an economic survival strategy for many black families. Upon investigation of one case involving a boy named Cecil, Officer Joy found that nearly everybody in one poor black Memphis neighborhood went to the railroad yards of the Broadway Coal Company and took coal for themselves or to sell cheaply to other neighbors. Officer Joy spoke to Mr. Wright, a special agent of the coal company, who stated that he had lost no less than one thousand tons of coal within the last six or eight months and that he had added another man on staff to catch some of the thieves. Cecil admitted stealing the coal because his mother had none. Since his father had deserted the family, the only source of income was the four or five dollars per week that his mother made from washing and ironing.[57] This case highlighted the link between the delinquent behavior of many black boys in Memphis and the precarious economic circumstances of their families. The overlap between delinquency and dependency, often hidden by the formal charges lodged against children, emerged in the details provided by some individual case files. One black male charged with larceny of some car tires said that he would not mind going to the Shelby County Industrial School because he did not get enough to eat at home.[58] Unlike boys who stole impulsively, the boys who gathered coal worked systematically to fulfill a specific need. Their collective efforts provoked a direct response from both the juvenile court and the larger business community in Memphis.

The second most common offense by delinquent boys was disorderly conduct, which encompassed a wide range of behaviors. Specific cases included breaking windows and other kinds of vandalism or property damage, creating disturbances or getting into fights, pulling false fire alarms, or annoying neighbors by swearing or throwing rocks ("chunking"). A typical case of disorderly conduct was that of Russell Walker, a white boy, whose neighbor complained to the juvenile court that he trespassed and destroyed her property, used bad language, and annoyed her. In court the neighbor stated that she was constantly wrangling with the neighborhood boys even though she had spoken to their parents. She claimed that Russell had thrown rocks and rotten eggs at her house. Russell's mother, however, said that she had placed the neighbor under a "peace order" because she had threatened to kill her children.[59] Russell's father simply affirmed his hope that the juvenile court could straighten out the whole affair and bring a little peace in the neighborhood. Another disorderly case involved Leroy Johnson, a black boy who, on a complaint from a theater owner, was arrested for creating a disturbance and "cursing everyone out." Leroy said that he got angry and cursed at the woman at the ticket office when she refused to refund his money. His mother said that he was a good boy and had permission to go to the movie. Judge Kelley ordered the boy to apologize to the ticket operator.[60]

The cases of boys accused of status offenses, like those of girls, were often more complicated from a behavioral standpoint, because they usually reflected deeply rooted problems in the boy's emotional life and family.[61] The status offenses of boys were more varied than those of girls. Sexual activity rarely constituted any part of a boy's offense, whereas truancy often was a factor. Truancy signified more than simply skipping school; it often indicated that other elements of a boy's life were unstable. Some parents of truants, especially black parents, could not afford to keep their sons in school because they could not pay for books or shoes or needed the income that came from the boy's job. Other parents did not care whether their sons attended school and simply neglected them. These parents' indifference was not always punished by the court, as indicated by a report of the Tennessee Child Welfare Commission in 1919 that criticized the poor enforcement of the compulsory attendance law in Memphis. Only 61 percent of the white children attended school for as long as sixty days, and only 42 percent of the black children did so.[62]

The situations of Tommie Barnes, white, and Clarence Watson, black, were typical of status offense cases in that family members initiated the complaint and the cases revealed serious intrafamilial conflict. Tommie Barnes's uncle complained to the court that Tommie ran away from home and would not attend school. Tommie did not get along with his stepfather. After Tommie's mother said that she "could not do anything with him," he went to live with his aunt and uncle. A slightly different picture of the family situation emerged from Tommie's point of view, however. His complaints were similar to those of many delinquent girls. In a letter to Judge Kelley, Tommie wrote, "My aunt don't believe in Picture Shows and swimming Pools. I want you to explain to her that they don't hurt anybody and you know that any young person enjoys these things every once in a while. And if you don't think they harm explain to her as I will abide strictly by your opinion." Kelley released the boy on probation to his aunt and uncle. In the case of Clarence Watson, the boy's mother complained to the court that he was hard to manage, did not go to school, and hung around with older boys who had a bad influence on him. She said that all her efforts had failed and she hoped that formal intervention by the juvenile court would help. She and her husband both worked and owned their house. Judge Kelley gave Clarence a severe lecture and released him to his mother. He later stole some newspapers and was put on probation to Officer Joy—without apparent effect, for his minor delinquencies continued for several years.[63]

Amid local and national perceptions of rising rates of juvenile crime that were clearly linked to a general sense of family crisis in the 1920s, many delinquent boys in Memphis came from working-class families that were generally able to provide them with shelter and stability. The overwhelming majority of male delinquents were not serious criminals; they were brought to court for nonviolent, relatively minor property offenses. The Memphis Juvenile Court, key to Progressivism and especially important for black children, served to keep young offenders like these out of the adult criminal justice system. It did not, however, aspire to play a very large role in addressing the predelinquent behaviors of status offenders. Rather, its main mission in practice was to soften the impact of the criminal justice system on small-time, young juvenile criminals.

ADJUDICATING MALE DELINQUENTS

Delinquent boys came to the attention of the juvenile court in various ways that differed significantly by race (see table 8). The most common complainants for both white and black males were law enforcement officials (police officers, special agents, probation officers).[64] They accounted for 50 percent of the complaints against white males and 41 percent of the complaints against black males. The second largest category of complainant was private citizen: 22 percent for white boys and 39 percent for black boys.[65] Unlike the case with delinquent girls, the families of delinquent boys played a much smaller role in initiating cases in the juvenile court. Parents and relatives accounted for only 14 percent of complaints against white boys and 8 percent of complaints against black boys. Not surprisingly, parents and school officials were the complainants for most status offenses, whereas law enforcement officers and private citizens were the complainants for most criminal offenses. These patterns in complainants and charges in turn corresponded with the boys' race: white boys predominated in status offenses while black boys predominated in criminal offenses.

Parents of delinquent boys, like those of delinquent girls, sometimes used the juvenile court's broad power to reinforce their own authority over their children. These parents clearly welcomed the court's intervention, often personified by Judge Kelley. One father complained to the court that his son was incorrigible. He had no specific act in mind on which to base the charge but was generally upset by the boy's demeanor and behavior. Another family appealed to the juvenile court for help because their son kept company with bad boys. The parents wanted the juvenile court to "scare" him a bit. One

TABLE 8. Complainant against Delinquent Boys ($N = 287$)

	WHITE		BLACK		TOTAL	
	N	%	N	%	N	%
Probation officer	3	2.4	1	0.6	4	1.4
Police	38	29.9	40	25.0	78	27.2
Special agents	23	18.1	24	15.0	47	16.4
School	8	6.3	12	7.5	20	7.0
Social service agency	1	0.8	0	0.0	1	0.3
Parents	16	12.6	9	5.6	25	8.7
Relative	2	1.6	3	1.9	5	1.7
Neighbor	5	3.9	8	5.0	13	4.5
Private citizen	28	22.0	62	38.8	90	31.4
Other	3	2.4	1	0.6	4	1.4
Total	127		160		287	
	SUMMARY					
Law	64	50.4	65	40.6	129	44.9
School/social services	9	7.1	12	7.5	21	7.3
Parents/relative	18	14.2	12	7.5	30	10.5
Other	36	28.3	71	44.4	107	37.3
Total	127		160		287	

white woman wrote to Judge Kelley, "I have heard of the good that you have done and are doing, also, I know that you are a mother . . . and this emboldens me to hope that you may be able to help me, or at least advise me."[66]

However, some parents of delinquent children resented the intrusion of the juvenile court authority into their families and flouted its power. The father of a boy named Harvey, who was white, voluntarily brought his son to the juvenile court, saying that he understood the truant officer was going to "have Harvey picked up" and that it would be best to show that he was anxious to cooperate with court officials. The chief probation officer held Harvey for the day to make him realize the seriousness of his truancy. However, when a follow-up officer visited the house to notify the family of their court date, Harvey's mother "attempted to 'ball out' officer about having boy in J.C. She stated that she had been told that old lady Jones got $5.00 for each case she could 'frame up' any charges against. Officer walked off and left her attempting to get up an argument." This case suggests that even within a single family, parental attitudes toward the juvenile court could differ substantially.[67]

Judge Kelley had three options for the disposition of delinquent boys: dismissal or release, noninstitutional supervision (probation), or institutional placement (see table 9). Unlike some other juvenile courts, the Memphis Juvenile Court never imposed corporal punishment as a penalty. Judge Kelley's own view was that "spanking is the lazy way, the antiquated way. . . . It is not the scientific, advanced method. . . . In my opinion, there are many better ways to reach a child's mental reactions than through its nervous system."[68] The placement decisions differed significantly by race. The majority of boys, 54 percent of white boys and 70 percent of black boys, were released outright, either because there was insufficient proof to demonstrate guilt or because it was the juvenile's first offense and Judge Kelley felt that a hearing would suffice to deter future criminal behavior. More than twice as many white as black boys were placed on probation: 30 percent versus 13 percent. Black and white boys were institutionalized at around the same rate (17 percent and 15 percent, respectively). Thus black delinquent boys were actually institutionalized only slightly more often than they were placed on probation (the key trend, however, was that most black boys were released outright). White boys, by contrast, were placed on probation twice as often as they were institutionalized. White status offenders had the highest rate of probation as well as the highest rate of institutional placement. Criminal offenders, particularly blacks, were most likely simply to be released.

The Memphis Juvenile Court, as we saw earlier, lacked the resources to carry out one of the fundamental components of the child-saving movement: probation. The low rate of probation for boys was similar to that of girls. The court readily admitted that it struggled with an inadequate probation staff; caseloads occasionally topped three hundred.[69] In addition to placing children on probation to officers paid by the court, Judge Kelley placed children on probation to volunteers such as Lance Forsdick of the YMCA, the principal at the Christian Brothers College, a man who was the city building inspector, and other trusted citizens of Memphis. Probation entailed two types of meetings: boys reported to the juvenile court at an appointed day and time to talk with a probation officer, and/or the officers visited the boys and their families at home. In 1924 Charles Chute of the National Probation Association complained that probation in Memphis was not intensive enough. "At present," he charged, "probation means little

TABLE 9. Disposition for Delinquent Boys ($N = 315$)

	WHITE		BLACK		TOTAL	
	N	%	N	%	N	%
Probation to parents	1	0.7	2	1.1	3	1.0
Probation to relative	5	3.6	0	0.0	5	1.6
Probation to other	6	4.4	6	3.4	12	3.8
Probation to officer	29	21.2	15	8.4	44	14.0
Tennessee Industrial School	10	7.3	0	0.0	10	3.2
State Training School-Nashville	1	0.7	0	0.0	1	0.3
State Training School-Pikeville	0	0.0	2	1.1	2	0.6
Shelby Co. Industrial School	8	5.8	26	14.6	34	10.8
Porter Home, Leath Orphange	1	0.7	0	0.0	1	0.3
Charles Wilson Home	0	0.0	2	1.1	2	0.6
Tenn. Children's Home Society	1	0.7	0	0.0	1	0.3
Dismissed, no proof	20	14.6	44	24.7	64	20.3
Dismissed, first offense	26	19.0	37	20.8	63	20.0
Dismissed at request	4	2.9	2	1.1	6	1.9
Released	24	17.5	41	23.0	65	20.6
Escaped	1	0.7	1	0.6	2	0.6
Total	137		178		315	

	SUMMARY					
Probation	41	30.1	23	13.0	64	20.4
Institutionalized	20	14.7	30	16.9	50	16.0
Foster care	1	0.7	0	0.0	1	0.3
Dismissed/released	74	54.4	124	70.1	198	63.3
Total	136		177		313	

*Removed 2 boys from sample who escaped from juvenile court

more than a suspended sentence." Further, Chute felt that the court was hampered because the probation officer was a woman (Beulah Wood Fite) who, despite her valiant efforts, was simply not as effective with older boys as a man could be.[70]

The Shelby County Industrial and Training School formed a crucial part of the juvenile corrections system in Memphis. The juvenile court sometimes used it as if it were a holding station and short-term jail. In addition, parents could commit their sons to the Industrial School without court intervention. Boys usually stayed between two and six months. A larger portion of black than white boys (15 percent versus 6 percent) was committed to the Industrial School in the 1920s, which is ironic considering that blacks were not even allowed into the institution until 1914. By the 1920s the Industrial School had become a predominantly black institution. This transformation in the function of the Industrial School highlights the changing nature of punishment meted out to white and black males by the juvenile justice system in Memphis. During the early years of institution building, black children were excluded from juvenile institutions and treatment programs, and their exclusion was itself a kind of punishment (in addition to being overtly discriminatory). Restriction of blacks from treatment opportunities continued during the Progressive Era, but dispositions increasingly came to include incarceration in custodial institutions.[71]

The very high rate of release and dismissal in the Memphis Juvenile Court, along with the low rate of probation and the large caseloads of probation officers, naturally raises serious questions about the court's effectiveness in rehabilitating delinquents, or even going through the motions of doing so. Just under 30 percent of the boys appeared in court later on new complaints.[72] The court employed increasingly severe measures each time a boy reappeared. He might be released with a warning the first time and placed on probation or put into the Industrial School the second time.

The problems of some repeat offenders seemed hopeless. Amos Morgan, a black boy, was in and out of the juvenile court for six years. His mother first complained in 1927 when he was ten that he was truant. Over the next few years, he was charged on various occasions with housebreaking, larceny, trespassing, and disorderly conduct. He was released to his mother, placed on probation, and sent to the Industrial School several times. Charles Lucas, a white boy, also had an extensive juvenile court record. First, at age fifteen, he stole a bicycle and rode a freight train to Mississippi, where he tried to sell the bike. Judge Kelley committed him to the Industrial School. A month later, having escaped from the Industrial School, he was charged with hopping a streetcar. He then escaped from detention and ran away from home. About three months later, the police brought him in for breaking into a store and stealing cigarettes, a few cans of peaches, and some money. In court he admitted that he also broke church windows and had robbed several other stores. On this last occasion, Judge Kelley committed him to the State Training and Agricultural School in Nashville. After release, when he was beyond juvenile court jurisdiction, he continued to steal and was sent to the workhouse in Memphis. Eventually he ended up in the state prison.[73]

Just as it did for female delinquents, the Child Guidance Clinic sometimes played an important role in the treatment of male delinquents in 1920s Memphis. Boys comprised most of the clinic's caseload. Robert Mason, an eleven-year-old white boy, was sent to the clinic because of truancy, lying, stealing, and antagonism to authority. His evaluation was typical of those for delinquent white boys. Dr. Williams wrote:

Causative Factors:

1. Home conditions in training—patterns set by the parents of opposition to authority, patterns of profanity, lying and dishonest dealing.

2. Undesirable companionship, inadequate supervision, patterns set by the vicious companions, paucity of proper recreational outlook.

3. A probable feeling of shame regarding the home conditions and behavior of mother, with an overcompensative defense and concealment of it all.

4. An antagonistic, almost paranoid reaction directed toward the world in general; this arising from his knowledge of the behavior of his mother and the fact that she is under criticism by society in general. He may not have this feeling but it must be remembered we have an intelligent boy who has rather keen insight into many things. Out of such paranoid, antagonistic individuals, criminals are made.

Dr. Williams also examined Willie Davis, age eighteen. He said of Willie:

Problems as Revealed:

1. General mental retardation due to inheritance.

2. Habits of idleness, low earning capacity, probably part of his general mental deficiency, further due to lack of proper training and supervision by parents.

3. Abnormal personality traits of cruelty, resentfulness, rages due to the weak inhibitions of his mental deficiency, bad patterns seen in the impulsive father.

4. Delinquent behavior of passing worthless checks, setting fires, stealing
are due to the early lack of training, suggestibility of the boy, habits of
idleness with small wants previously readily supplied by the father. Early
stealing from father not corrected. Some of these acts are determined by his
attitude of revenge.[74]

These clinic assessments, often formulaic and pessimistic, reflected the
eclectic blend of psychological and psychiatric ideas that were characteristic
of mental health thinkers in the 1920s and that were evident in better-known
child guidance clinics in cities such as Boston, Chicago, Philadelphia, and
Los Angeles.[75]

The racial ideology of the Memphis Juvenile Court and of Judge Kelley were most observable in treatment decisions. From the data available,
it appears that the juvenile court did not systematically or overtly punish
black male delinquents more harshly than white male delinquents. Rather,
the juvenile court invested fewer personnel, less money, and less time in
black children. This pattern of slighting the needs of black children was
most evident in the use of probation. Even though blacks always made up
the majority of male delinquents, the court employed three white probation
officers and only one black one during most of the 1920s. Blacks more often
experienced the least therapeutic options: release or incarceration.

Instances of overtly prejudicial treatment of black children certainly existed in the Memphis Juvenile Court. To some black boys, the rules of race
relations must have appeared especially arbitrary. For example, in 1922 the
sister of a boy named Ollie complained to the juvenile court that Ollie would
not work or go to school, and that she wanted him sent to reform school.
Judge Kelley thereupon sent him to the State Training and Agricultural
School for Boys in Pikeville. About two weeks after Ollie arrived at the reform school, the superintendent wrote to Judge Kelley: "you sentenced a
colored boy by the name of Ollie, col., to this institution, convicted of Delinquency and given a sentence of 1 year. According to law it will be impossible
for us to keep this boy on this charge. If you cannot send us a commitment
showing him convicted of a felony, we will have to release him." The chief
probation officer wrote back to the superintendent as follows:

> The Judge asks that I say that the boy, Ollie, colored, was sent to your
> Insitution [sic] for making a very obscene remark to a white school girl. He
> had also been guilty of some other minor offense.
> We realized that you possibly could not keep him on this charge but as

there was no other place to send him we thought you might keep him a few weeks for the general effect it would have on the negro boys in the Colored Detention Home and we appreciate your forbearance in the matter.

The Judge asks especially if you dismissed him not to tell him that he is being dismissed because you could not hold him but give him a good sound lecture and tell him you are dismissing him through the orders of Judge Kelley or for good behavior or any similar excuse you say fit to give.[76]

Some black delinquent boys also claimed that they experienced unfair treatment by law enforcement officials before arriving in court. One boy said that the police drove over his leg, then abused him and slapped his face. The police responded that they had to chase the boy because he would not stop. Another black child told court officials that the officer threatened to beat him if he did not admit to stealing a bicycle. In a similar case, a boy was arrested after a neighborhood man was robbed, and the police initially identified the boy on the basis of a general description. Even though the man could not identify the boy, the officers searched him and found that he was carrying a razor, whereupon they sent him to the juvenile court on a weapons charge.[77] In the case of three black brothers, the arresting police officers "stated that they had no proof on the boys of larceny and had brought them in on a disorderly conduct charge. That they, however, felt reasonably sure that the boys had stolen something and were trying to make them confess to it."[78] Some black delinquents continued to spend time in the city jail.[79] No doubt black boys, just like white boys, often lied to court officials in trying to make the most of their situations. But too many diverse allegations of discriminatory treatment by police appear in the case files to doubt that racial prejudice by law enforcement was real, especially in how children were initially processed into the juvenile court. Thus, even though the juvenile court itself does not appear to have demonstrated systematic prejudice toward black children, it operated within a context of police racism that almost surely led to discriminatory treatment.

The Memphis Juvenile Court embodied many of the most progressive aspects of the juvenile justice movement in America. Judge Kelley believed in the curative powers of probation (even if the court could not regularly employ it), and the court attempted to integrate the diagnostic methods of the Child Guidance Clinic. The juvenile court was not, at least not in obvious ways, an instrument of systematic racial discrimination in its punishment of black male delinquents. At the same time, however, the Memphis Juvenile Court as a whole was not strongly oriented to providing preventive treatment for delinquent boys, white or black. Resource constraints were real. Most of the families of delinquent boys were left to sort out their problems on their own.

Analysis of individual case file data illuminates important patterns in the family characteristics, offenses, and court processing of delinquent children in the Memphis Juvenile Court in the 1920s. White and black delinquents came primarily from working-class families with strong ties to the labor market and traditional ideas about appropriate behavior for their children. Memphis child welfare officials were primarily concerned with the sexual behavior of white girls; they left the fate of black girls largely, but not entirely, in the hands of their parents or other private citizens. Parents collaborated with juvenile justice officials in the regulation of adolescent female sexuality.

Black and white delinquent boys experienced the justice system in Memphis both similarly and differently. The court segregated detention facilities, officer duties, and hearing and record-keeping procedures. It also invested fewer of its scarce treatment resources in black than white children. Importantly, black delinquents, especially boys, were charged with criminal offenses at higher rates than white delinquents. However, the court itself did not obviously punish black delinquents more harshly than white delinquents. Delinquents in Memphis, white and black alike, received neither much punishment nor much treatment from the city's juvenile justice system.

Conclusion

NEW STUDIES OF SOCIAL WELFARE, especially those using family case records, have tended to challenge previous interpretations that stressed the overbearing power of child-serving institutions. As the case records from the Memphis Juvenile Court have revealed, court probation officers initiated hardly any cases. Members of the community had considerable impact in shaping operations of social welfare institutions, including the juvenile court. Parents, neighbors, and concerned citizens actively sought the juvenile court's assistance with personal family disputes, using it to enforce their own views of proper child rearing. To be sure, the juvenile court also played an overtly coercive role in trying to control juvenile delinquency, but the juvenile court was much more than an agent of law enforcement. It was also a source of support and counsel for troubled families. Social welfare and juvenile justice policy emerged from the interplay among many competing actors with diverse motivations.

The growth of the child welfare network in Memphis revealed a system that was shaped more by individual personalities, patterns of voluntary associational life, and community-building aspirations than by bureaucracy or deliberate state building. The levels of cooperation achieved between strong private activism and developing public institutions reflected historical patterns of the local community. Much social welfare history, written primarily about northeastern cities, has chronicled the growth of public responsibility and the withering away of early private organizations. As historians continue to examine southern child welfare, however, they will have to reconsider the relationship between private and public initiatives. The strength of private networks and the importance of personal connections in Memphis persisted well into the twentieth century. Their longevity suggests a system of welfare provision that was an ingrained regional variation due to strong community responsibility rather than simply a developmental stage in a single nationwide process.

The urban South was not uniformly an exception to national developments in child welfare and juvenile justice. Claims by historians about distinctive patterns of southern life resulting from the legacy of slavery, climate, or rural isolation and dependence on an agricultural economy have shaped how much of the region's history has been written. However, the Memphis Juvenile Court and the child welfare network had much in common with Progressive Era courts in other regions of the country: for example, the important roles of upper- and middle-class white and black reformers, the incorporation of psychiatric evaluations and therapeutic casework, an increasingly professional staff, and concern with efficiency in rendering social services. As an urban court, the Memphis Juvenile Court, like those in Boston, Chicago, and Los Angeles, also had at its disposal a network of agencies and services that collectively provided families with valuable emergency assistance such as food, fuel, shelter, and medical care. Similar to their counterparts elsewhere, the Memphis Juvenile Court probation officers were overwhelmed by their caseloads and clients' needs and barely managed to carry out their duties. Although the court in Memphis, like those in other cities, could not come close to solving its clientele's underlying problems, it could often make tangible contributions toward their short-term family stability.

Women's roles in welfare work have also undergone considerable reexamination by historians. Recent scholarship about the role of southern black women and their self-help community efforts has not only broadened the concept of social welfare but also demonstrated that blacks took active measures to provide for their own communities what was not available from the white-dominated community. This scholarship generally complements what has been written about the role of white women and the creation of the maternal state. While black women worked mostly within the private sphere of social welfare provision, many white women worked in public service and contributed to the development of social welfare policy. The founding of a national Children's Bureau and the female dominion of child welfare that surrounded it had local counterparts in Memphis and elsewhere. Drawing on a strong local female reform network, Judge Camille Kelley, along with many other white and black women in social service, guided the juvenile court and child welfare policy in Memphis for thirty years.

During the last fifteen years, state legislatures and the public have sharply questioned the desirability of a separate system of justice for juveniles. States lowered the age at which children can be tried as adults for certain crimes, for example. Today the Supreme Court is deciding whether states can use the death penalty for juveniles, and a twelve-year-old Florida boy was sentenced to life in prison for killing a playmate. Although debates about "super-predators" have subsided, Americans are still dealing with the legacy of the policies that emerged in the late twentieth century. The history of juvenile justice has long fluctuated with changing perceptions of juvenile crimes and the desirability of harsh punishment or lenient treatments for them. The Memphis Juvenile Court during the 1920s (a time when, similar to the 1990s, the public was deeply concerned about rising crime rates and changing family structures) mainly faced nonviolent minor property crimes rather than the violent personal crimes that were common in the 1990s. Yet even during the early years of last century, the Memphis Juvenile Court had uneven success in restoring family stability or ending the careers of young delinquents. Due to limited resources, probation officers generally had minimal contact with their clients, and custodial institutions offered few real rehabilitative programs. The juvenile court was not an autonomous institution. As an expression of its community, the court's limitations surely reflected the larger public's reluctance to enact fundamental social changes in order to assist working-class youth to work out their problems.

This study highlights the need for further research in two main areas of child welfare history: race relations and the handling of nonsupport cases. First, the racial dimensions of other juvenile court operations need to be examined more fully. Knowing how other racially diverse juvenile courts dealt with the problems of poor racial minorities in the past offers a more useful comparison to modern juvenile courts and can, compared to other studies, inform national social policy as America becomes increasingly diverse. Although the Memphis Juvenile Court incarcerated black males only slightly more often than white males, case files suggest that from the beginning of the juvenile court's history, blacks experienced greater intimidation and more discriminatory treatment from the police. However, keeping in mind both context and chronology, I have suggested that the segregation of blacks within a *juvenile* system was better than their exclusion; at the very least, juvenile court protected black boys (and girls) from the brutal *adult* criminal system of the South. But now as an increasing number of black juveniles are diverted to the adult system, modern juvenile justice has more and more in common with nineteenth-century conditions before the existence of juvenile courts. The degree to which the status of the court's clientele as children outweighs the importance of their race or crime goes to the heart of the goals of the juvenile court movement, has led some scholars to call for the abolition of the juvenile court, and requires additional investigation.

The limited assistance provided by the juvenile court to dependent black children also needs further examination. Only 15 percent of dependency cases in the Memphis Juvenile Court were black compared to 56 percent of delinquency cases. The few black cases in my study suggest, however, that background factors contributing to dependency among black children were similar to those for white children. Clearly black families did not seek the juvenile court's assistance to the same degree as did white families, perhaps because the former associated the juvenile court with coercion. Why else this may have been so, and whether the juvenile court would have embraced them had they come forward more willingly, are significant questions for further empirical investigation.

Second, the Memphis Juvenile Court's jurisdiction over nonsupport cases offers a fascinating new opportunity to explore the social welfare function of the juvenile court in early-twentieth-century urban America. Since nearly every case involved parents in some capacity, the extent to which juvenile court was always a *family* court sheds light on the wide range of problems juvenile court officers encountered. Nonsupport cases most explicitly delved into economic relationships between married working-class women and men, a subject historians know very little about. It was perhaps in these cases that the court's direct role in providing emergency intervention for troubled families was most evident. The extraordinary range of difficult family situations that court probation officers encountered should caution scholars, and the public, to be mindful of the often impossible mission asked of the juvenile court.

The juvenile court I studied no longer exists, but perhaps it should. Since its beginning, the juvenile court has always operated somewhere in between the state and the society, the ideal and the reality, the world of the law and the world of institutions driven by day-to-day necessity. It has also operated between the ideals of punishment and social justice. Existing between two worlds in this way, it is perhaps no surprise that the juvenile court was deeply flawed, satisfying no one completely. However, the strength of the Memphis

Juvenile Court in the 1920s lay in its role as an important gateway to social services for white and black poor children and their families. The juvenile court was a family court. It was the community's court. Since that time, expanded local and state governments and other institutions have eclipsed the power of the juvenile court, leaving only criminal matters to be decided by juvenile court judges. If the juvenile court resumed its status as a gateway to social services, and was not just a criminal court, it might fulfill its original goal. It could actually help poor children and their families.

Appendix

SOURCES AND SAMPLING PROCEDURES

This study draws on the unpublished records of the Memphis and Shelby County Juvenile Court. The most tantalizing sources for the analysis of juvenile court clientele are the confidential social files. They provide information about the children and their families in three broad areas: background characteristics, offense characteristics, and court processing. The other important sources are the minute books, which list the official cases the judge heard each day.[1] The minute books contain basic information about each case and allow us to examine the flow of cases through the court.

The social files usually consist of three parts. The first part includes records of the case generated internally by court personnel. These records include a general information sheet (Environment and Family History Blank), a typewritten report of the initial investigation of the juvenile's social environment and family history (the number of persons in the house, rent cost, number of rooms, sanitary condition, religion, occupation, wages, and mental or physical defects of household members), and reports of subsequent developments in the case, such as new offenses. The case accounts contain transcripts of court testimony and interviews with children, parents, neighbors, and social workers involved in the case. The probation officer in charge of handling the case usually compiled this record.

The second part of the social files consists of two kinds of correspondence: official and personal. The juvenile court officers wrote letters to children, their parents, local orphanages and charities, the local reform school, and state institutions such as the Tennessee Industrial School. They also wrote to employers, other juvenile courts in the country, and the police department. Personal correspondence includes letters from children and their parents to Judge Kelley or to the probation officer. Parents and relatives also had neighbors or people of local authority write testimonials on their behalf.

The social files also have miscellaneous records. These include police notes and legal documents such as subpoenas and appearance bonds, receipts for the release of children from court, and results of medical exams. Court officers sometimes saved interesting newspaper stories about their clients. One case contains a newspaper article about a woman who was accused of murdering her first two husbands. Some cases also have the results of psychiatric exams done by the Memphis Child Guidance Clinic.

These case files chronicle extraordinarily complex stories of individual families. The files not only describe the background and court experience of the clientele but also illuminate the citywide welfare network. Correspondence between local agencies such as the Associated Charities, St. Peter's Orphanage, or the YWCA shows that they cooperated with the juvenile court as well as with each other. The Memphis Juvenile Court also corresponded with regional child-caring agencies such as the Mississippi Children's Home, national child welfare organizations, and other juvenile courts. Letters from California, Chicago, New York, and St. Louis indicate the court's connection to a national network. Thus the social files are useful for their range and rich details.

The second set of the juvenile court records I used in this study is the minute books. They contain a daily log of court hearings. The minutes include only basic information such as name, age, race, sex, crime (dependency, delinquency, or nonsupport), length of sentence or probation, and where the child was sent. Each page of these ledger books has roughly ten cases with the judge's ruling. Court officials recorded black cases with red ink and white cases with black ink; the minute books show that the court heard black and white cases on separate days. The court also heard nonsupport cases on special days of the week.[2] As do the social files, the minute books reveal as much about the operation of the court as about the clients themselves.

To analyze the juvenile court's operations and its clientele, I chose to sample cases from three years during the 1920s: 1921, 1925, and 1929. Using the minute book listing of each new case, I took a systematic sample of cases (every third case) for each year.[3] The sample had a total of 737 cases: 240 from 1921, 250 from 1925, and 247 from 1929.[4] I used the child's name in the minute book to locate the corresponding social files. I collected information on thirty-three variables for each case, using a data collection instrument derived from Steven Schlossman's and Mary Odem's studies of the Los Angeles Juvenile Court.[5] Unfortunately, many cases did not have elaborate social files. In these instances, the minute books provided me with only basic information on a case.[6]

The total N for each table varies somewhat because of inconsistencies in data availability for each case. My data collection strategy was generally conservative. For example, for the variables criminal history, illness, alcoholism, and sex abuse, I recorded a positive response only when I located a specific reference in the case files. Unless specifically mentioned, I assumed that no such problems existed (if a charge was later recanted, however, I still included it). No doubt my data underestimates the prevalence of these variables in each family's history.

Occupational data was very incomplete, and my coding strategy was less conservative. In tabulating male employment, for example, instead of leaving out all of the "unknowns" I included them in the category of "Employed, hours indeterminate." This made sense, in my judgment, because these families, for the most part, were not homeless and had some stability. By including the "unknowns" in the employed but indeterminate category, I assumed that the chief adult male in residence had at least minimal employment, even if only seasonal day labor. In tabulating female employment data, however, I made the opposite decision. I left out the "unknowns" because I could not assume that most mothers were minimally employed. If they were, the probation officers would almost surely have gone out of their way to record that fact.

I divided occupations of parents into seven categories: professional, proprietary, clerical, skilled, semiskilled, unskilled, and domestic and personal service.[7] Professionals included druggists, nurses, and ministers. Proprietary occupations included barbers, contractors, restaurant owners, and operators of rooming houses. Clerical included salesmen, office workers, and retail sales. Domestic and personal service included porters, waiters and waitresses, chauffeurs, janitors, cooks, and laundresses. Other occupational possibilities included housewife, farmer, or no regular occupation (usually due to a poorhouse or prison sentence or to an illness). Farmers were classified as unskilled labor because in the urban market their skills were of limited use.

Most of the children came from working-class families. Working class is defined as a household with a resident guardian whose occupation was unskilled, semiskilled, or skilled, or someone with no regular occupation. The semiskilled category had the largest range of occupations. In many cases the job skills were impossible to determine, and the boundary between semiskilled and unskilled was fluid. Semiskilled work included truck drivers, saw filers, and night watchmen. The most common occupation in this category was a factory worker of some kind. Local factories employed people who manufactured snuff, candy, awnings, rugs and shades, mattresses, and bags. Shipping and packing factories also required manual laborers. Unskilled workers included peddlers, timbermen/loggers, river men, butchers, and general laborers. Skilled workers included carpenters, painters, foremen in factories, tailors, plumbers, mechanics, switchmen, and bakers.

Because of my sampling procedure, the total number of children is slightly more than the total number of families or cases. The court usually assigned consecutive case numbers to each person in the same family. Since I followed the daily entry of case numbers and chose every third entry, I occasionally counted more than one member of the same family in my sample. In many of the court's dependency cases, more than one sibling was brought into court. Moreover, dependency charges for a child often accompanied nonsupport charges against a father. However, delinquency charges against more than one sibling for the same event almost never happened.[8] The number of such cases that affected my sample is very small, but the methodological point highlights important differences in the nature of the two kinds of cases. Dependency (and nonsupport) charges reflected long-term family situations and often entailed numerous appearances in court by more than one sibling. Delinquency charges usually represented single events by children who sometimes committed their crime with a companion.

Each type of case had different sample sizes. The analysis of dependency in the Memphis Juvenile Court is based on a sample of 205 children. The analysis of female delinquency in Memphis is based on a sample of 65 cases, 30 white girls and 35 black girls. These girls represent 17 percent of the delinquency cases in the sample, approximately the same portion of girls to boys as in other cities. The analysis of male delinquency is based on a sample of 315 cases taken from the Memphis Juvenile Court. Boys made up about 80 percent of the delinquency cases, again, a percentage that is similar to other juvenile courts.

DEFINITIONS

In Tennessee the Public Act of 1911 defined a dependent child as one who was under age seventeen and was

> destitute or homeless or abandoned or dependent upon the public for support, or has not proper parental care or guardianship or who is found begging or receiving or gathering alms (whether actually begging or under pretext of selling or offering anything for sale) or being in any street, road, or public place for the purpose of so begging, gathering, or receiving alms, or who is found living in any saloon, disorderly house, bawdyhouse, or house of ill fame, or with any vicious or disreputable person, or whose home, by reason of neglect, cruelty, drunkenness, or depravity on the part of its parents, guardian, or other person in whose care it may be, is an unfit place for such a child, and any child under the age of fourteen years who is found begging, peddling, or selling any article, or singing or playing any musical instrument, upon the streets or giving any public entertainment, or who accompanies or is used in aid of any person so doing.

The act also defined a delinquent child as one who is under the age of seventeen

> who violates any law of the state or any city or town ordinance, or who is incorrigible, or who is a persistent truant from school, or who associates with criminals or reputed criminals or vicious or immoral persons, who is growing up in idleness or crime, or who frequents, visits or is found in any disorderly house, bawdy-house, or house of ill fame, or any house or place where fornication is enacted, or in any place where spirituous liquors or wine or intoxicating liquors or malt liquors are sold at retail, exchanged or given away, or who patronizes, frequents, visits, or is found in any gaming house or in any place

where any gaming device is or shall be operated, or who wanders about the streets in the nighttime without being on any lawful business or occupation, or who habitually wanders about any railroad yards or tracks or climbs on any moving train or enters any car or engine without authority, or who habitually uses vile, obscene, vulgar, profane, or indecent language, or is guilty of immoral conduct in any public place or about any schoolhouse.[9]

Nonsupport was defined as follows in 1915: "It is a misdemeanor for any person legally chargeable with the care of a child under the age of sixteen years willfully and without good cause to neglect or fail to provide for such child according to his means, or to leave it destitute, or in danger of becoming a public charge. There shall be a presumption, rebuttable in character, that the person so charged is possessed of means adequate to such support."[10]

In the minute books of the Memphis Juvenile Court (the recording of formal hearings), all children in dependency cases were formally adjudged "dependent." However, multiple meanings of dependency and neglect complicated the work of juvenile court officers. The terms "dependent" and "neglected" had similar but not identical technical meanings. Dependency usually referred to the inability of those legally responsible for a child to provide care or the nonexistence of such people, which left the child entirely without care. Dependency implied a desperate condition, such as orphanage or extreme destitution, that was not blamed on a specific individual. Neglect, however, introduced the notion of culpability and usually implied improper guardianship, willful neglect, or abuse by an adult who was responsible for the child. These formal distinctions, however, generally meant little in everyday life. Family members, social service agency workers, and community members embraced many other kinds of informal definitions. I use the term "dependent" generically to cover dependent, neglected, and abused children unless a case was specifically one of neglect or abuse.[11]

Notes

INTRODUCTION

1. Platt, *Child Savers*, 73–74.

2. Tiffin, *In Whose Best Interest?* 20–22; Schlossman, *Love and the American Delinquent*, 67–69.

3. Schlossman, *Love and the American Delinquent*, 14–17; Grossberg, *Governing the Hearth*, 236–37, 291–94; Feld, *Bad Kids*, 52–53 and chapter 8; Clapp, *Mothers of All Children*, 113, 143; Butterfield, *All God's Children*, 155; Rosenheim et al., *Century of Juvenile Justice*, 116, 362–64, 368–69.

4. For discussions of the concept of *parens patriae*, see Schlossman, *Love and the American Delinquent*, 58; Rothman, *Conscience and Convenience*, 236. Scholars generally refer to juvenile courts without using an article ("the") in order to emphasize the distinction from criminal court. I think many readers will be more comfortable with *the* juvenile court, so I have chosen to use the term in this way.

5. Schlossman, *Love and the American Delinquent*, 58–62.

6. Rothman, *Conscience and Convenience*, 218–19.

7. Tiffin, *In Whose Best Interest?* 226–28.

8. Ibid., 228. See Tanenhaus, "Growing Up Dependent" for a discussion of these issues in Chicago.

9. Shelden, "Rescued from Evil," 238–40.

10. Chambers, "Towards a Redefinition of Welfare History."

11. For examples of studies overestimating the juvenile court's autonomy, see Platt, *Child Savers*; Rothman, *Discovery of the Asylum*; Rothman, *Conscience and Convenience*; Mennel, *Thorns and Thistles*.

12. Gordon, *Heroes of Their Own Lives*; Odem, *Delinquent Daughters*.

13. Several unpublished doctoral dissertations deal with juvenile justice in the South. See Shelden, "Rescued from Evil"; William B. Jones, "Treatment of Juvenile Offenders in Tennessee"; Hardy, "Comparative Study of Institutions"; Lisenby, "Administrative History of Public Programs"; Curtis, "Juvenile Court Movement in Virginia"; Polansky, " 'For It Made Me a Lady.' "

14. Rothman, *Conscience and Convenience*, 206; Schlossman, *Love and the American Delinquent*, 57.

15. Feld, *Bad Kids*, 83–90.

16. Honey, *Southern Labor*, 14.

17. See Zunz, *Changing Face of Inequality*, and Schneider, *In the Web of Class* on the importance of religion in welfare services. See Schlossman's *Love and the American Delinquent* on the importance of ethnicity. Also see Haws, *Age of Segregation*.

18. Klewer, *Memphis Digest*, 49–51.

19. Honey, *Southern Labor*, 45–49; Carter, "Southern Political Style," 58–61.

20. This bias is especially true for criminal justice history. See Rothman, *Discovery of the Asylum*. On southern criminal justice, see Hindus, *Prison and Plantation*; Ayers, *Vengeance and Justice*; Oshinsky, "*Worse than Slavery*"; Donald R. Walker, *Penology for Profit*; and Zimmerman, "Penal Systems."

21. See Gordon, "Social Insurance and Public Assistance"; Katz, *In the Shadow of the Poorhouse*; Orloff, *Politics of Pensions*; Skocpol and Ikenberry, "Political Formation."

22. Grantham, *Southern Progressivism*, 217–30.

23. Woodward, *Origins of the New South*; Miller, *Memphis during the Progressive Era*; Chatfield, "Southern Sociological Congress."

24. Works about black women's social welfare efforts include Neverdon-Morton, *Afro-American Women*; Salem, *To Better Our World*; Hine, " 'We Specialize in the Wholly Impossible' "; Berkeley, " 'Colored Ladies Also Contributed.' "

25. Three recent books have laid the groundwork for research about southern social welfare. See Green, *Before the New Deal*, *The New Deal and Beyond*, and *This Business of Relief*.

26. However, visions of welfare differed by race. Gordon, "Black and White Visions of Welfare."

27. On blacks gaining access to public welfare, see Rabinowitz, *Race Relations in the Urban South*, chapter 6.

28. Herbert Lou wrote in 1927 that "there are women judges in Chicago, Ill.; Memphis, Johnson City, Tenn.; Plattsburg, N.Y.; Danville, Boyce, Va.; Miami, Fla.; and the District of Columbia. In the Domestic Relations Court of Birmingham, Ala., a woman judge tries adult cases. Women judges sit in a few other courts which also hear children's cases." Lou, *Juvenile Courts in the United States*, 78. Miriam Van Waters, although not formally designated a judge, also played a prominent national role in juvenile justice. See Freedman, *Maternal Justice*.

29. For discussions about maternalism, see Clapp, "Welfare and the Role of Women"; Clapp, *Mothers of All Children*; Freedman, *Maternal Justice*; Gordon, "Putting Children First," 63–86; Ladd-Taylor, "Toward Defining Maternalism"; Ladd-Taylor, *Mother-Work*; Koven and Michel, "Womanly Duties"; Michel and Rosen, "Paradox of Maternalism"; Skocpol, *Protecting Soldiers and Mothers*; Knupfer, *Reform and Resistance*.

30. Muncy, *Creating a Female Dominion*, xv; Gordon, "Social Insurance and Public Assistance," 48.

31. Odem, *Delinquent Daughters*, 156.

32. See the appendix for a more detailed discussion of sources and sampling procedures. The juvenile court also heard a category of cases that applied to adults only. Wives initiated nonsupport petitions against their husbands when they failed or refused to support her and/or the couple's children.

CHAPTER 1. The City of Memphis and Progressive Social Reform

1. Goldfield, *Cotton Fields and Skyscrapers*, 4–5, 95. For discussions of cultural transference of values of rural migrants to the urban environment, see Kenneth K. Bailey, *Southern White Protestantism*; Flynt, "Religion in the Urban South"; Shelton, *Enduring South*; Botsch, *We Shall Not Overcome*; Anderson, "Agrarian Attitudes"; Grantham, *Southern Progressivism*, 410–11.

2. William A. Link, *Paradox of Southern Progressivism*, xi–xii, 7–10; Berkeley, " 'Like a Plague of Locust,' " 193, 209–10; Green, *This Business of Relief*, 138–39.

3. Grantham, *Southern Progressivism*, 276; Goldfield, *Cotton Fields and Skyscrapers*, 98–102.

4. Grantham, *Southern Progressivism*, 78–79.

5. Kirby, *Rural Worlds Lost*, xv, 119.

6. Honey, *Southern Labor*, 14; Capers, *Biography of a River Town*, 111.

7. Capers, *Biography of a River Town*, 107; Berkeley, " 'Like a Plague of Locust,' " 21.

8. Goldfield, *Cotton Fields and Skyscrapers*, 54–55.

9. Berkeley, " 'Like a Plague of Locust,' " 20, 40, 58–59; Capers, *Biography of a River Town*, 107, 111.

10. Capers, *Biography of a River Town*, 138, 142, 149.

11. Sigafoos, *Cotton Row to Beale Street*, 50–51.

12. Williams, "Two Black Communities in Memphis," 33; Capers, *Biography of a River Town*, 177–78; Berkeley, " 'Like a Plague of Locust,' " 192–93.

13. Melton, "Blacks in Memphis," 5–9; Berkeley, " 'Like a Plague of Locust,' " 350–51.

14. Woodward, *Origins of the New South*, 299; Melton, "Blacks in Memphis," 22, 120; Capers, *Biography of a River Town*, 125.

15. Miller, *Mr. Crump of Memphis*, 28; Biles, *Memphis in the Great Depression*, 135; Berkeley, " 'Like a Plague of Locust,' " 302–41.

16. Brownell, "Commercial-Civic Elite."

17. Woodward, *Origins of the New South*, 116–21.

18. *Memphis Chamber of Commerce Journal* (April 1920): 89; Sigafoos, *Cotton Row to Beale Street*, 91–93.

19. *Memphis Chamber of Commerce Journal* (April 1920): 89; *Memphis News Scimitar*, October 12, 1924.

20. Sigafoos, *Cotton Row to Beale Street*, 71.

21. *Memphis Chamber of Commerce Journal* (April 1920): 89; Biles, *Memphis in the Great Depression*, 50–51.

22. Miller, *Memphis during the Progressive Era*, 45–47; *Memphis Chamber of Commerce Journal* (April 1920): 89; Sigafoos, *Cotton Row to Beale Street*, 72.

23. Peter Gottlieb, "Rethinking the Great Migration," in Trotter, *Great Migration in Historical Perspective*, 71; Sigafoos, *Cotton Row to Beale Street*, 72–75; Capers, *Biography of a River Town*, 219, 221–23; Miller, *Memphis during the Progressive Era*, 43–44.

24. Robert Sigafoos defines a cotton factor in *Cotton Row to Beale Street*, 67.

25. Capers, *Biography of a River Town*, 220–21; Sigafoos, *Cotton Row to Beale Street*, 67.

26. Honey, *Southern Labor*, 21–22.

27. Ibid., 30–32.

28. Sigafoos, *Cotton Row to Beale Street*, 72–73, 83, 141–42, 145.

29. Honey, *Southern Labor*, 24, 29–30.

30. Ibid., 30–31; Melton, "Blacks in Memphis," 76; Berkeley, " 'Colored Ladies Also Contributed.' "

31. Melton, "Blacks in Memphis," 84–88.

32. U.S. Bureau of the Census, *Fifteenth Census of the United States, 1930*, 920. These findings are similar to those in Norfolk, Virginia, described by Lewis, *In Their Own Interests*; Honey, *Southern Labor*, 34.

33. U.S. Bureau of the Census, *Thirteenth Census of the United States, 1910*, 48, 758.

34. Kirby, *Rural Worlds Lost*, 233–37.

35. Industrial production workers did not outnumber farmers in the South until the late 1940s, and the rural South in the Progressive Era was much as it had been in the 1870s. Ibid., xiv. Earl Lewis shows that Norfolk served as an urban magnet for the surrounding rural hinterland of Virginia and North Carolina in much the same way as Memphis did for Tennessee and Mississippi. Earl Lewis, "Expectations, Economic Opportunities, and Life in the Industrial Age: Black Migration to Norkfolk, Virginia, 1910–1945," in Trotter, *Great Migration in Historical Perspective*, 22–24.

36. Miller, *Memphis during the Progressive Era*, 7–8; Biles, *Memphis in the Great Depression*, 13; Capers, *Biography of a River Town*, 205.

37. Grossman, *Land of Hope*, 28–29; Lewis, "Expectations, Economic Opportunities," 23; Kirby, *Rural Worlds Lost*, 53; Sigafoos, *Cotton Row to Beale Street*, 97–98.

38. Kirby, *Rural Worlds Lost*, 276–77.

39. Ibid., 294, 305.

40. Melton, "Blacks in Memphis," 20.

41. Gottlieb, *Making Their Own Way*, 22–32; Grossman, *Land of Hope*, 30–33.

42. Grossman, *Land of Hope*, 30–31, 33; Kirby, *Rural Worlds Lost*, 276–81; Gottlieb, "Rethinking the Great Migration," 72–73.

43. Lewis, "Expectations, Economic Opportunities," 25–26.

44. Rabinowitz, *Race Relations in the Urban South*, 112–13, 182, 196–97; Lewis, *In Their Own Interests*, 18.

45. Sigafoos, *Cotton Row to Beale Street*, 103–4.

46. Jacqueline Jones, *Labor of Love*, 154; Lewis, "Expectations, Economic Opportunities," 26; Grossman, *Land of Hope*, 31.

47. Biles, *Memphis in the Great Depression*, 12–13; Miller, *Memphis during the Progressive Era*, 7; Honey, *Southern Labor*, 15.

48. See Hindus, *Prison and Plantation*; Ayers, *Vengeance and Justice*, 234–35.

49. Biles, *Memphis in the Great Depression*, 6, 10–11, 13–14, 28.

50. Grantham, *Southern Progressivism*, 277.

51. Biles, *Memphis in the Great Depression*, 20.

52. Rosen, "Business, Democracy, and Progressive Reform"; Grantham, *Southern Progressivism*, 279.

53. See Hall, "O. Delight Smith's Progressive Era," 167; Wiebe, *Search for Order*; Skowronek, *Building a New American State*.

54. Miller, *Memphis during the Progressive Era*, 13.

55. Grantham, *Southern Progressivism*, 287–88; Biles, *Memphis in the Great Depression*, 29.

56. Miller, *Mr. Crump of Memphis*, 35–41.

57. Ibid., 58, 63.

58. Grantham, *Southern Progressivism*, 284–87; Miller, *Mr. Crump of Memphis*, 71.

59. Miller, *Mr. Crump of Memphis*, 105–6.

60. Ibid., 86–87.

61. Melton, "Blacks in Memphis," 29, 39–41.

62. Lamon, *Black Tennesseans*, 207–8; Melton, "Blacks in Memphis," 42–43.

63. Lamon, *Black Tennesseans*, 45; Melton, "Blacks in Memphis," 104; Honey, *Southern Labor*, 45–49.

64. Miller, *Memphis during the Progressive Era*, 92.

65. See also Wyatt-Brown, *Southern Honor*; Ownby, *Subduing Satan*; Ayers, *Vengeance and Justice*.

66. Miller, *Mr. Crump of Memphis*, 106–15.

67. Phillips, "Rowlett Paine's First Term"; Lanier, *Memphis in the Twenties*, 19–20.

68. Miller, *Mr. Crump of Memphis*, 130.

69. *Memphis News Scimitar*, October 30, 1923; November 5, 1923; Jackson, *Ku Klux Klan in the City*, 47–48.

70. Miller, *Mr. Crump of Memphis*, 138.

71. Biles, *Memphis in the Great Depression*, 22–23; Lanier, *Memphis in the Twenties*, 32–33; Phillips, "Rowlett Paine's First Term."

72. Jackson, *Ku Klux Klan in the City*, 240, 247–49.

73. *Memphis News Scimitar*, November 5, 1923.

74. A United States Bureau of Education survey ranked Tennessee schools forty-fourth in the country. *Commercial Appeal*, May 30, 1920; Phillips, "Rowlett Paine's First Term"; Sigafoos, *Cotton Row to Beale Street*, 131.

75. *Memphis Chamber of Commerce Journal* (March 1923): 18; *Memphis Press-Scimitar*, September 29, 1929.

76. *Memphis News Scimitar*, February 21–22, 1925; *Memphis Press-Scimitar*, July 16, 1927.

77. Cash, *Mind of the South*, 266; Grantham, *Southern Progressivism*, 410–11; Lanier, *Memphis in the Twenties*, 16–17.

78. Arthur S. Link, "Progressive Movement in the South"; Keller, *Regulating a New Society*, chapters 1, 5, 6.

79. Chatfield, "Southern Sociological Congress," 24, 41, 82, 97.

80. Ibid., 104–6.

81. Woodward, *Origins of the New South*, 406.

82. William A. Link, *Paradox of Southern Progressivism*, 306–10.

83. Ibid., xi–xii.

84. Odem, *Delinquent Daughters*, 8, 11, 19, 37.

85. Wedell, *Elite Women*, 72–73; *Memphis Press-Scimitar*, April 29, 1927; January 21, 1929.

86. Odem, *Delinquent Daughters*, 28–30.

87. Dittmer, *Black Georgia in the Progressive Era*, 110; Kirby, *Darkness at the Dawning*, 4; Cartwright, *Triumph of Jim Crow*, 255–59; Kousser, *Shaping of Southern Politics*; Rabinowitz, *Race Relations in the Urban South*, 331–34, 339; McMillen, *Dark Journey*, xv.

88. William A. Link, *Paradox of Southern Progressivism*, 322.

89. See Hindus, *Prison and Plantation*; Wyatt-Brown, *Southern Honor*; Ayers, *Vengeance and Justice*, 9–33; and, for welfare policies, Wisner, *Social Welfare in the South*.

CHAPTER 2.   Child Welfare and the Establishment of the Juvenile Court

1. Schlossman, *Love and the American Delinquent*, 57.

2. Klewer, *Memphis Digest*, 49–51.

3. Sara A. Brown, "Institutions," in Clopper, *Child Welfare in Tennessee*, 521.

4. Three counties initially had juvenile courts in 1905: Shelby, Davidson, and Knox. The next year the population requirement was raised and applied only to Shelby and Davidson counties.

5. The Board of State Charities served only for show, since its reports rarely made substantive criticism and instead usually found everything "in apple-pie order." Tennessee Board of State Charities, *Report of the Board of State Charities of Tennessee to the Fiftieth General Assembly 1896*, 6, 10; *Report of the Board of State Charities of Tennessee to*

the *Fifty-third General Assembly 1903*, 8; *Biennial Report of the Board of State Charities of Tennessee 1915*, 8–9. See also Grantham, *Southern Progressivism*, 218–19; Shivers, "Social Welfare Movement in the South," 239–45.

6. Brown, "Institutions," 536, 539.

7. Department of Institutions of Tennessee, *Biennial Report, 1924–1926*, 264, 269–73; Brown, "Institutions," 526–28, 537–39.

8. Shelden, "Rescued from Evil," 108–9.

9. Shelden, "History," 97; Shelden, "Rescued from Evil," 124.

10. Shelden argues that the majority of people involved in founding the reformatory were members of the upper class, businessmen, or their wives. Shelden, "Rescued from Evil," 130–34.

11. There is discrepancy among my sources about whether the state actually provided money for the Shelby County Industrial and Training School. William Miller says the appropriation bill was killed in the Senate because it felt that east Tennessee should not support a west Tennessee institution. Randall Shelden says the seventy-five thousand dollars was appropriated. It is clear that a combination of private contributions and county money paid for the reform school. Miller, *Memphis during the Progressive Era*, 106; Shelden, "Rescued from Evil," 123–29, 134–41; Shelden, "History," 96–106.

12. Miller, *Memphis during the Progressive Era*, 107–8.

13. Quoted in Shelden, "Rescued from Evil," 135.

14. Shelden, "History," 99.

15. Brown, "Institutions," 546; *Commercial Appeal*, March 20, 1920.

16. Girls were never sent to the Shelby County Industrial and Training School. They usually went to the Convent of the Good Shepherd or to an orphanage.

17. Shelden, "History," 100–101.

18. Board of Inspectors of the Tennessee Penitentiary. Main Prison, Convict Record Books K–T. Volumes 99 (1900–1904), 100 (1904–12).

19. Shelden, "History," 102.

20. Brown, "Institutions," 546.

21. *Memphis News Scimitar*, March 20, 1920.

22. *Commercial Appeal*, March 21, 1920.

23. Ibid., March 24, 1920.

24. Shelden, "History," 104–5.

25. Membership form, Playground Association of Memphis. Suzanne Scruggs Papers.

26. *Memphis Press*, May 12, 1910.

27. Quoted in Shelden, "Rescued From Evil," 35.

28. Lee Hanmer (Playground Association of America) to Suzanne Scruggs, July 14, 1908. Suzanne Scruggs Papers; *Memphis Press*, May 12, 1910.

29. Quoted in Shelden, "Rescued From Evil," 35.

30. Much of the historical interpretation of the playground movement focuses on reformers' attempts to Americanize new immigrant populations during the first decade of the twentieth century. Immigrants, however, used playgrounds for their own purposes. Rosenzweig, *Eight Hours for What We Will*, 146–52.

31. Suzanne Scruggs to Memphis Park Commission, September 10, 1908. Suzanne Scruggs Papers.

32. Miller, *Memphis during the Progressive Era*, 84–86.

33. Donzelot, *Policing of Families*.

34. Rothman, *Conscience and Convenience*, 236–38, 243–245; Schlossman, *Love and the American Delinquent*, 137–41.

35. Despite the popularity of the court and its rapid acceptance as a public solution to juvenile delinquency, it remained an urban phenomenon. According to a U.S. Children's Bureau study, in 1918 there were 321 courts with separate juvenile hearings and probation services. Only 42 served rural areas and the rest served populations of five thousand or more. Since the greater proportion of children lived in rural areas, the court was unavailable to them. Tiffin, *In Whose Best Interest?* 226. About four out of five children in Tennessee lived in rural communities. Raymond G. Fuller, "Recreation," in Clopper, *Child Welfare in Tennessee*, 307.

36. Ashcraft, *Public Care*, 33–35; Tennessee Department of Public Welfare, *Handbook of Laws*, 337–43.

37. The first draft of the juvenile court bill was drawn up by Marion Griffin, secretary to the Juvenile Court Committee of the Playground Association and Tennessee's first woman lawyer. *Memphis Press*, April 9, 1909. On women lawyers in Tennessee, see *Memphis News Scimitar*, March 22, 1925.

38. Mabel Brown Ellis, "Juvenile Courts," in Clopper, *Child Welfare in Tennessee*, 443–44; Shelden, "Rescued from Evil," 182.

39. By the 1920s the Nineteenth Century Club was perhaps the largest female social organization in Memphis. It was not restrictive enough to be strictly "elite." Municipal activism may have begun with a core of elite women but gradually came to include many who were not. *Social Register of Memphis*, 1925. See Lobes, "Hearts All Aflame."

40. Wedell, *Elite Women*, 48–52, 85–87, 102–4, 132; *Commercial Appeal*, March 30, 1913; *Memphis Press-Scimitar*, April 29, 1927. As many other studies have shown, the volunteer service work of these women laid the groundwork for political opportunities and eventually gave way to professional and public careers for women. Thus Judge Camille Kelley eclipsed Suzanne Scruggs. Lubove, *Professional Altruist*; Kunzel, "Professionalization of Benevolence"; Brumberg and Tomes, "Women in the Professions."

41. On the life and work of Suzanne Scruggs, see Wedell, *Elite Women*, 109–34.

42. Berkeley, " 'Colored Ladies Also Contributed.' " Other works about black women's social welfare work include Neverdon-Morton, *Afro-American Women*; Salem, *To Better Our World*; Hine, " 'We Specialize in the Wholly Impossible.' "

43. Gordon, "Black and White Visions of Welfare," 168–69; Berkeley, " 'Colored Ladies Also Contributed,' " 196.

44. Inter Racial League, *Inter Racial Blue Book*, 7–9.

45. *Memphis Press*, January 12, 1909; *Commercial Appeal*, May 6 and 7, 1907; January 26, 1910. Indeed, as late as 1914, four years after the juvenile court opened, boys and some girls under age sixteen were sent to the State Prison in Nashville. These children were mostly black and were probably charged with at least a felony. Board of Inspectors of the Tennessee Penitentiary. Main Prison, Convict Record Books K–T. Volumes 99 (1900–1904), 100 (1904–12), 101 (1912–17).

46. *Commercial Appeal*, February 23, 1910; August 21, 1910. Making the juvenile court a city court rather than a county one meant that the mayor appointed the judge. Leroy Leflore suggests that Mayor Crump was behind the change from county to city jurisdiction. Leflore, Turner, and Jones, "History of the Juvenile Court."

47. *Commercial Appeal*, August 21, 1910; A. M. Hildebrand to the Advisory Board of the Juvenile Court, September 14, 1910; A. M. Hildebrand to Mary West, September 26, 1910. Suzanne Scruggs Papers.

48. Kelley, "Burglar Four Years Old," 318.

49. Ellis, "Juvenile Courts," 416–17; Ashcraft, *Public Care*, 33–35.

50. Ellis, "Juvenile Courts," 444; Ashcraft, *Public Care*, 33–35.

51. The bills also included state provision of care for feebleminded children; public provision of hospital care for dependent pregnant women; a nonsupport law; a statewide playground law; permission for children under sixteen to be accompanied by a woman when going before a grand jury; shielding girls who were "victims of social wrong" from testifying publicly; appropriation of money for investigation of crimes against children; allowing women to hold the office of juvenile court judge; enabling women to serve on school boards; and making all laws pertaining to children statewide in scope. Unspecified newspaper article from Memphis Public Library (probably *Commercial Appeal*), March 31, 1913.

52. Memphis Juvenile Court Advisory Board, "First Report of Juvenile Court Advisory Board," February 23, 1910. Suzanne Scruggs Papers.

53. Kelley, "Burglar Four Years Old," 318–19.

54. There is some evidence that Hooks opened a detention home or industrial school for black children before the establishment of the juvenile court. Church, *Nineteenth Century Memphis*, 43–44; *Memphis Press*, July 13, 1910.

55. Memphis Juvenile Court Advisory Board, "First Report of Juvenile Court Advisory Board," February 23, 1910; Julia Hooks to Suzanne Scruggs, December 15, 1910. Suzanne Scruggs Papers; *Memphis Press*, July 13, 1910; Shelden, "Rescued from Evil," 188–89.

56. Kelley, "Burglar Four Years Old," 318–19.

57. The municipal code stated: "There shall be maintained in the City of Memphis two detention homes for juvenile delinquents, dependents and those confided to the care of the Municipal Juvenile Court—one to be maintained exclusively for white children, and the other exclusively for colored children. Said places of detention shall be operated and maintained by the Judge of the Municipal Juvenile Court by and with the consent of the Board of Visitors and Supervisors, and provision shall be made in the budget of the Juvenile Court for the necessary expenses connected therewith." The municipal code also specified provision for white and black probation officers but left their duties up to the judge. Klewer, *Memphis Digest*, 24, 49–51, 92.

58. Chute, "Juvenile Court of Memphis," 6; *Memphis News Scimitar*, December 3, 1928.

59. Hastings H. Hart (Russell Sage Foundation) to Suzanne Scruggs, August 29, 1910; October 22, 1910; Cora M. Bain (Probation Officer Louisville, Kentucky) to Suzanne Scruggs, May 7, 1910. Suzanne Scruggs Papers.

60. Ellis, "Juvenile Courts," 446–47.

61. Ellis, "Memphis and Her New Judge," 285; Shelby County Quarterly Court Minutes, January 8, 1917; *Memphis Press-Scimitar*, May 1, 1930; *Commercial Appeal*, April 6, 1920; April 15, 1937; Leflore, Turner, and Jones, "History of the Juvenile Court."

62. *Memphis Press*, October 27, 1910; December 29, 1910.

63. Ibid., December 29, 1910.

64. During passage in the legislature, the bill was made optional, not compulsory. Mabel Brown Ellis, "Mothers' Pensions," in Clopper, *Child Welfare in Tennessee*, 511–13. Joanne Goodwin has found that many mothers' pension programs expected women to earn at least some of their own money while being assisted. Goodwin, *Gender and the Politics of Welfare Reform*, chapter 5.

65. Ellis, "Mothers' Pensions," 512–17. By 1920 only four counties in Tennessee had pensions available and, outside Shelby County, none had large appropriations or administrative personnel.

66. Leflore, Turner, and Jones, "History of the Juvenile Court"; Tennessee Board of

State Charities, *Biennial Report of the Board of State Charities of Tennessee 1915*, 48; Ellis, "Juvenile Courts," 452; Ellis, "Memphis and Her New Judge," 285.

67. *Memphis Press-Scimitar*, November 10, 1950.

68. Wheeler, *One Woman, One Vote*, 18–19.

69. *Commercial Appeal*, March 18, 1920.

70. Ibid., January 15, 1920; *Memphis News Scimitar*, November 9–10, 1920; September 29, 1921.

71. *Commercial Appeal*, March 20, 1920; *Memphis News Scimitar*, March 22, 1920.

72. Neither court had jurisdiction over adults since the law made no provision for trying adults for contributing to delinquency. Chute, "Juvenile Court of Memphis," 1, 14–15; Turner, *Your Juvenile Court*, 2.

73. *Memphis News Scimitar*, October 10, 1922.

74. Ibid., November 23, 1920; *Commercial Appeal*, October 28, 1934; Memphis Chamber of Commerce, *Memphis Chamber of Commerce Journal* (February 1920). On the importance of the personality of judges in administration of juvenile justice during this time period, see Rothman, *Conscience and Convenience*, chapter 7.

75. Camille Kelley's role in the adoption scandal that erupted in the early 1950s over the practices at the Tennessee Children's Home in Memphis remains unclear but seems to have played a role in the timing of her resignation. For a further discussion of the "baby selling," see Austin, *Babies for Sale*.

76. *Memphis News Scimitar*, January 14, 1920.

77. Austin, *Babies for Sale*, 29–30; Kelley, *Delinquent Angels*, 5.

78. Kelley, *Friend in Court*, 1–4; *Memphis News Scimitar*, November 23, 1920.

79. *Memphis News Scimitar*, January 14, 1920; May 12, 1922; *Commercial Appeal*, May 1, 1920.

80. York, "Municipal Mother," 19. See also Schlossman, "Before Home Start."

81. At the time, Kathryn Sellers of the Washington, D.C., Juvenile Court was the only other woman judge, although women were referees on other courts. *Memphis News Scimitar*, November 23, 1920; *Memphis Press-Scimitar*, April 30, 1930.

82. *Memphis News Scimitar*, November 23, 1920; Roark, "Judge Kelley," 62.

83. *Memphis Press-Scimitar*, March 14, 1927.

84. Kelley, *Friend in Court*, 98.

85. Kelley, "Making the World Safe," 175.

86. *Memphis News Scimitar*, May 12, 1922; Anne Firor Scott, *Southern Lady*; Schlossman, "Before Home Start," 447, 450–52.

87. *Memphis Press-Scimitar*, April 30, 1930; Roark, "Judge Kelley," 9, 62; *Memphis Commercial Appeal*, February 13, 1938; See Odem and Schlossman, "Guardians of Virtue"; Schlossman and Wallach, "Crime of Precocious Sexuality"; Shelden, "Sex Discrimination."

88. *Memphis Press-Scimitar*, February 14, 1930.

89. Kelley, "Making the World Safe," 146.

90. *Memphis News Scimitar*, May 6, 1926; *Memphis Press-Scimitar*, September 7, 1929; Roark, "Judge Kelley," 9, 62.

91. *Memphis Press-Scimitar*, September 7, 1929; Kelley, *Friend in Court*, 154–67.

92. Kelley, *Friend in Court*, 26, 85–86.

93. Beulah Wood Fite to Charles L. Chute (National Probation Association), October 21, 1932. Juvenile Court of Memphis and Shelby County, Memphis, Tennessee.

94. Kelley, *Friend in Court*, 15–16, 37, 75.

95. Case no. 7735 (1926).

96. Chute, "Juvenile Court of Memphis," 3, 7; case no. 10477 (1929).

97. *Memphis Press-Scimitar*, November 23, 1927. For more on Judge Lindsey, see Mennel, *Thorns and Thistles*; Slater, "Judge Benjamin Barr Lindsey"; Larsen, *Good Fight*.

98. *Memphis Press-Scimitar*, December 9, 1929.

99. Kelley, *Friend in Court*, 8–9; Ernest Cole (National Probation Association) to Camille Kelley, February 21, 1928. Juvenile Court of Memphis and Shelby County, Memphis, Tennessee; *Memphis Press-Scimitar*, May 2, 1928; July 18, 1933.

100. *Memphis Press-Scimitar*, January 21, 1929; September 29, 1937; December 4, 1953; March 10, 1954.

101. Ibid., April 15, 1937; August 26, 1937; September 29, 1937; *Memphis Commercial Appeal*, April 15, 1937; November 10, 1950; Roark, "Judge Kelley," 62.

102. Freedman, *Maternal Justice*, 77, 84–90.

103. Ibid., 100–103, 180, 249.

104. City of Memphis, *Memphis City Directory*, 1928, 1929; Juvenile Court Staff List, Juvenile Court of Memphis and Shelby County, Memphis, Tennessee.

105. *Memphis Press-Scimitar*, March 11, 1929.

106. *Commercial Appeal*, April 15, 1937.

107. These years of service are approximations pieced together from case file references, newspaper announcements, and investigations of the National Probation Association, especially Chute, "Juvenile Court of Memphis."

108. *Commercial Appeal*, April 6, 1920; *Memphis News Scimitar*, May 4, 1922; July 11, 1922; Chute, "Juvenile Court of Memphis," 4–5. This string of female chief probation officers is quite curious. The same woman who recommended Camille Kelley to Mayor Paine also suggested Ada Turner to the Juvenile Court Advisory Board. Upon Turner's resignation in 1922, the chairman of the Advisory Board said that in all probability a man would be selected to fill the position. Supposedly, a Mr. M. W. Davies was chief probation officer for part of 1923. That a man did not fill the position until the political scandal in 1937 attests to a strong female network of power in Memphis at this time.

109. Gutman, *Black Family in Slavery and Freedom*, 230–39.

110. Case no. 7598 (1925); case no. 7556 (1925); case no. 7610 (1925).

111. Juvenile Court Correspondence, January 26, 1928; Klewer, "Memphis Municipal Code" and "Charter and Legislative Acts," in *Memphis Digest*, 49, 91; *Memphis Press-Scimitar*, April 5, 1929.

112. Rabinowitz, "From Exclusion to Segregation."

113. Muncy, *Creating a Female Dominion*.

CHAPTER 3. The Juvenile Court and the Progressive Child Welfare Network

1. Shivers, "Social Welfare Movement in the South"; Wisner, *Social Welfare in the South*; Rabinowitz, "From Exclusion to Segregation"; Grantham, *Southern Progressivism*.

2. Some historians have argued that scholarship devoted to "bringing the state back in" underestimates how much the private sector and forces outside the state shaped twentieth-century urban welfare even in cities such as Chicago that were considered to be at the vanguard of welfare reform. Cmiel, *Home of Another Kind*, 4.

3. Berkeley, " 'Like a Plague of Locust,' " 185, 195, 210.

4. Grantham, *Southern Progressivism*, 218–19.

5. *Memphis News-Scimitar*, April 5, 1925.

6. Biles, *Memphis in the Great Depression*, 55–57.

7. Eric Schneider finds the same type of network among those working with juvenile delinquency in Boston. See Schneider, *In the Web of Class.*

8. Sigafoos, *Cotton Row to Beale Street*, 86; Shivers, "Social Welfare Movement in the South," 130, 152.

9. Social Agencies' Endorsement Committee of the Chamber of Commerce Minutes, December 4, 1919; February 12, 1920; May 14, 1920, United Way of Greater Memphis, Memphis, Tennessee.

10. Sigafoos, *Cotton Row to Beale Street*, 137.

11. Social Agencies' Endorsement Committee Minutes, February 12, 1920.

12. Ibid., June 10, 1920; Green, *This Business of Relief*, 138.

13. Council of Social Agencies Minutes, October 12, 1920, United Way of Greater Memphis, Memphis, Tennessee.

14. Council of Social Agencies Minutes, December 16, 1920.

15. *Memphis News Scimitar*, November 24, 1920; Green, *This Business of Relief*, 144–45, 185–86.

16. Memphis Chamber of Commerce, *Memphis Chamber of Commerce Journal* (April 1923): 9.

17. Ibid., (July 1923): 13.

18. Council of Social Agencies Minutes, April 1927, October 1927.

19. *Memphis Press-Scimitar*, October 17–26, 1927.

20. Ibid., April 21, 1928.

21. Ibid., October 12, 1929; January 24, 1930; April 1, 1930.

22. Social Agencies' Endorsement Committee Minutes, January 8, 1920; Green, *This Business of Relief*, 137–38.

23. Social Agencies' Endorsement Committee Minutes, February 12, 1920; *Memphis News Scimitar*, April 6, 1925.

24. In some cases, the segregation of welfare services was indeed quite rigid. Several times in 1925 white ambulances that arrived first at emergency scenes refused to take injured blacks to a hospital. One man bled to death while another lay in the street until an ambulance for blacks arrived. This callousness was too much even for Memphis, and the newspaper ran an editorial condemning the city. Nevertheless, this incident highlights the parallel, segregated welfare networks in Memphis. *Memphis News Scimitar*, April 9, 1925; August 10, 1925.

25. Case no. 4578 (1921).

26. *Memphis Press-Scimitar*, May 31, 1928; *Commercial Appeal*, January 28, 1923; *Memphis Press-Scimitar*, 1928.

27. Council of Social Agencies Minutes, June 4, 1925; "Chairman & Co-Chairman appointed for different Committees," Council of Social Agencies, June 12, 1930.

28. Council of Social Agencies Minutes, February 11, 1926. In 1929 the Nominating Committee of the Memphis Council of Social Agencies consisted of three women. They submitted female nominees for president and first and second vice president and male nominees for treasurer and secretary. As exciting as this may have been, Mrs. Riddick, the nominee for president, withdrew her name. The council wound up with only one female officer, the second vice president, who was its first female executive. Council of Social Agencies Minutes, April 10, 1929; May 9, 1929; June 13, 1929.

29. This concern was common among those involved in social service during the early twentieth century. On the growth of social work training programs for whites and

blacks in the South during the 1920s and the importance of the Red Cross in social work education, see Shivers, "Social Welfare Movement in the South," 187, 205–16, 269–71, 376.

30. *Memphis Press-Scimitar*, June 25, 1927; May 17, 1927; Grantham, *Southern Progressivism*, 227–30.

31. Chafe, "Women's History and Political History," 117–118; Cott, *Grounding of Modern Feminism*, chapters 1–3.

32. William A. Link, *Paradox of Southern Progressivism*, 321.

33. Thomas Bernard and Barry Feld make a similar argument. See Bernard, *Cycle of Juvenile Justice*, 83 and Feld, *Bad Kids*, 6–10, 290–92. A former director of the Children's Bureau in Memphis, Samuel T. Rutherford, told me that he believed the juvenile court operated as a social welfare agency until the mid-1950s. A combination of the creation of the Department of Public Welfare, and the Tennessee Children's Home Society adoption scandal, along with reform in adoption legislation and the resignation of Judge Kelley, redefined and limited the social welfare role of the juvenile court. Samuel T. Rutherford, telephone interview with author, April 6, 1993.

34. Although Eric Schneider finds a network among delinquency agencies in Boston, he argues that the juvenile court was incidental to it. This situation was certainly not the case in Memphis. Schneider, *In the Web of Class*, 149.

35. Sara A. Brown, "Institutions," in Clopper, *Child Welfare in Tennessee*, 545.

36. Sara A. Brown, "Home Finding," in Clopper, *Child Welfare in Tennessee*, 605; *Memphis Press-Scimitar*, November 9, 1938; *Commercial Appeal*, February 16, 1938; Council of Social Agencies Minutes, January 10, 1924.

37. Kelley, *Friend in Court*, 260, 258.

38. All the names of family members have been changed in order to protect their confidentiality. The case file numbers are original.

39. Case no. 8204 (1927).

40. Council of Social Agencies Minutes, March 1928, January 1929, September 1929. In 1876 the Women's Christian Association opened a Mission Home for women "fallen from virtue." In 1909 it became the Ella Oliver Refuge. The Bethany Training Home was founded in 1916. *Commercial Appeal*, July 9, 1935; Wedell, *Elite Women*, 37–42.

41. Council of Social Agencies Minutes, December 1924; Wedell, *Elite Women*, 48–50.

42. Case no. 7625 (1925).

43. Council of Social Agencies Minutes, July 1928, March 1929.

44. *Commercial Appeal*, August 18, 1932. That child welfare institutions were significantly more developed in cities than in rural areas was clearly documented by Mabel Brown Ellis, "Juvenile Courts," in Clopper, *Child Welfare in Tennessee*.

45. Case no. 9580 (1928); case no. 10191 (1928).

46. Brown, "Institutions," 545.

47. Tennessee Department of Institutions and Public Welfare, *Report on Juvenile Correctional Institutions*, 18–20.

48. For a history of the child guidance clinic movement, see Horn, *Before It's Too Late*, 13–14 and Kathleen W. Jones, *Taming the Troublesome Child*, chapters 3–5.

49. Horn, *Before It's Too Late*, 4; Kathleen W. Jones, *Taming the Troublesome Child*, 9–10.

50. Council of Social Agencies Minutes, April 14, 1921.

51. *Memphis News Scimitar*, January 8, 1924; January 11, 1924; February 24, 1924; April 10, 1924; April 13, 1924. There was no relationship between the Commonwealth Fund, a private philanthropy in New York, and the Community Fund, the central fund of Mem-

phis social services. Nor was there a relationship between the National Committee for Mental Hygiene and the Community Fund. There was much overlap, however, within the social service community of Memphis, so that people who were officers of the Council of Social Agencies might also have positions in the administration of the Community Fund and its annual fund-raising drives.

52. It is impossible to determine how many children the court sent to the clinic, since my information about the clinic comes from individual juvenile court case files rather than clinic records. The case files contain evaluations that show that, in addition to juvenile court, other social service agencies and schools referred children to the clinic.

53. *Memphis News Scimitar*, November 10, 1926.

54. Ibid., November 13, 1926; December 3, 1926.

55. Council of Social Agencies Minutes, December 2, 1926.

56. *Memphis Press-Scimitar*, December 23, 1926.

57. Council of Social Agencies Minutes, April 23, 1927.

58. Case no. 5376 (1925); case no. 5377 (1925); case no. 5378 (1925).

59. Executive Committee of the Council of Social Agencies Minutes, May 6, 1921, United Way of Greater Memphis, Memphis, Tennessee.

60. Case no. 4615 (1921); case no. 5376 (1925).

61. Case no. 7303 (1925).

62. *Memphis Press-Scimitar*, September 2–7, 1929; September 12–13, 1929; September 18, 1929; October 16, 1929; December 9, 1929.

63. Ibid., December 9, 1929.

64. *Memphis Chamber of Commerce Journal* (April 1923 and September 1924); *Memphis Press-Scimitar*, October 13, 1928.

65. "Charles Wilson Home," April 8, 1931. Located with Council of Social Agencies Minutes.

66. Case no. 7691 (1925).

67. Tennessee State Planning Commission, *Study of State Institutions*, 49; Thurston, *Dependent Child*, 39; Smith, "Child Care Institutions"; Cmiel, *Home of Another Kind*, 18–19, 97–98; Hacsi, *Second Home*, 104, 113–20.

68. Orphanages in Memphis for white children were St. Peter's Orphanage, which was first established around 1841; the Protestant Widows and Orphans Asylum, which opened in the early 1850s and later changed its name to the Leath Orphan Asylum and then the Porter Home and Leath Orphanage; the Church Home that was run by the Episcopal church and founded in 1865; and the American Christian Home. The following are founding dates for black orphanages: Old Ladies and Orphans Home, 1894; Orange Mound Negro Orphanage, 1914; Industrial Settlement Home, 1915; Charles Wilson Home, 1924.

69. Shivers, "Social Welfare Movement in the South," 95–96; Berkeley, " 'Like a Plague of Locust,' " 210; Salem, *To Better Our World*, 69–73.

70. Brown, "Institutions," 529; Tennessee Industrial School, *Fifth Biennial Report of the Tennessee Industrial School 1897*, 74–80; *Tenth Biennial Report of the Tennessee Industrial School 1907*, 13–14; Tennessee Planning Commission, *Study of State Institutions*, 47; Tennessee Board of State Charities, *Biennial Report of the Board of State Charities of Tennessee 1915*, 24; *Memphis Press-Scimitar*, March 5, 1930.

71. Judge Kelley did not commit black children to the Tennessee Industrial School, and later reports made no mention of a black division. Tennessee Department of Institutions, *Second Biennial Report of Tennessee Board of Control 1917–1918*, 10.

72. Much research remains to be done on the history of foster care and the treatment of dependent children. For a start, see Cmiel, *Home of Another Kind*; Hacsi, *Second Home*; Tanenhaus, "Growing Up Dependent."

73. *Memphis News Scimitar*, August 31, 1924. The charter of the Tennessee Children's Home Society permitted the expenditure of private funds on programs for temporary institutional care and foster placement to both white and black children in free, boarding, and adoptive homes. Public funds from the state, however, were expended only for white children admitted to the society's custody. Tennessee Department of Public Welfare, *Handbook of Laws*, 330.

74. Council of Social Agencies Minutes, December 10, 1925; *Memphis Press-Scimitar*, March 1, 1929.

75. Quoted in Katz, *In the Shadow of the Poorhouse*, 68.

76. Jean Proutt, "Publicity—before and After" (paper presented for the Associated Charities, Memphis, Tennessee, 1925). Memphis Room, Memphis Public Library, Memphis, Tennessee; Grantham, *Southern Progressivism*, 226–27.

77. Francis H. McLean, "Study of the Work of the Associated Charities" (study presented to the Associated Charities, Memphis, Tennessee, 1925). Memphis Room, Memphis Public Library, Memphis, Tennessee; *Annual Report of the Associated Charities of Memphis, 1922–1923*, 2–4.

78. *Memphis News Scimitar*, December 2, 1923.

79. Ibid., October 14, 1921; case no. 7408 (1925); case no. 10173 (1929); Grantham, *Southern Progressivism*, 229; Shivers, "Social Welfare Movement in the South," 190–92. The Federation of Jewish Welfare Agencies provided social service and financial assistance for Jewish families in Memphis. Organized in 1906, the Jewish Charities shifted from addressing immediate financial and housing needs to concerns about family stability and assimilation into American life. In the 1920s the federation created the Family Welfare Committee, which made friendly home visits, helped in budget planning, and gave family counseling. Stella Lowenstein, longtime superintendent of social service and very active in Memphis social work, said that more families looked on the federation as a place for family rehabilitation rather than charity. Meyers, "Evolution of the Jewish Social Service Agency," 19, 26, 52–54, 99; *Annual Report of Federation of Jewish Welfare Agencies*, 1935.

80. The Inter Racial League, *Inter Racial Blue Book*.

81. Case no. 7177 (1925).

82. For a discussion of the origins of the Institute for Juvenile Research, see Horn, *Before It's Too Late*, 13–14, 57; Kathleen W. Jones, *Taming the Troublesome Child*, 38–41.

83. Social Agencies' Endorsement Committee Minutes, April 26, 1921.

84. McLean, "Study of the Work of the Memphis Associated Charities," 7.

85. Council of Social Agencies Minutes, February 11, 1927.

86. *Memphis Press-Scimitar*, February 14, 1930.

CHAPTER 4. Juvenile Justice and the Treatment of Dependent Children

1. The history of child neglect and dependency is, at best, uneven. Thurston, *Dependent Child*; Lisenby, "An Administrative History of Public Programs; Tiffin, *In Whose Best Interest?*; Ashby, *Saving the Waifs*; Gordon, *Heroes of Their Own Lives*; Tanenhaus, "Growing Up Dependent."

2. Tiffin, *In Whose Best Interest?* 45–57; Kathleen W. Jones, *Taming the Troublesome Child*, 35–37.

3. In Tennessee, county courts had the exclusive right to apprentice three classes of children: those abandoned by their father, orphans without property, and illegitimate children. Children could not be bound out without the mother's consent unless she was unable or unfit to care for them. As late as 1910 Davidson County Court (Nashville) apprenticed black boys and made dispositions of white bastard children. Institutions had no power to apprentice children. However, recall (from chapter 2) that in the early 1920s several grand jury investigations showed that the Shelby County Industrial and Training School was illegally apprenticing boys, particularly blacks, to local farmers. Apprenticeship Records of Davidson County Court, 1881–1910, Metropolitan Archives, Nashville, Tennessee; W. H. Swift, "The Child and the State," in Clopper, *Child Welfare in Tennessee*, 39–40.

4. First opened in Savannah (1738); New Orleans (1739); and Charleston, South Carolina (1790), orphanages for white and black children in the South grew steadily in number during the nineteenth century. Ashcraft, *Public Care*, 13–19; Salem, *To Better Our World*, 73, 83–84; Jacobs and Davies, *More than Kissing Babies?* 69; Zmora, *Orphanages Reconsidered*, 9; Hacsi, *Second Home*, 17–18; Shivers, "Social Welfare Movement in the South," 97.

5. Gutman, *Black Family in Slavery and Freedom*, 226–28, 470.

6. Zmora, *Orphanages Reconsidered*, 10, 14; Hacsi, *Second Home*, 190–91.

7. Rebecca J. Scott, "Battle over the Child," 193–95.

8. Ibid., 200–202.

9. Katz, *In the Shadow of the Poorhouse*, 124–25; Tiffin, *In Whose Best Interest?* chapter 4.

10. Gordon, *Pitied but Not Entitled*, 37–64; Shivers, "Social Welfare Movement in the South," 311–14; Ashcraft, *Public Care*, 25–27; Tiffin, *In Whose Best Interest?* 121–34.

11. Tanenhaus, "Growing Up Dependent."

12. For the full legal definition of dependency in Tennessee, see the appendix.

13. Honey, *Southern Labor*, 24–26; Kirby, *Rural Worlds Lost*, 280, 286–87.

14. Case no. 10380 (1929).

15. Case no. 4311 (1921); case no. 4335 (1921).

16. Swift, *Manufacturing "Bad Mothers,"* 40; Cmiel, *Home of Another Kind*; Zmora, *Orphanages Reconsidered*, 48, 69; Hacsi, *Second Home*, 104–6, 214.

17. Case no. 7616 (1925).

18. Case no. 7493 (1925).

19. Case no. 4503 (1921); case no. 10083 (1929).

20. Case no. 7613 (1925).

21. Michael Grossberg argues that during the nineteenth century, judges established hegemony over domestic relations and became the new patriarchs. I prefer Linda Gordon's rather narrow definition of patriarchy as "male dominance in which fathers control families and families are the units of social and economic power." See Grossberg, *Governing the Hearth*, 289–302, and Gordon, *Heroes of Their Own Lives*, vi–vii.

22. Case no. 10422 (1929).

23. Case no. 7517 (1925); case no. 4645 (1921).

24. Case no. 10185 (1929); case no. 4639 (1921).

25. Lewis, *In Their Own Interests*, 23; Jacqueline Jones, *Labor of Love*, 102, 126–27, 228–29.

26. Mabel Brown Ellis, "Juvenile Courts," in Clopper, *Child Welfare in Tennessee*, 494.

27. Lisenby, "Administrative History of Public Programs," 286–87; Shivers, "Social Welfare Movement in the South," 269, 383.

28. Sanders, *Negro Child Welfare*, 189–93, 201.

29. Rabinowitz, "From Exclusion to Segregation."

30. See O'Neill, *Divorce in the Progressive Era*; May, *Great Expectations*.

31. An additional 10 percent lived with their father alone.

32. For a more extensive discussion of single mothers and dependency, see Luker, *Dubious Conceptions*; Gordon, *Pitied but Not Entitled*, 15–35.

33. Gordon, *Pitied but Not Entitled*, 19–23; Jacqueline Jones, *Labor of Love*, 113–14.

34. Common examples of criminal activity included vagrancy, theft, forgery, bootlegging, drunkenness, and immorality.

35. Case no. 7027 (1925); case no. 10461 (1929); case no. 7393 (1925); case no. 10404 (1929).

36. These figures underestimate the incidence of these problems, because I recorded only those cases that I could positively identify. Current research indicates that child abuse is vastly underreported. National Research Council, *Understanding Child Abuse and Neglect*, 78–94. See also Gordon, *Heroes of Their Own Lives*, 1.

37. Case no. 9898 (1929).

38. Breeden, "Disease as a Factor," 1–28.

39. William A. Link, *Paradox of Southern Progressivism*, 230–31; Kirby, *Rural Worlds Lost*, 186–87; H. H. Mitchell, "Health," in Clopper, *Child Welfare in Tennessee*, 67–89. See also Ethridge, *Butterfly Caste*.

40. *Memphis Press-Scimitar*, February 4, 1927. Also, more people in Tennessee died of tuberculosis than any other disease. However, by 1928 Tennessee had dropped to fifth place on the national death chart. Ibid., January 24, 1928. Tennessee also had the second highest United States death rate from malaria. Mitchell, "Health," 77.

41. Mitchell, "Health," 75; Jacqueline Jones, *Labor of Love*, 123.

42. Case no. 10359 (1925); case no. 7270 (1925).

43. Case no. 9871 (1929). This arrangement, much like that of Elsie Jones discussed earlier, prompted an anonymous call to the juvenile court that "three little girls by the name of Rogers were living in a negro house." When the probation officer talked to Mrs. Rogers, she could see nothing wrong with leaving the children at Betty Rollins's home and was quite indignant at the court's interference.

44. See also Glenn, "From Servitude to Service Work"; Hunter, "Domination and Resistance"; Kirby, *Rural Worlds Lost*, 288. This practice of hiring black women to help with domestic work provided nonfarm wages to rural black women as well.

45. Kirby, *Rural Worlds Lost*, 277–81; Lewis, *In Their Own Interests*, 32–33; case no. 6956 (1925); case no. 7583 (1925); case no. 7619 (1925); case no. 10458 (1929).

46. Chambers, "Towards a Redefinition of Welfare History," 421–22; Gutman, *Black Family in Slavery and Freedom*, 226–28.

47. Case no. 7372 (1925).

48. Linda Gordon characterizes the first general agent of the Massachusetts Society for the Prevention of Cruelty to Children as a "virtual ambulance chaser," and Steven Schlossman suggests that probation officers drummed up their own business in the Milwaukee Juvenile Court. Gordon, *Heroes of Their Own Lives*, 37; Schlossman, *Love and the American Delinquent*, 153–54, 256.

49. Case no. 4407 (1921); Gordon, *Heroes of Their Own Lives*, 154.

50. Case no. 9850 (1929).

51. Much like Miriam Van Waters in the Los Angeles Juvenile Court, Judge Kelley was clearly a product of conservative social and cultural forces in interpreting the boundaries

of acceptable female behavior in the 1920s. Van Waters, however, self-consciously rejected the sexual double standard and aggressively sought penalties for female and male sexual misconduct and tried to make men assume responsibility for their illegitimate children. Freedman, *Maternal Justice*, 86–87.

52. The greater portion of police referrals for girls than boys resulted partly because the girls' guardians were arrested twice as often for crimes as the boys' guardians.

53. Case no. 10428 (1929).

54. Interestingly, boys petitioned by social service agencies were more likely to be placed on probation, whereas girls were more likely to be committed to an institution. Since girls generally came from less stable families, agency caseworkers may have felt that they needed more protection than boys. Agencies probably also came in contact with many families that required the kind of immediate assistance that orphanages offered.

55. Case no. 7024 (1925).

56. Case no. 9975 (1929); case no. 10477 (1929); case no. 4087 (1921).

57. Case no. 7009 (1925).

58. Case no. 4431 (1921).

59. Case no. 7222 (1925); case no. 9886 (1929); case no. 7619 (1925); case no. 4578 (1921).

60. Case no. 7318 (1925).

61. Case no. 7442 (1925).

62. Case no. 7324 (1925).

63. Case no. 7523 (1925).

64. Case no. 4204 (1921).

65. Case no. 7150 (1925); case no. 7697 (1925); case no. 4645 (1921).

66. Case no. 6956 (1925); case no. 7027 (1925); case no. 7297 (1925); case no. 10164 (1929).

67. Case no. 7523 (1925).

68. Case no. 9898 (1929).

69. Case no. 7694 (1925).

70. Case no. 10083 (1929).

71. Case no. 7351 (1925); case no. 10083 (1929); case no. 10338 (1929); case no. 9895 (1929).

72. Gordon, *Heroes of Their Own Lives*, 250–88.

73. Case no. 7553 (1925); case no. 7294 (1925); case no. 9841 (1929).

74. The problem of ambiguous and biased definitions of neglect still continues among child welfare researchers and social workers today. Neglect currently refers to the presence of deficiencies in caretaker obligations that harm the child's psychological and/or physical health. Child neglect includes a range of behaviors such as educational, supervisory, medical, physical, and emotional neglect, and abandonment. Four general categories of child maltreatment are recognized today by practitioners: physical abuse, sexual abuse, neglect, and emotional maltreatment. Swift, *Manufacturing "Bad Mothers,"* 88–100, 151–71; National Research Council, *Understanding Child Abuse and Neglect*, 57–72.

CHAPTER 5. Juvenile Justice and the Treatment of Delinquent Children

1. Kelley, *Friend in Court*, 97. For the legal definition of delinquency in Tennessee, see the appendix. See also Teitelbaum, "Status Offenses and Status Offenders," in Rosenheim et al., *Century of Juvenile Justice.*

2. Sanders, *Negro Child Welfare*, 191.

3. On the history of boys' crimes, see Schlossman, *Love and the American Delinquent,* 205; Schneider, *In the Web of Class,* 164–68.

4. Brandt, *No Magic Bullet,* 128–29; Alexander, "*Girl Problem,*" 1–4; Odem, *Delinquent Daughters,* 95–127; Freedman, *Maternal Justice,* 77–90; Peiss, *Cheap Amusements*; Beth Bailey, *From Front Porch to Back Seat.*

5. Alexander, "*Girl Problem,*" 4, 22–24; Odem, *Delinquent Daughters,* 158–60.

6. Fass, *Damned and the Beautiful,* 95, 116.

7. *Memphis News Scimitar,* January 4, 1922.

8. Odem and Schlossman, "Guardians of Virtue"; Schlossman and Wallach, "Crime of Precocious Sexuality."

9. Brandt, *No Magic Bullet,* 8–9, 14–17, 21–23, 29, 31.

10. Ibid., 129–30.

11. Ruth Alexander finds that black parents, just as white parents, used courts and custodial institutions in New York to maintain family control. Alexander, "*Girl Problem,*" 49.

12. Jacqueline Jones, *Labor of Love,* 149–50; Odem, *Delinquent Daughters,* 28–30.

13. U.S. Bureau of the Census, *Fourteenth Census of the United States, 1920,* 960; U.S. Bureau of the Census, *Fifteenth Census of the United States, 1930,* 890.

14. Case no. 10395 (1929).

15. *Memphis Press-Scimitar,* April 30, 1930; Schlossman and Wallach, "Crime of Precocious Sexuality," 84.

16. Case no. 10341 (1929).

17. Case no. 7152 [7153] (1925); case no. 7544 (1925).

18. Case no. 4624 (1921); case no. 10489 (1929).

19. Marchand, *Advertising the American Dream,* 66–69; Chesney-Lind and Shelden, *Girls, Delinquency, and Juvenile Justice,* 43; Fass, *Damned and the Beautiful,* 230–34.

20. Williamson, *Crucible of Race,* chapter 7.

21. Case no. 10374 (1929); case no. 7607 (1925).

22. Steven Schlossman explores this issue in *Love and the American Delinquent,* chapter 9. Child welfare officials at the time recognized this linguistic charade. Sara A. Brown, "Institutions," in Clopper, *Child Welfare in Tennessee,* 530.

23. The different terminology for similar behavior often reflected different complainants. White and black family members were most likely to complain that girls were incorrigible, while police or agencies, those outside the family, would be most likely to encounter girls who had run away.

24. Case no. 10510 (1929); case no. 10314 (1929); case no. 7135 (1925); case no. 6953 (1925).

25. Mabel Brown Ellis, "Juvenile Courts," in Clopper, *Child Welfare in Tennessee,* 432.

26. Case no. 4186 (1921); case no. 4482 (1921).

27. Mary Odem makes this argument for Los Angeles. Odem, *Delinquent Daughters,* 48, 135, 159–60.

28. See Benson, *Counter Cultures.*

29. Julia Blackwelder makes this argument for San Antonio. See Blackwelder, *Women of the Depression,* 64–66.

30. Case no. 4189 (1921); case no. 7321 (1925).

31. Fass, *Damned and the Beautiful,* 108–9.

32. Some of the girls were victims of considerable familial stress. At least 7 percent of the girls experienced discernible sexual abuse, 9 percent had a family member with a criminal history, and 7 percent had a guardian with a history of alcoholism. Illness in the

family was the most common kind of family problem. Almost half of the white families were known to a social service agency by the time they appeared in court. However, only 11 percent of the black families had prior contact with an agency.

33. Odem, *Delinquent Daughters*, 38–62, 167–76.

34. Fass, *Damned and the Beautiful*, 120 and chapter 6.

35. Chute, "Juvenile Court of Memphis," 2. The few existing annual reports of the Memphis Juvenile Court note the number of unofficial hearings the court conducted in addition to the officially listed court hearings. In 1920 about 40 percent of the total caseload was handled unofficially; in 1930 about 50 percent of the cases were unofficial. "Memphis Juvenile Court Annual Report, 1920," "Memphis Juvenile Court Annual Report 1930," at the Juvenile Court of Memphis and Shelby County, Memphis, Tennessee. Judge Kelley also said that unofficial work by probation officers made up much of the court's work. Kelley, *Friend in Court*, 258. On unofficial cases, see also Rothman, *Conscience and Convenience*, 249–50; Schlossman, *Love and the American Delinquent*, 147–53; Wolcott, "Cops and Kids."

36. Case no. 4786 (1921).

37. After the clinic closed, clinical investigations were limited to a physical exam. Judge Kelley believed strongly in the benefits of psychological analysis for juvenile delinquents, and around 1929 she was able to hire Altye Barbour to conduct mental examinations of all children in court.

38. Case no. 4786 (1921); case no. 7544 (1925).

39. Case no. 5376 (1922).

40. Chute, "Juvenile Court of Memphis," 13.

41. Mary Odem shows that the Los Angeles Juvenile Court officials were quite thorough in their examination procedures and knew far more about the sexual behavior and physical condition of their delinquent females than officials at the Memphis Juvenile Court knew about their girls. The incidence of venereal disease appeared to be lower among white girls in the Memphis Juvenile Court than in the Los Angeles Juvenile Court. Odem, *Delinquent Daughters*, 143–45.

42. The Memphis Juvenile Court committed twice as many females as males to correctional institutions. See Shelden, "Sex Discrimination," 69. Higher rates of female institutionalization have also been described in Chicago, Los Angeles, Milwaukee, and Boston. See Breckinridge and Abbott, *Delinquent Child and the Home*, 40; Odem, *Delinquent Daughters*, 146–47, 156; Schlossman, *Love and the American Delinquent*, 178–79, 203; Schneider, *In the Web of Class*, 160–64.

43. Chute, "Juvenile Court of Memphis," 7–8; Ellis, "Juvenile Courts," 452–54, 500–503.

44. Memphis Chamber of Commerce, *Memphis Chamber of Commerce Journal* (March 1922): 36–37; *Memphis News Scimitar*, April 21, 1922.

45. Case no. 8204 (1927).

46. Case no. 7424 (1925).

47. Case no. 7215 (1925).

48. Chute, "Juvenile Court of Memphis," 16; Camille Kelley to Mildred Scoville (Commonwealth Fund), February 16, 1926; *Memphis News Scimitar*, March 4, 1925.

49. About 25 percent of the white female status offenders and 20 percent of black female status offenders appeared in the juvenile court at least once again. Among criminal offenders the rates were 3 and 8 percent for white and black females, respectively.

50. Lombroso maintained that females were congenitally less likely to commit crimes because of their sedentary nature and role as caretakers. He also speculated that women's

crimes centered on "a preoccupation with sex matters." Chesney-Lind and Shelden, *Girls, Delinquency, and Juvenile Justice*, 56.

51. Mennel, *Thorns and Thistles*, 80–85, 91–92; Schlossman, *Love and the American Delinquent*, 67–69; Ruth, *Inventing the Public Enemy*, 12–13.

52. Horn, *Before It's Too Late*, 14–18; Mennel, *Thorns and Thistles*, 195; Ruth, *Inventing the Public Enemy*, 16–17; Kathleen W. Jones, *Taming the Troublesome Child*, 38–61.

53. Chesney-Lind and Shelden, *Girls, Delinquency, and Juvenile Justice*, 63, 78.

54. *Memphis Press-Scimitar*, September 7, 1929.

55. Ruth, *Inventing the Public Enemy*, 11, 30–32; Horn, *Before It's Too Late*, 37; Kathleen W. Jones, *Taming the Troublesome Child*, chapters 4, 5, 7; *Memphis News Scimitar*, January 6, 1924; March 25, 1925; Kelley, *Friend in Court*, 122–24.

56. The incidence of delinquency among middle-class boys has received little historical attention. Vaz, *Middle-Class Juvenile Delinquency*.

57. Case no. 7048 (1925); case no. 10455 (1929).

58. Case no. 4365 (1921).

59. A "peace order" appears to have been a restraining order or some kind of protection from abuse that citizens could obtain from one of the other Memphis courts.

60. Case no. 10134 (1929); case no. 9960 (1929).

61. About 25 percent of the white families and 19 percent of the black families were known to some other social service agency in Memphis before they appeared in the juvenile court. Anecdotal evidence shows that a large number of families had no church affiliation. It is not surprising that families without ties to private support networks should seek or be referred to public modes of assistance. Zunz, *Changing Face of Inequality*, 259–79; Katz, *In the Shadow of the Poorhouse*, 59–63; Chambers, "Towards a Redefinition of Welfare History," 422.

62. Case no. 10458 (1929); Gertrude H. Folks, "Schools," in Clopper, *Child Welfare in Tennessee*, 162–69.

63. Case no. 4678 (1921); case no. 4287 (1921).

64. An important component of law enforcement in Memphis consisted of private police. The Memphis Retailers' Association, Memphis Streetcar Railroad, Illinois Central Railroad, Broadway Coal Company, and the *Commercial Appeal* and *News Scimitar* newspapers all hired private police called "special agents."

65. The category of private citizen included witnesses and victims who had no relationship to the child or any specific professional affiliation. Random individuals who happened to witness a crime often called the police or juvenile court to report delinquent children. Some private citizens were victims of juvenile crime, either as owners of small stores that were robbed or vandalized, or as subjects of verbal abuse, robbery, or physical attack.

66. Case no. 7466 (1925); case no. 10113 (1929); case no. 9933 (1929).

67. Case no. 4233 (1921). For a discussion of the multiple uses of institutions by clientele, see Gordon, "Family Violence, Feminism, and Social Control."

68. Roark, "Judge Kelley," 9.

69. *Memphis News Scimitar*, March 4, 1925; "Annual Report of Memphis Juvenile Court, 1934"; Chute, "Juvenile Court of Memphis," 3–5, 7–9.

70. Chute, "Juvenile Court of Memphis," 7–9.

71. Despite unequal treatment, the juvenile justice system did seek to protect black children and was not as aggressively discriminatory as the adult criminal justice system. Black male adolescents were not incarcerated to the same degree as black male adults. For discussions of incarceration trends and racism in southern penology, see Adamson,

"Punishment after Slavery"; Ayers, *Vengeance and Justice*, chapters 2 and 6; Zimmerman, "Penal Systems and Penal Reform."

72. The portion of boys who appeared in court again was almost the same for status and criminal offenders and for white and black boys.

73. Case no. 10478 (1927); case no. 10299 (1929).

74. Case no. 5672 (1921); case no. 4320 (1921).

75. According to Margo Horn, the focus on behaviorism gave way to a model that included separate roles for emotions and personality, or a psychodynamic model of therapy. Horn, *Before It's Too Late*, 135–39.

76. Case no. 4584 (1921).

77. Case no. 7282 (1925); case no. 7264 (1925); case no. 7463 (1925).

78. Case no. 3981 (1921).

79. Case no. 10477 (1929); case no. 7152 (1925); case no. 10501 (1929); case no. 9969 (1929); case no. 9868 (1929). Keeping children in jail was, of course, illegal because the Public Act of 1911, which created the juvenile justice system in Tennessee, forbid children from being in contact with or confined with adult convicts.

APPENDIX

1. The juvenile court processed many cases "unofficially" under a variety of circumstances. Sometimes these cases involved a court appearance without a formal record; other times the court handled parts of complicated cases unofficially; presumably, too, entire cases were unofficial. Passing references in case files indicate that these shadow cases existed, but it is impossible to determine how many unofficial cases passed through the court.

2. In addition to the two types of children's cases, the juvenile court also heard a third kind of case that involved adults. In nonsupport cases, the juvenile court acted as an arbitrator of relations between mothers and fathers. Wives brought nonsupport charges against their husbands, and the court tried to enforce a standing order for payment. I chose not to analyze the nonsupport data since these were primarily adult cases.

3. In 1921 the juvenile court administered the mothers' pension, but I excluded these cases from the sample since this study is concerned with juvenile cases. Later that year the Probate Court took over mothers' pensions.

4. These included 138 nonsupport cases. Therefore, the sample initially had a total of 599 children.

5. Odem and Schlossman, "Guardians of Virtue."

6. Access to case files is by permission of the Juvenile Court of Memphis and Shelby County. Case file numbers in the footnote citations are the actual docket numbers followed by the year the case began, but all names have been changed to protect the confidentiality of the families.

7. These categories are taken from the occupation statistics of the United States Census. See also Trotter, *Black Milwaukee*.

8. Since I eliminated fourteen cases of duplication, my analysis is based on calculations for 585 children.

9. Tennessee Department of Public Welfare, *Handbook of Laws*, 337.

10. Ibid., 334.

11. Lou, *Juvenile Courts in the United States*, 55; Tiffin, *In Whose Best Interest?* 39; Fraser and Gordon, "Genealogy of Dependency."

Bibliography

PRIMARY SOURCES

Archival Sources
Tennessee State Library and Archives, Nashville. Board of Inspectors of the Tennessee Penitentiary. Main Prison, Convict Record Books K–T. Volumes 99 (1900–1904), 100 (1904–12), 101 (1912–17).
Public Library of Nashville and Davidson County, Metropolitan Archives, Nashville, Tennessee. Annual Reports of Humane and Juvenile Court Commission, 1921–43. Miscellaneous Apprenticeship Records of Davidson County Court, 1881–1910.
Memphis Public Library, Memphis Room, Memphis, Tennessee. City of Memphis. Minute Books, Criminal Court, 1914, 1924. Memphis Associated Charities. *Annual Reports.* Memphis: Hood Printing Co., 1911–30. Memphis Chamber of Commerce. *Memphis Chamber of Commerce Journal.* Memphis: Pilcher Printing Co., 1918–25. Memphis Church Home. *Annual Reports.* Sewanee, Tenn.: University Press, 1920, 1924, 1930, 1931. *Social Register of Memphis.* Suzanne Scruggs Papers, 1908–20.
Juvenile Court of Memphis and Shelby County, Memphis, Tennessee. Legal Files, 1911–30. Minute Books, 1910–30. Social Files, 1913–30. Annual Reports, 1920, 1921, 1929, 1930, 1934.
United Way of Greater Memphis, Memphis, Tennessee. Executive Committee of Memphis Council of Social Agencies Minutes, 1920–32, 1934–39. Memphis Council of Social Agencies Minutes, 1920–34. Memphis Council of Social Agencies, Miscellaneous Correspondence and Reports. Social Agencies' Endorsement Committee of the Chamber of Commerce Minutes, 1919–23.

Newspapers
Memphis Commercial Appeal, 1910–30.
Memphis News Scimitar, 1920–26.
Memphis Press-Scimitar, 1926–30.
Memphis Press, 1909–10.

Books and Articles
Breckinridge, Sophonisba, and Edith Abbott. *The Delinquent Child and the Home: A Study of the Delinquent Wards of the Juvenile Court of Chicago.* New York: Russell Sage, 1912.
Chute, Charles L. "The Juvenile Court of Memphis, Tennessee. Report of a Survey." New York: National Probation Association, 1924.
Clopper, Edward N., ed. *Child Welfare in Tennessee.* New York: National Child Labor Committee, 1920.

Ellis, Mabel Brown. "Memphis and Her New Judge." *The Survey* (May 22, 1920): 285–86.

Hiller, Francis H. *Treatment of Juvenile Offenders in Nashville, Tennessee. Report of a Survey.* New York: National Probation Association, 1930.

Inter Racial League. *The Inter Racial Blue Book.* Memphis: Early-Freeburg, 1926.

Kelley, Camille. *A Friend in Court.* New York: Dodd, Mead and Co., 1942.

———. *Delinquent Angels.* Kansas City, Mo.: Brown-White-Lowell Press, 1947.

———. "Making the World Safe for the Children." *Memphis Chamber of Commerce Journal* (July 1920): 146, 175.

Kelley, Florence. "A Burglar Four Years Old in the Memphis Juvenile Court." *The Survey* 32 (June 20, 1914): 318–19.

Klewer, Edward B. *The Memphis Digest.* Memphis: S. C. Toof and Co., 1931, 1937, 1949.

Lou, Herbert. *Juvenile Courts in the United States.* Chapel Hill: University of North Carolina Press, 1927.

Roark, Eldon F. "Judge Kelley, First Woman Juvenile Court Judge in the South." *Holland's* (September 1931): 9, 62.

Sanders, Wiley Britton. *Negro Child Welfare in North Carolina.* Chapel Hill: University of North Carolina Press, 1933.

Thurston, Henry W. *The Dependent Child.* New York: Columbia University Press, 1930.

Turner, Kenneth. *Your Juvenile Court.* Memphis: Juvenile Court of Memphis and Shelby County, 1991.

Van Waters, Miriam. *Parents on Probation.* New York: New Republic, 1927.

———. *Youth in Conflict.* New York: Republic Publishing Company, 1925.

York, Mary. "A Municipal Mother." *Woman's Journal* 13 (November 1928): 19.

Government Documents

Tennessee Board of State Charities. *Annual and Biennial Reports,* 1896–1922.

Tennessee Department of Institutions. *Biennial Reports,* 1918–40.

Tennessee Department of Institutions and Public Welfare. *Report on Juvenile Correctional Institutions.* Nashville: Tennessee Department of Institutions and Public Welfare, 1938.

Tennessee Department of Public Welfare. *Handbook of Laws: Containing Social Welfare Legislation Needed by the Field Staff for Reference.* Nashville: Tennessee Department of Public Welfare, Division of Research and Statistics, 1946.

Tennessee Industrial School. *Reports,* 1887–1914.

Tennessee Reformatory for Boys. *Biennial Reports,* 1912–13.

Tennessee State Planning Commission. *A Study of State Institutions. Tennessee Industrial School.* Nashville: Tennessee State Planning Commission, 1937.

U.S. Bureau of the Census. *Thirteenth Census of the United States, 1910: Population.* Washington, D.C.: Government Printing Office, 1913.

———. *Fourteenth Census of the United States, 1920: Population.* Washington, D.C.: Government Printing Office, 1922.

———. *Fifteenth Census of the United States, 1930: Population.* Washington, D.C.: Government Printing Office, 1933.

SECONDARY SOURCES

Adamson, Christopher R. "Punishment after Slavery: Southern State Penal Systems, 1865–1890." *Social Problems* 30 (June 1983): 555–69.

Alexander, Ruth M. *The "Girl Problem": Female Sexual Delinquency in New York, 1900–1930*. Ithaca: Cornell University Press, 1995.

Alonzo, Frank. "The History of the Mississippi Youth Court System." *Journal of Mississippi History* 39 (1977): 133–53.

Anderson, Clifford B. "Agrarian Attitudes Toward the City, Business, and Labor in the 1920s and 1930s." *Mississippi Quarterly* 14 (Fall 1961): 183–89.

Ashby, Leroy. *Saving the Waifs: Reformers and Dependent Children, 1890–1917*. Philadelphia: Temple University Press, 1984.

Ashcraft, Virginia. *Public Care: A History of Public Welfare Legislation in Tennessee*. Knoxville: University of Tennessee, 1947.

Austin, Linda. *Babies for Sale: The Tennessee Children's Home Adoption Scandal*. Westport, Conn.: Praeger, 1993.

Ayers, Edward L. *Vengeance and Justice: Crime and Punishment in the Nineteenth Century American South*. New York: Oxford University Press, 1984.

Bailey, Beth. *From Front Porch to Back Seat: Courtship in Twentieth-Century America*. Baltimore: Johns Hopkins University Press, 1988.

Bailey, Kenneth K. *Southern White Protestantism in the Twentieth Century*. New York: Harper and Row, 1964.

Beifuss, Joan Turner. *At the River I Stand: Memphis, the 1968 Strike, and Martin Luther King*. Memphis: B and W Books, 1985.

Benson, Susan Porter. *Counter Cultures: Saleswomen, Managers, and Customers in American Department Stores, 1890–1940*. Urbana: University of Illinois Press, 1988.

Berkeley, Kathleen C. " 'Colored Ladies Also Contributed': Black Women's Activities from Benevolence to Social Welfare, 1866–1896." In *The Web of Southern Social Relations: Women, Family, and Education*, edited by Walter Fraser, Frank Saunders, and Jon Wakelyn, 181–203. Athens: University of Georgia Press, 1985.

———. " 'Like a Plague of Locust': Immigration and Social Change in Memphis, Tennessee, 1850–1880." PhD diss., University of California at Los Angeles, 1980.

Biles, Roger. *Memphis in the Great Depression*. Knoxville: University of Tennessee Press, 1986.

Blackwelder, Julia Kirk. *Women of the Depression: Caste and Culture in San Antonio, 1929–1939*. College Station: Texas A and M University Press, 1984.

Botsch, Robert Emil. *We Shall Not Overcome: Populism and Southern Blue Collar Workers*. Chapel Hill: University of North Carolina Press, 1980.

Brandt, Allan M. *No Magic Bullet: A Social History of Venereal Disease in the United States since 1880*. New York: Oxford University Press, 1987.

Breeden, James O. "Disease as a Factor in Southern Distinctiveness." In *Disease and Distinctiveness in the American South*, edited by Todd L. Savitt and James Harvey Young, 1–28. Knoxville: University of Tennessee Press, 1988.

Bremner, Robert, ed. *Care of Dependent Children in the Late Nineteenth and Early Twentieth Centuries*. New York: Arno Books, 1974.

Brownell, Blaine A. "The Commercial-Civic Elite and City Planning in Atlanta, Memphis, and New Orleans in the 1920s." *Journal of Southern History* 41 (August 1975): 339–68.

Brumberg, Joan Jacobs, and Nancy Tomes. "Women in the Professions: A Research Agenda for American Historians." *Reviews in American History* 10 (June 1982): 275–96.

Bryant, Keith. "The Juvenile Court Movement: Oklahoma as a Case Study." *Social Science Quarterly* 49 (1968): 368–76.

Butterfield, Fox. *All God's Children: The Bosket Family and the American Tradition of Violence.* New York: Knopf, 1995.

Capers, Gerald M. *The Biography of a River Town. Memphis: Its Heroic Age.* Chapel Hill: University of North Carolina Press, 1939.

Carter, Dan. "Southern Political Style." In *Age of Segregation: Race Relations in the South, 1890–1945,* edited by Robert Haws, 58–61. Jackson: University of Mississippi Press, 1978.

Cartwright, Joseph H. *The Triumph of Jim Crow: Tennessee Race Relations in the 1880s.* Knoxville: University of Tennessee Press, 1976.

Cash, W. J. *The Mind of the South.* New York: Alfred A. Knopf, 1941.

Chafe, William H. "Women's History and Political History: Some Thoughts on Progressivism and the New Deal." In *Visible Women: New Essays on American Activism,* edited by Nancy Hewitt and Suzanne Lebsock, 101–18. Urbana: University of Illinois Press, 1993.

Chambers, Clarke A. *Seedtime of Reform: American Social Service and Social Action, 1918–1933.* Minneapolis: University of Minnesota Press, 1963.

———. "Towards a Redefinition of Welfare History." *Journal of American History* 73 (September 1986): 407–33.

Chatfield, E. Charles, Jr. "The Southern Sociological Congress, 1912–1920: The Development and Rationale of a Twentieth Century Crusade." MA thesis, Vanderbilt University, 1958.

Chesney-Lind, Meda, and Randall G. Shelden. *Girls, Delinquency, and Juvenile Justice.* Pacific Grove, Calif.: Brooks/Cole Publishing Company, 1992.

Church, Roberta. *Nineteenth Century Memphis Families of Color, 1850–1900.* Memphis: Murdock Print Co., 1987.

Clapp, Elizabeth J. *Mothers of All Children: Women Reformers and the Rise of Juvenile Courts in Progressive Era America.* University Park: Pennsylvania State University Press, 1998.

———. "Welfare and the Role of Women: The Juvenile Court Movement." *Journal of American Studies* 28 (1994): 359–83.

Cmiel, Kenneth. *A Home of Another Kind: One Chicago Orphanage and the Tangle of Child Welfare.* Chicago: University of Chicago Press, 1995.

Cobb, James C. *The Most Southern Place on Earth: The Mississippi Delta and the Roots of Regional Identity.* New York: Oxford University Press, 1992.

Cobb, James C., and Michael Namorato, eds. *The New Deal and the South.* Jackson: University of Mississippi Press, 1984.

Costin, Lela, Howard Krager, and David Stoesz. *The Politics of Child Abuse in America.* New York: Oxford University Press, 1995.

Cott, Nancy. *The Grounding of Modern Feminism.* New Haven: Yale University Press, 1987.

Crow, Jeffery, ed. *Race, Class, and Politics in Southern History: Essays in Honor of Robert Durden.* Baton Rouge: Louisiana State University Press, 1989.

Curtis, George. "The Juvenile Court Movement in Virginia." PhD diss., University of Virginia, 1973.

Dittmer, John. *Black Georgia in the Progressive Era, 1900–1920.* Urbana: University of Illinois Press, 1977.

Donzelot, Jacques. *The Policing of Families.* New York: Pantheon, 1979.

Epperson, Jane Ann. "A Study of the Tennessee Industrial School." MA thesis, University of Chicago, 1937.

Ethridge, Elizabeth W. *The Butterfly Caste: A Social History of Pellagra in the South.* Westport, Conn.: Greenwood Press, 1972.

Faist, Thomas. *The Unfulfilled Dream: A History of Race Relations and Civil Rights in Memphis since the Civil War.* Memphis: by the author, 1982.

Fass, Paula S. *The Damned and the Beautiful: American Youth in the 1920s.* New York: Oxford University Press, 1977.

Feder, Elizabeth. "The Elite of the Fallen: The Origins of a Social Policy for Unwed Mothers, 1880–1930." PhD diss., Johns Hopkins University, 1991.

Feld, Barry C. *Bad Kids: Race and the Transformation of the Juvenile Court.* New York: Oxford University Press, 1999.

Flynt, Wayne. "Religion in the Urban South: The Divided Mind of Birmingham, 1900–1930." *Alabama Review* 30 (April 1977): 108–34.

Fraser, Nancy, and Linda Gordon. "A Genealogy of Dependency: Tracing a Keyword of the U.S. Welfare State." *Signs* 19 (Winter 1994): 309–36.

Freedman, Estelle B. *Maternal Justice: Miriam Van Waters and the Female Reform Tradition.* Chicago: University of Chicago Press, 1996.

Gittens, Joan. *Poor Relations: The Children of the State in Illinois, 1818–1990.* Urbana: University of Illinois Press, 1994.

Glenn, Evelyn Nakano. "From Servitude to Service Work: Historical Continuities in the Racial Division of Paid Reproductive Labor." *Signs* 18 (Autumn 1992): 1–43.

Goldfield, David R. *Cotton Fields and Skyscrapers: Southern City and Region, 1607–1980.* Baton Rouge: Louisiana State University Press, 1982.

Goodwin, Joanne L. *Gender and the Politics of Welfare Reform: Mothers' Pensions in Chicago, 1911–1929.* Chicago: University of Chicago Press, 1997.

Gordon, Linda. "Black and White Visions of Welfare: Women's Welfare Activism, 1890–1945." *Journal of American History* 78 (September 1991): 559–90.

———. "Family Violence, Feminism, and Social Control." *Feminist Studies* 12 (Fall 1986): 453–78.

———. *Heroes of Their Own Lives: The Politics and History of Family Violence, Boston, 1880–1960.* New York: Viking Press, 1988.

———. *Pitied but Not Entitled: Single Mothers and the History of Welfare.* New York: Free Press, 1994.

———. "Putting Children First: Women, Maternalism, and Welfare in the Early Twentieth Century." In *U.S. History as Women's History: New Feminist Essays,* edited by Linda K. Kerber, Alice Kessler-Harris, and Kathryn Kish Sklar, 63–86. Chapel Hill: University of North Carolina Press, 1995.

———. "Social Insurance and Public Assistance: The Influence of Gender in Welfare Thought in the United States, 1890–1935." *American Historical Review* 97 (February 1992): 19–54.

Gottlieb, Peter. *Making Their Own Way: Southern Blacks' Migration to Pittsburgh, 1916–30.* Urbana: University of Illinois Press, 1987.

Grantham, Dewey W. *Southern Progressivism: The Reconciliation of Progress and Tradition.* Knoxville: University of Tennessee Press, 1983.

Green, Elna C. *This Business of Relief: Confronting Poverty in a Southern City, 1740–1940.* Athens: University of Georgia Press, 2003.

———, ed. *Before the New Deal: Social Welfare in the South, 1830–1930.* Athens: University of Georgia Press, 1999.

————, ed. *The New Deal and Beyond: Social Welfare in the South Since 1930.* Athens: University of Georgia Press, 2003.

Grossberg, Michael. *Governing the Hearth: Law and Family in Nineteenth-Century America.* Chapel Hill: University of North Carolina Press, 1985.

Grossman, James R. *Land of Hope: Chicago, Black Southerners, and the Great Migration.* Chicago: University of Chicago Press, 1989.

Gutman, Herbert G. *The Black Family in Slavery and Freedom, 1750–1925.* New York: Pantheon, 1976.

Hacsi, Timothy A. *Second Home: Orphan Asylums and Poor Families in America.* Cambridge: Harvard University Press, 1997.

Hall, Jacquelyn Dowd. "O. Delight Smith's Progressive Era: Labor, Feminism, and Reform in the Urban South." In *Visible Women: New Essays on American Activism,* edited by Nancy Hewitt and Susan Lebsock, 166–98. Urbana: University of Illinois Press, 1993.

Hardy, John G. "A Comparative Study of Institutions for Negro Juvenile Delinquents in Southern States." PhD diss., University of Wisconsin, 1946.

Harris, David. "Racists and Reformers: A Study of Progressivism in Alabama, 1896–1911." PhD diss., University of North Carolina, 1967.

Hawes, Joseph M. *Children in Urban Society: Juvenile Delinquency in Nineteenth-Century America.* New York: Oxford University Press, 1971.

Haws, Robert, ed. *Age of Segregation: Race Relations in the South, 1890–1945.* Jackson: University of Mississippi Press, 1978.

Hilliard, David Moss. "The Development of Public Education in Memphis, Tennessee, 1848–1945." PhD diss., University of Chicago, 1946.

Hindus, Michael S. *Prison and Plantation: Crime, Justice, and Authority in Massachusetts and South Carolina, 1767–1878.* Chapel Hill: University of North Carolina Press, 1980.

Hine, Darlene Clark. " 'We Specialize in the Wholly Impossible': The Philanthropic Work of Black Women." In *Lady Bountiful Revisited: Women, Philanthropy, and Power,* edited by Kathleen D. McCarthy, 70–93. New Brunswick: Rutgers University Press, 1990.

Holl, Jack. *Juvenile Reform in the Progressive Era: William R. George and the Junior Republic Movement.* Ithaca: Cornell University Press, 1971.

Honey, Michael K. *Southern Labor and Black Civil Rights: Organizing Memphis Workers.* Chicago: University of Illinois Press, 1993.

Horn, Margo. *Before It's Too Late: The Child Guidance Movement in the United States, 1922–1945.* Philadelphia: Temple University Press, 1989.

Hunter, Tera W. "Domination and Resistance: The Politics of Wage Household Labor in New South Atlanta." *Labor History* 34 (Spring/Summer 1993): 205–20.

Jackson, Kenneth T. *The Ku Klux Klan in the City, 1915–1930.* New York: Oxford University Press, 1967.

Jacobs, Francine Helene, and Margery W. Davies, eds. *More than Kissing Babies?: Current Child and Family Policy in the United States.* Westport, Conn.: Auburn House, 1994.

Jones, Jacqueline. *Labor of Love, Labor of Sorrow: Black Women, Work, and the Family, from Slavery to the Present.* New York: Vintage Books, 1985.

Jones, Kathleen W. *Taming the Troublesome Child: American Families, Child Guidance, and the Limits of Psychiatric Authority.* Cambridge, Mass.: Harvard University Press, 1999.

Jones, William B. "The Treatment of Juvenile Offenders in Tennessee: A Study of Incarceration." PhD diss., Vanderbilt University, 1939.

Katz, Michael B. *In the Shadow of the Poorhouse: A Social History of Welfare in America.* New York: Basic Books, 1986.

Keller, Morton. *Regulating a New Society: Public Policy and Social Change in America, 1900–1933*. Cambridge, Mass.: Harvard University Press, 1994.

Kirby, Jack Temple. *Darkness at the Dawning: Race and Reform in the Progressive South*. Philadelphia: Lippincott, 1972.

———. *Rural Worlds Lost: The American South, 1920–1960*. Baton Rouge: Louisiana State University Press, 1987.

Knupfer, Anne Meis. *Reform and Resistance: Gender, Delinquency, and America's First Juvenile Court*. New York: Routledge, 2001.

Kousser, J. Morgan. *The Shaping of Southern Politics: Suffrage Restriction and the Establishment of the One-Party South, 1880–1910*. New Haven: Yale University Press, 1974.

Koven, Seth, and Sonya Michel. "Womanly Duties: Maternalist Politics and the Origins of Welfare States in France, Germany, Great Britain, and the United States, 1880–1920." *American Historical Review* 95 (October 1990): 1076–1108.

———, eds. *Mothers of a New World: Maternalist Politics and the Origins of Welfare States*. New York: Routledge, 1993.

Kretzman, Martin. "The Kid's Judge: Institutional Innovation in the Early Denver Juvenile Court under Judge Ben B. Lindsey, 1901–1927." PhD diss., University of Denver, 1997.

Kunzel, Regina G. "The Professionalization of Benevolence: Evangelicals and Social Workers in the Florence Crittendon Homes, 1915–1945." *Journal of Social History* 22 (Fall 1988): 21–43.

Ladd-Taylor, Molly. *Mother-Work: Women, Child Welfare, and the State, 1890–1930*. Urbana: University of Illinois Press, 1994.

———. "Toward Defining Maternalism in U.S. History." *Journal of Women's History* 5 (Fall 1993): 110–13.

Lamon, Lester C. *Black Tennesseans, 1900–1930*. Knoxville: University of Tennessee Press, 1977.

Lanier, Robert A. *Memphis in the Twenties: The Second Term of Mayor Rowlett Paine, 1924–1928*. Memphis: Zenda Press, 1979.

La Pointe, Patricia. *From Saddlebags to Science: A Century of Health Care in Memphis, 1830–1930*. Memphis: Health Sciences Museum Foundation of the Memphis and Shelby County Medical Society Auxiliary, 1984.

Larsen, Charles. *The Good Fight*. Chicago: Quadrangle Books, 1972.

Lee, David. *Tennessee in Turmoil: Politics in the Volunteer State, 1920–1932*. Memphis: Memphis State University Press, 1979.

Leflore, Leroy, Eugene Turner, and John C. Jones. "A History of the Juvenile Court of Memphis and Shelby County." Paper presented to Center for Study of Crime, Delinquency, and Corrections, Southern Illinois University, 1980.

Leiby, James. *A History of Social Welfare and Social Work in the United States*. New York: Columbia University Press, 1978.

Lewis, Earl. *In Their Own Interests: Race, Class, and Power in Twentieth-Century Norfolk, Virginia*. Berkeley: University of California Press, 1991.

Link, Arthur S. "The Progressive Movement in the South, 1870–1914." *North Carolina Historical Review* 23 (April 1946): 172–95.

Link, William A. *The Paradox of Southern Progressivism, 1880–1930*. Chapel Hill: University of North Carolina Press, 1992.

Lisenby, William Foy. "An Administrative History of Public Programs for Dependent Children in North Carolina, Virginia, Tennessee, and Kentucky, 1900–1942." PhD diss., Vanderbilt University, 1962.

Lobes, Loretta Sullivan. "Hearts All Aflame: Women and the Development of New Forms of Social Service, 1870–1930." PhD diss., Carnegie Mellon University, 1996.

Lubove, Roy. *The Professional Altruist: The Emergence of Social Work as a Career, 1880–1930.* Cambridge, Mass.: Harvard University Press, 1965.

Luker, Kristin. *Dubious Conceptions: The Politics of Teenage Pregnancy.* Cambridge, Mass.: Harvard University Press, 1996.

Marchand, Roland. *Advertising the American Dream: Making Way for Modernity, 1920–1940.* Berkeley: University of California Press, 1985.

May, Elaine Tyler. *Great Expectations: Marriage and Divorce in Post-Victorian America.* Chicago: University of Chicago Press, 1980.

McCarthy, Kathleen D., ed. *Lady Bountiful Revisited: Women, Philanthropy, and Power.* New Brunswick: Rutgers University Press, 1990.

McMillen, Neil R. *Dark Journey: Black Mississippians in the Age of Jim Crow.* Urbana: University of Illinois Press, 1989.

Melton, Gloria Brown. "Blacks in Memphis, Tennessee, 1920–1955: A Historical Study." PhD diss., Washington State University, 1982.

Mennel, Robert M. *Thorns and Thistles: Juvenile Delinquents in the U.S., 1820–1940.* Hanover: University of New Hampshire Press, 1973.

Meyers, Lawrence. "Evolution of the Jewish Service Agency in Memphis, Tennessee, 1847 to 1963." MA thesis, Memphis State University, 1965.

Michel, Sonya, and Robyn Rosen. "The Paradox of Maternalism: Elizabeth Lowell Putnam and the American Welfare State." *Gender and History* 4 (Autumn 1992): 364–86.

Miller, William D. *Memphis during the Progressive Era, 1900–1917.* Memphis: Memphis State University Press, 1957.

———. *Mr. Crump of Memphis.* Baton Rouge: Louisiana State University Press, 1964.

Mintz, Steven, and Susan Kellogg. *Domestic Revolutions: A Social History of American Family Life.* New York: Free Press, 1988.

Muncy, Robyn. *Creating a Female Dominion in American Reform, 1890–1935.* New York: Oxford University Press, 1991.

National Research Council. *Understanding Child Abuse and Neglect.* Washington, D.C.: National Academy Press, 1993.

Neverdon-Morton, Cynthia. *Afro-American Women of the South and the Advancement of the Race, 1895–1925.* Knoxville: University of Tennessee Press, 1989.

Odem, Mary. *Delinquent Daughters: Protecting and Policing Adolescent Female Sexuality in the United States, 1885–1920.* Chapel Hill: University of North Carolina Press, 1995.

Odem, Mary E., and Steven Schlossman. "Guardians of Virtue: The Juvenile Court and Female Delinquency in Early Twentieth Century Los Angeles." *Crime and Delinquency* 37 (April 1991): 186–203.

O'Neill, William L. *Divorce in the Progressive Era.* New Haven: Yale University Press, 1967.

Orloff, Anne Shola. *Politics of Pensions: A Comparative Analysis of Britain, Canada, and the United States, 1880–1940.* Madison: University of Wisconsin Press, 1993.

Oshinsky, David M. *"Worse Than Slavery": Parchman Farm and the Ordeal of Jim Crow Justice.* New York: Free Press, 1996.

Ownby, Ted. *Subduing Satan: Religion, Recreation, and Manhood in the Rural South, 1865–1920.* Chapel Hill: University of North Carolina Press, 1990.

Peiss, Kathy. *Cheap Amusements: Working Women and Leisure in Turn-of-the-Century New York.* Philadelphia: Temple University Press, 1986.

Phillips, Virginia. "Rowlett Paine's First Term as Mayor of Memphis, 1920–1924." MA thesis, Memphis State University, 1958.

Platt, Anthony M. *The Child Savers: The Invention of Delinquency*. Chicago: University of Chicago Press, 1969.

Polakow, Valerie. *Lives on the Edge: Single Mothers and Their Children in the Other America*. Chicago: University of Chicago Press, 1993.

Polanksy, Lee. "'For It Made Me a Lady': The Georgia Training School for Girls and the Delinquent Girl, 1914–1922." PhD diss., Emory University, 2002.

Rabinowitz, Howard N. "From Exclusion to Segregation: Health and Welfare Services for Southern Blacks, 1865–1890." *Social Service Review* 48 (September 1974): 327–54.

———. *Race Relations in the Urban South, 1865–1890*. Urbana: University of Illinois Press, 1980.

Rafter, Nicole Hahn. *Partial Justice: Women in State Prisons, 1800–1935*. Boston: Northeastern University Press, 1985.

Rodgers, Daniel T. "In Search of Progressivism." *Reviews in American History* 10 (December 1982): 113–32.

Rosen, Christine Meisner. "Business, Democracy, and Progressive Reform in the Redevelopment of Baltimore after the Great Fire of 1904." *Business History Review* 63 (Summer 1989): 283–328.

Rosenheim, Margaret K., Franklin E. Zimring, David S. Tanenhaus, and Bernardine Dohrn, eds. *A Century of Juvenile Justice*. Chicago: University of Chicago Press, 2002.

Rosenzweig, Roy. *Eight Hours for What We Will: Workers and Leisure in an Industrial City, 1870–1920*. New York: Cambridge University Press, 1983.

Rothman, David J. *Conscience and Convenience: The Asylum and Its Alternatives in Progressive America*. Boston: Little, Brown and Company, 1980.

———. *The Discovery of the Asylum: Social Order and Disorder in the New Republic*. Boston: Little, Brown and Company, 1971.

Ruth, David E. *Inventing the Public Enemy: The Gangster in American Culture, 1918–1934*. Chicago: University of Chicago Press, 1996.

Ryerson, Ellen. *The Best-Laid Plans: America's Juvenile Court Experiment*. New York: Hill and Wang, 1978.

Salem, Dorothy C. *To Better Our World: Black Women in Organized Reform, 1890–1920*. Brooklyn: Carlson, 1990.

Schlossman, Steven. "Before Home Start: Notes Toward a History of Parent Education in America, 1897–1929." *Harvard Educational Review* 46 (August 1976): 436–67.

———. *Love and the American Delinquent: The Theory and Practice of "Progressive" Juvenile Justice, 1825–1920*. Chicago: University of Chicago Press, 1977.

Schlossman, Steven, and Alexander Pisciotta. "Identifying and Treating Serious Juvenile Offenders: The View from California and New York in the 1920s." In *Intervention Strategies for Chronic Juvenile Offenders: Some New Perspectives*, edited by Peter Greenwood, 7–38. New York: Greenwood Press, 1986.

Schlossman, Steven, and Susan Turner. "Status Offenders, Criminal Offenders, and Children 'at Risk' in Early Twentieth-Century Juvenile Court." In *Children at Risk in America*, edited by Roberta Wollons, 32–57. Albany: State University of New York Press, 1993.

Schlossman, Steven, and Stephanie Wallach. "The Crime of Precocious Sexuality: Female Juvenile Delinquency in the Progressive Era." *Harvard Educational Review* 48 (February 1978): 65–94.

Schneider, Eric C. *In the Web of Class: Delinquents and Reformers in Boston, 1810s–1930s*. New York: New York University Press, 1992.

Schultz, J. Lawrence. "The Cycle of Juvenile Court History." *Crime and Delinquency* 19 (October 1973): 457–76.

Scott, Anne Firor. "Most Invisible of All: Black Women's Voluntary Associations." *Journal of Southern History* 56 (February 1990): 3–22.

———. *Natural Allies: Women's Associations in American History*. Urbana: University of Illinois Press, 1991.

———. *The Southern Lady: From Pedestal to Politics, 1830–1930*. Chicago: University of Chicago Press, 1970.

Scott, Rebecca J. "The Battle over the Child: Child Apprenticeship and the Freedman's Bureau in North Carolina." In *Growing Up in America: Children in Historical Perspective*, edited by N. Ray Hiner and Joseph M. Hawes, 193–202. Urbana: University of Illinois Press, 1985.

Shannon, Irwin. "Juvenile Delinquency: A Statistical Study of 1,778 Cases of Juvenile Delinquency in Nashville, Tennessee." MA thesis, Vanderbilt University, 1928.

Shelden, Randall G. "A History of the Shelby County Industrial and Training School." *Tennessee Historical Quarterly* 51 (Summer 1992): 96–106.

———. "Rescued from Evil: Origins of the Juvenile Justice System in Memphis, Tennessee, 1900–1917." PhD diss., Southern Illinois University, 1976.

———. "Sex Discrimination in the Juvenile Justice System, Memphis, Tennessee, 1900–1917." In *Comparing Male and Female Offenders*, edited by Margarite Warren, 55–72. Beverly Hills: Sage, 1981.

Shelton, John Reed. *The Enduring South: Subcultural Persistence in Mass Society*. Lexington, Mass.: D. C. Heath, 1972.

Shivers, Lyda Gordon. "The Social Welfare Movement in the South: A Study in Regional Culture and Social Organization." PhD diss., University of North Carolina, 1935.

Shockley, Gary. "A History of the Incarceration of Juveniles in Tennessee, 1796–1970." *Tennessee Historical Quarterly* 43 (Fall 1984): 229–49.

Sigafoos, Robert A. *Cotton Row to Beale Street: A Business History of Memphis*. Memphis: Memphis State University Press, 1979.

Sitkoff, Harvard. *A New Deal for Blacks, the Emergence of Civil Rights as a National Issue: The Depression Decade*. New York: Oxford University Press, 1978.

Skocpol, Theda. *Protecting Soldiers and Mothers: The Political Origins of Social Policy in the United States*. Cambridge, Mass.: Belknap Press, 1992.

Skocpol, Theda, and John Ikenberry. "The Political Formation of the American Welfare State in Historical and Comparative Perspective." *Comparative Social Research* 6 (1983): 87–148.

Skowronek, Stephen. *Building a New American State: The Expansion of National Administrative Capacities, 1877–1920*. New York: Cambridge University Press, 1982.

Slater, Peter. "Judge Benjamin Barr Lindsey and the Denver Juvenile Court during the Progressive Era." MA thesis, Brown University, 1965.

Smith, Julie L. "Child Care Institutions and the Best Interest of the Child: Pittsburgh's Protestant Orphan Asylum and Home for Friendless Children, 1832–1928." PhD diss., Carnegie Mellon University, 1994.

Sutton, John. *Stubborn Children: Controlling Delinquency in the United States, 1640–1981*. Berkeley: University of California Press, 1988.

Swift, Karen J. *Manufacturing "Bad Mothers": A Critical Perspective on Child Neglect*. Toronto: University of Toronto Press, 1995.

Tanenhaus, David S. "Growing Up Dependent: Family Preservation in Early Twentieth-Century Chicago." *Law and History Review* 19 (2001): 547–82.

———. "Policing the Child: Juvenile Justice in Chicago, 1870–1925." PhD diss., University of Chicago, 1997.

Thomas, Bernard J. *The Cycle of Juvenile Justice.* New York: Oxford University Press, 1992.

Tiffin, Susan. *In Whose Best Interest? Child Welfare Reform in the Progressive Era.* Westport, Conn.: Greenwood Press, 1982.

Tindall, George B. *The Emergence of the New South, 1913–1945.* Baton Rouge: Louisiana State University Press, 1967.

Trattner, Walter I. *From Poor Law to Welfare State: A History of Social Welfare in America.* New York: Free Press, 1984.

Trotter, Joe William, Jr. *Black Milwaukee: The Making of an Industrial Proletariat, 1915–45.* Urbana: University of Illinois Press, 1988.

———, ed. *The Great Migration in Historical Perspective.* Bloomington: Indiana University Press, 1991.

Tucker, David M. *Black Pastors and Leaders: Memphis, 1819–1972.* Memphis: Memphis State University Press, 1975.

Vaz, Edmund, ed. *Middle-Class Juvenile Delinquency.* New York: Harper and Row, 1967.

Walker, Donald R. *Penology for Profit: A History of the Texas Prison System, 1867–1912.* College Station: Texas A and M University Press, 1988.

Walker, Randolph Meade. *The Metamorphosis of Sutton E. Griggs: The Transition from Black Radical to Conservative, 1913–1933.* Memphis: Walker Publishing, 1990.

Wallace, Ellen. "History of Legal Provisions for the Poor and of Public Welfare Administration in Tennessee." MA thesis, University of Chicago, 1927.

Wedell, Marsha. *Elite Women and the Reform Impulse in Memphis, 1875–1915.* Knoxville: University of Tennessee Press, 1991.

Wheeler, Marjorie Spruill, ed. *One Woman, One Vote: Rediscovering the Woman Suffrage Movement.* Troutdale, Ore.: NewSage Press, 1995.

Wiebe, Robert H. *The Search for Order, 1877–1920.* New York: Hill and Wang, 1967.

Williams, Charles, Jr. "Two Black Communities in Memphis, Tennessee: A Study in Urban Socio-Political Structure." PhD diss., University of Illinois at Urbana-Champaign, 1982.

Williamson, Joel. *The Crucible of Race: Black-White Relations in the American South since Emancipation.* New York: Oxford University Press, 1984.

Wisner, Elizabeth. *Social Welfare in the South: From Colonial Times to World War I.* Baton Rouge: Louisiana State University Press, 1970.

Wolcott, David. "Cops and Kids: The Police and Juvenile Delinquency in Three American Cities, 1890–1940." PhD diss., Carnegie Mellon University, 2000.

Wood, Sharon. "Wandering Girls and Leading Women: Sexuality and Urban Public Life, 1880–1910." PhD diss., University of Iowa, 1994.

Woodward, C. Vann. *Origins of the New South, 1877–1913.* Baton Rouge: Louisiana State University Press, 1951.

Wyatt-Brown, Bertram. *Southern Honor: Ethics and Behavior in the Old South.* New York: Oxford University Press, 1982.

Zelizer, Viviana A. *Pricing the Priceless Child: The Changing Social Value of Children.* New York: Basic Books, 1985.

Zimmerman, Hilda Jane. "Penal Systems and Penal Reform in the South since the Civil War." PhD diss., University of North Carolina at Chapel Hill, 1947.

Zmora, Nurith. *Orphanages Reconsidered: Child Care Institutions in Progressive Era Baltimore.* Philadelphia: Temple University Press, 1994.

Zunz, Olivier. *The Changing Face of Inequality: Urbanization, Industrial Development, and Immigrants in Detroit, 1880–1920.* Chicago: University of Chicago Press, 1982.

Index